Fans!

How We Go Crazy Over Sports

Fans!

How We Go Crazy Over Sports

MICHAEL ROBERTS

THE NEW REPUBLIC BOOK COMPANY, INC.

Washington, D.C.

Published in 1976 by
The New Republic Book Company, Inc.
1220 Nineteenth St. N.W.
Washington, D.C. 20036

Library of Congress Cataloging in Publication Data

Roberts, Michael, 1945-
    Fans, how we go crazy over sports.

    Includes index.
    1. Sports—Public opinion.   2. Sports—Psychological
aspects.   I. Title.
GV706.R57   301.15'43'796   76-26880
ISBN 0-915220-20-2

Printed in the United States of America

To Deb and Gretch

The chain of events that brought me to this gratifying moment leads directly back to David Sanford, managing editor of *The New Republic*, and I thank him. I am also grateful (now that the bleeding over the typewriter long into the night is finished) to Marty Peretz and Bob Myers, respectively *capo di tutti capi* and *consigliere* at TNR, for shamelessly badgering an unsuspecting three-column-a-week sports-writer into such a project; to Joan Tapper, a sensitive editor who went beyond the call of duty with timely pep talks (with special thanks for enjoining me from titling Chapter Five "Plimpton Contemplating a Busted Homer").

Friends too numerous to list contributed anecdotes and steered me to accounts of useful incidents. Dave Burgin and John Clendenon, who successively ran the sports department of the *Washington Star*, indirectly contributed a great deal by fostering several projects from which I drew ideas. Special thanks also to Peter Sherman and Dan Norman.

I only wish it were possible to acknowledge everything I owe Frimette and Harold Roberts, my parents. Hannah and Charles Salmanson, my mother-in-law and father-in-law, have been unfailing in their support and encouragement. Deb, my wife, contributed to the book in many ways, not the least of which was making me back up my assertions. Last, and least, Gretchen saw to it that, no matter how pressing the work, I got fresh air several times a day.

Contents

Introduction

In October 1973 I saw a short newspaper story about a Colorado man who had attempted suicide by shooting himself in the head. His note referred to the Denver Broncos, a pro football team that had fumbled seven times that day while losing to the Chicago Bears. The Bears had recovered five of the fumbles. The county sheriff's office refused to identify the fan but disclosed the contents of the suicide note: "I have been a Broncos fan since the Broncos were first organized, and I can't stand their fumbling anymore."

Poor marksmanship was all that averted a human sacrifice to the football gods; maybe they were appeased by the gesture itself. The man who had been willing, in his frustration, to give his life for the Broncos apparently survived. I never learned anything else of his fate—whether he recovered and swore off football or plugged himself again the next time Denver turned in a sloppy game. At any rate, the two paragraphs on his deed, tucked in among the serious stuff about who won and who lost and who was about to sign a big contract, gave the people who edit or read sports pages a brief laugh. I may have laughed, too—I don't remember—but, thinking about it from time to time, I became ever more intrigued with the hold spectator sports and jock-heroes have on their followers.

Those thoughts were the origin of this book. But fans' devotions were not the only subject I found myself exploring. Jock worship does not exist in a vacuum. It affects every facet of life, from commerce to religion to justice to international politics.

FANS!

The leading contemporary example is Muhammad Ali's impact on the world. Ali looms large, unavoidably, in these pages, because of the incalculable consequences of his inconsequential deeds. Those consequences are what make his activities the antithesis of my idea of *sport:* play for its own sake or its health benefits. Athletics conducted for money, the glory of an institution, or the vicarious gratification of nonparticipants are not sport.

What shaped up, as I fiddled with that concept, is a sports book that is not, strictly speaking, a book about sports. It is not about games themselves or athletes themselves or how they accomplish their feats or what they think (except when they use their pedestals as platforms for haranguing others to think as they do) or what they eat for breakfast (unless the menu is dictated by commercial considerations).

As much as anything, it grew out of a bemused sportswriter's existence, since I wouldn't have been required to spend much of my time from 1972 to 1975 studying the behavior described herein if it hadn't been for an accidental tenure as sports columnist for the *Washington Star.* Before the demise of the *Washington Daily News* threw me on the mercy of the *Star,* I had been a horse-racing writer, not a sportswriter. The distinction is not carelessly drawn. Racing is not a sport in the same sense as everything else spectators and promoters lump together under the rubric, although for the sake of convenience it is invariably put in the same category.

For reasons obscure to me, for instance, racing coverage in most newspapers appears at the end of the sports section, just past the box scores and hole-in-one reports from local country clubs, and just before the stock-market tables. Actually it has much more in common with the latter than the former. The investor who places his wager on a stock issue is motivated not by sentiment or loyalty to industry based in his home town, but by honest, uncluttered greed. So it is at the races—the patron's thoughts, like the participant's, are fixed on personal enrichment.

From the hindsight of an ex-sportswriter, that seems eminently reasonable. The spectacle of galloping thoroughbreds is not responsible for guiding adolescents in the ways of virtue. No public consensus obliges jockeys to set the right example by refraining from strong drink, fornication, and tobacco. Even the fastest horses are seldom deified, fawned over, or asked to endorse candidates for elective office.

Now and then, of course, a fuss *is* made over a particularly fine specimen. Man O'War was immensely popular; his funeral, in Lexington, Kentucky, drew a big crowd (of humans), and the downtown merchants draped their storefronts in black. Secretariat beer mugs and T-shirts moved briskly after the honoree won the 1973 Triple Crown and was featured on the covers of the national newsmagazines. (As for what can happen when a horse metamorphoses from betting object to generalized sports hero, a William Morris man once said, "I became known as 'Secretariat's agent.' Now, I also happen to be Gregory Peck's agent, and I represent Sophia Loren and Danny Thomas. But I became known as Secretariat's agent. That's something to think about.") Every year on the first Saturday in May thousands at Churchill Downs and millions watching on television obligingly get misty-eyed when the band strikes up "My Old Kentucky Home" during the post parade for the Derby.

But these are aberrations. Misty eyes at racetracks are usually outnumbered by jaundiced ones about a thousand to one. Like anyone else on the beat I got used to seeing things from a comfortably cynical perspective. The switch to a new milieu—in which any band of mercenaries could command the devotion of a mass of people by stitching the name of a city or university across their jerseys—called for a reshuffling of sensibilities.

In turn came the realization that it's hard for a layman to conceive of an unhappy sportswriter. By unanimous agreement of friends and neighbors in other occupations, nothing else was anywhere near so glamorous or exciting. Sportswriting can be both of those for anyone in the right frame of mind. After all, writing about the game is indisputably the next best thing to being big, strong, and agile enough to win the glory directly. You get to spend time in private with some of the most exalted figures in America, to actually converse with them, to have them address you by your first name.

Since the duties require passing in and out of locker rooms and ball park player entrances, there is even an outside chance of being mistaken for a you-know-what and asked for an autograph. One colleague strongly resembled (from the neck up, at least) a famous halfback whose team he covered; to pass through the mob outside the stadium after the games he had to sign the halfback's name on the scraps of paper thrust at him.

Heady stuff, but a taste of the jock's life is a bonus. Merely living like a sportswriter has its compensations, because promoters feel they can never do enough for reporters assigned to their events. The bigger the event, the more at stake in the cultivation of goodwill, the more lavish the care and feeding of the scribes.

The outstanding example I encountered was the one National Football League championship game I covered. That was Super Bowl VIII (the NFL is so acutely conscious of its own grandeur that Super Bowls are designated with Roman numerals, like Popes and Lincoln Continentals) in Houston. As is customary, the NFL provided a room at its headquarters hotel where accredited media people could get free drinks at almost any time of day during the week before the game. Meals were available too—sumptuous buffets, actually—as part of a service by which those of us who wished to make a pretense of daily reporting were bused to one team's hotel for breakfast interviews and to the other's for lunch. The box lunch handed out on game day would have done honor to a Beverly Hills soiree, and came packed in a carrying bag, stamped with the NFL logo, that became one's property upon consumption of its contents.

At all times there were NFL publicity men stationed in convenient places with piles of mimeographed articles, against the chance I might find myself so busy playing in the Super Bowl press golf tournament that it became necessary to retype a handout and turn it in under my own byline. Should some other diversion further impose on my time, the league could also arrange for the retyping job.

For sportswriters and other hangers-on, the climax of any Super Bowl week is not Super Sunday, when the game takes place, but Super Friday Night, when the big party is held. The size and tone are a point of NFL pride. To do it properly a year earlier, in Los Angeles, the league

Introduction

had booked the *Queen Mary*—the whole ship—then docked at Long Beach. In anticipation of Houston some of us joked that the only way Commissioner Pete Rozelle could top himself was to rent the Astrodome.

In this instance life imitated low humor. The floor of the roofed stadium was done up like a western movie set. At various intervals whole steers were being barbecued. Miss Texas was on display, rhinestones glittering blindingly from her tiara; she even favored us with a few country selections on her fiddle. Bars were spaced a few yards apart around the perimeter of the floor, and every sportswriter and sportscaster in town (along with every hooker and freeloader in the Southwest) was filling up on free booze while NFL publicity men, decked out in denim duds and ten-gallon hats, roamed the make-believe cowtown making sure everyone got enough to drink.

So what's not to like? Admittedly, it sounds like a pretty good deal. But by the time I whooped it up with those twenty thousand or so other inhabitants of what Robert Lipsyte calls "SportsWorld," some of the doubts I've mentioned were already nagging me. Maybe it wasn't the utopia everyone took it for. Maybe it was too far removed from reality, or maybe it had become its own reality. There were moments that had given me pause.

One of the most memorable occurred at the American League baseball playoffs in Oakland, California. October 1973—a momentous time in United States history. Richard Nixon was already in Dutch, but the immediate heat was on his associate Mr. Agnew. The news had just gotten out that federal prosecutors had put a cynical construction on what the vice-president called "commonly accepted" fund-raising methods.

Before the action started at Oakland Coliseum, I stood around with some other writers watching the telecast of the National League game in New York on a press-box monitor. Suddenly baseball faded out and the screen was filled by the image of Spiro Agnew. I reached to turn up the volume, but my hand stopped in midair. No volume control on the monitor. *No sound* at all, I realized for the first time. We jock-journalists were expected to know what was going on without being told. Only, here was something a little more complicated than keeping track of balls and strikes. Was Agnew out? Was he announcing he'd fight the case in court? Had Nixon resigned and Agnew become president? In seconds the vice-presidential portrait dissolved back into the features of a batter digging in at home plate in Shea Stadium, leaving us without a clue as to what might be going on in real life.

Probably did resign, I mused; probably some NBC color commentator was at that very moment riffling through his record book and informing the TV audience that this was the *first* playoff game ever played with the vice-presidency vacant.

Then the press-box public-address system boomed suspensefully: "For your information. . ."—a very pregnant pause—". . .the Mets are leading Cincinnati, two to one. . . ."

A longer pause followed, then: "For your further information, Vice-President Agnew has resigned." Well, all right, at least the basic fact was confirmed. Still, a few of us were eager to know a little more about this unprecedented national cataclysm. "Gentlemen, here is some information," came the hoped-for announcement a few minutes later. "World Series credentials may be obtained at the desk at. . ."

I heard no more about the vice-presidency at Oakland Coliseum that day. And now that I think about it, I shouldn't have been surprised.

Fans!

How We Go Crazy Over Sports

The Redskin Chronicles and Other Fan Tales

There may never have been a more opportune time for a foreign power to attack the United States than the afternoon of January 14, 1973. A football game was being played in Los Angeles, California. This was a special game, called the Super Bowl, contested for the championship of the National Football League. Winning it, most Americans thought, was the most thrilling thing the players could ever experience. Most Americans behaved as if it were also the most thrilling thing that could happen to the residents of the metropolitan area in which the winning team was franchised. The populations poised on the brink of sheer, soaring ecstasy that day were those of Miami, Florida, and Washington, D.C.

That's what made it an ideal time for foreign aggression. No populace invested more emotion in an NFL team than Washington's, and Washington's populace was, literally, the government of the United States. And if ever the whole government was charged up to watch a ballgame, this was the time—an enemy could count on it. From the White House downtown, to the Capitol up the Hill, to the Pentagon just across the Tidal Basin, to the CIA a few miles down the George Washington Parkway in the suburban Northern Virginia woods, all psychic energy was trained on the Redskins' attempt to bring home to their backers a year's worth of smug superiority.

More rapt than all the senators, congressmen, brass, and spooks, if such a thing were possible, was the president of the United States. After

1

agonizing over a decision, he had chosen not to go to Los Angeles to see the game in person. His reason: To accommodate his security retinue, 100 other fans would have to be deprived of their seats. In retrospect this would be seen as one of the more magnanimous acts of Richard Nixon's incumbency. Tube-bound Nixon was sure to be, however. And if he hadn't whiled away the days up to game time diagraming plays for the Redskins, it was only because the last play he had suggested to a Super Bowl contender had resulted in an intercepted pass. Many VIPs would attend the game, of course. In fact, the more clout, the more likely its possessor would have access not only to the Super Bowl but to enough regular-season games to have developed a particularly strong affinity for the team.

This was great tribute to the Redskins, but no more so than their accomplishment of something politicians had been promising for years. For three hours, at least, the streets of Washington would be free from fear. There would be no muggers, no muggees. There would be no traffic. There would be nobody in restaurants and movie theaters. Water pressure would be dangerously unbalanced during time-outs, when untold numbers of toilets were flushed in near unison. Television sets in 750,000 of the area's 920,000 households were expected to be turned to the game, and there was always the chance that inhabitants of the aberrant 170,000 would be guests in the others. The two daily papers, the *Post* and the *Star*, had dispatched about fifteen reporters and photographers across the continent.

Journalistically the Redskins' progress had been treated with the intensity worthy of a presidential impeachment story. The morning after the playoff victory that put Washington in the Super Bowl, both papers ran eight-column headlines across their front pages (*Post:* "We're a Winner at Last;" *Star:* "How Sweet It Is"). The *Post* had deemed the game account too important to be handled by a mere sportswriter; the byline above the piece, which also ran the width of Page One, was that of David S. Broder, dean of Washington political analysts. (His lead: "For the first time since World War II, Washington is a winner. The Nation's Capital ended 30 years of sports humiliation and heartbreak. . . .") In an editorial the *Star* spoke of "a tide in the affairs of men" and predicted that the team was on its way to "making Washington Number 1." A TV station had sent four correspondents to file up-to-the-minute bulletins. Regular programming had been interrupted even early in the week to show the team getting on a bus to ride to the airport to catch a plane to Los Angeles. On Super Bowl eve the station showed an hour-long special on "the growing excitement gripping Redskin fans," and followed up the next morning with a half-hour documentary on the life of one of the running backs.

Any other city blessed with a Super Bowl team might have reacted similarly. What was remarkable in Washington was the negligible difference between this response to the Super Bowl and the attention paid any other Redskins game. Washingtonians had long ago collectively decided that nothing was more important; the Redskins' activities controlled the rhythm of their comings and goings, the threads of their conversations, the moods of their Monday mornings in fall and winter.

Their thrall was typified in William Raspberry, a well-respected columnist whose work appeared on the op-ed page of the *Post* and generally concerned education and other vital topics. One day, Raspberry opened his innermost feelings to readers: "You wouldn't leave your loose change lying around a kleptomaniac. You wouldn't entice an alcoholic friend into a saloon. So please don't talk to me about the Washington Redskins . . . I have made a shocking discovery that I am hooked." Referring to a defeat by the Dallas Cowboys, he described "the fitful sleep haunted by the 'if onlys.' Everybody you meet talks endlessly about the Redskins and their playoff hopes . . . my insane sleepless anguish over George Allen's strategy . . ."

Officially the police had nothing to say about the correlation between crime and football, but a precinct cop told the *Post*, "Crime goes away on Redskin day. We don't expect anything until 7:00 P.M." What then? "It depends on whether they win or lose." If the department was reticent about arrest figures, it might be because cops weren't chasing robbers with everyday ardor.*

*That seemed to be a consequence of televised football in New York. In February 1975 the *New York Post* reported the city's arrest rate declined sharply on Monday nights, when a

FANS!

In an announcement, the need for which was disconcerting to nervous flyers, airport authorities once disclosed that even though a game was being telecast, watching it was forbidden to the men in the control tower. Too distracting, they said. The set was kept in the radio room, so word of the Redskins' fate could be passed in between takeoff and landing instructions.

Effects on the output of the hundreds of thousands on the federal payroll weren't easy to gauge. With many government employees, it was hard to tell whether they were not working for a reason or simply not working. Some said Monday morning was just like any other day at the office. Many said discussions of the ball game *did* take precedence over all else. "The work just slows down, it's gotta slow down," said one. "Any other morning you start working right away, but the day after the game the first hour is definitely devoted to it." Another said, "Nobody works for about two hours." Another, "Through lunchtime." Another, "Monday morning and throughout the rest of the day." Some were sure the taxpayers had a better chance of getting their money's worth when the Redskins won. "I'm happier," one lawyer said, "and when I'm happy I'll do more work."

On Capitol Hill, interest was no less intense. "That's the total subject in the cafeterias—the Capitol dome could be burning," a Hill-watcher said. He referred to the War Lords, a claque of the seniormost congressmen's aides. "They have great in-depth conversations. They'll come in at 8:30 and stay till 10:30, 11, till everybody's had his say about the game."

A curious item turned up in the *Washington Star* in 1974: After successfully managing a bill to increase the capacity of RFK Stadium by eight thousand Redskins seats, Rep. Kenneth J. Gray (D-Ill.) had been able to arrange for thirty-five to forty of his colleagues to buy season tickets. Questioned about this, Gray described the preceding hellish months during which he had been pestered ceaselessly by fellow congressmen demanding tickets.

"game of the week" was telecast nationally. The newspaper surmised that New York's finest were trying to avoid spending the crucial hours in night court. A survey showed that on sixteen Monday nights during football season in 1974 there had been an average of 39.9 arrests. On ten preceding Monday nights the average was 48.5.

4

The Redskin Chronicles

In October 1975 when investigative reporters exposed indiscreet relationships between public officials and defense contractors, they discovered, incidentally, that planes-and-weapons-makers considered Redskins tickets an effective bribe: One of Northrop Corporation's favorite ways to butter up congressmen was to get them tickets and invite them to lavish prekickoff bashes. The punchline was that the Defense Department was being billed for everything.

Over a two-year period (1971-1973) Northrop spent $14,343: $8,336 for the tickets and the rest for parking at the stadium and sumptuous brunches at an exclusive Capitol Hill establishment called the 116 Club, in honor of the 116 lobbyists who comprised its membership. Beneficiaries of the hospitality included (in addition to the congressmen and their aides) high civilian and military officials of the defense establishment. In the interest of supporting the home team they had been willing to overlook civil-service regulations and Defense Department directives forbidding Pentagon employees to accept gifts from companies doing business with the government. (At the time Northrop was competing for a contract to build a lightweight fighter plane that could bring the nation's thirteenth-largest defense contractor up to $6 billion in sales.) While no one could doubt the wisdom of these rules, it was naive to think any mortal in Washington had the self-control to refuse a proffered Redskins ticket. If there was blame to assign, it was to Northrop for creating the temptation; Northrop had sized up the situation with the cool amorality of a dope dealer and now was dangling heroin in front of junkies. "These episodes," syndicated columnist Mary McGrory wrote, "do not add greatly to football's reputation as a wholesome pastime." It was obvious that McGrory was one of the few Washingtonians indifferent to the burgundy-and-gold heroes, which was to say that in the eyes of the majority she simply didn't understand football. "Not to possess Redskins tickets spells a fatal absence of status," she informed readers, as if they didn't already know.

Members of the city council had rejoiced publicly when a special box was provided for them at RFK Stadium, with free passes for themselves and guests. "It's befitting for the elected officials," Councilwoman Willie Hardy said. The box had been built by order of the D.C. Armory Board, whose appropriations were controlled by the council. Whether this circumstance had anything to do with the provision of tickets was left unanswered. Sterling Tucker, chairman of the council, described them as "some little courtesies" that ought to be extended to such dignitaries: "The pressures on public officials are enormous and the pay doesn't match it. Anything we can do to add to the pleasure of that work, I am not opposed to it." (Tucker's salary was $32,000, the other council members', $22,000.) This was an issue, it turned out later in the year, that was sweeping the country. When the St. Louis Board of Aldermen proposed a resolution to congratulate the Cardinals on their NFL divisional championship, there were five nay votes. The dissenters cited the fact that the Cardinals had stopped giving two free tickets to each alderman.

The St. Louis championship was a tainted one, anyway. In November 1975 the Cardinals had beaten the visiting Redskins with a touchdown pass on the last play of the game; the receiver, Mel Gray, leaped to take in the pass, crossed the goal line in midair, and fumbled the ball when jostled by a defender as he descended. Two officials signaled touchdown; another declared the pass incomplete. They conferred for several suspenseful minutes. Then, to the raucous delight of the St. Louis crowd, they gave the touchdown and the victory to the Cardinals, ruling that Gray had possession when he entered the end zone.

But according to the book, "both feet must touch the ground while the player has possession of the ball." And the *Washington Post,* which was just as distraught over the defeat as its readers, had photos to prove that Gray's catch had not conformed to the rule. The *Post* ran its sequence the following Tuesday morning, across the full width of the front page, about six inches deep, directly under the banner and above a story about President Ford's economic summit meeting in France. In the critical shot Redskin Pat Fischer was driving his shoulder into Gray's. The ball was squirting out of Gray's grasp. His left toe was touching the ground, but his entire right foot was indisputably several inches above the synthetic grass.

All of Washington now considered itself the victim of a hometown job. Everyone talked about it, and one citizen did something about it.

He filed suit in U.S. district court, asking that the game be stricken from the league standings and treated as if it had never been played. The NFL, taking no chances, was represented by Washington's biggest legal guns, Covington and Burling. After listening to thirty minutes of oral argument Judge George L. Hart, Jr., a Mary McGrory fellow traveler, dismissed the suit as "frivolous." (The *Sporting News* heaved a sigh of relief: "The mind boggles at the thought of every judgment call being subject to judicial review.")

Frivolous, maybe, but most fans were still simmering. As the *Wall Street Journal* was later to report, "NFL officials are discovering that Redskin rooters aren't typical fans. Many are high-powered politicians. . . ." The NFL officials had come to town to testify on a bill that would permanently prevent games on network television from being blacked out in the home team's area if tickets had sold out by seventy-two hours before game time. The very impetus for the bill was thought by many to have been desperation. During the original hearings three years earlier several senators and congressmen had cited their inability to get tickets. In arguing against the law, Joe Robbie, managing partner of the Miami Dolphins, had said, "We would cheerfully contribute our share to construct enough extra seats in RFK so all members of Congress could see the Redskins without the need for legislation." As coincidence would have it, Pete Rozelle, commissioner of the NFL, was summoned to testify on the permanent bill the week after the St. Louis contretemps. From a committeeman's seat in a hearing room of the World's Greatest Deliberative Body, Sen. Warren Magnuson (D-Wash.) peered down at the commissioner and asked, "Is there anything that can be done about the great robbery?"

If legislators weren't afraid to wear their feelings on their sleeves, neither were the newspapers too rigid to sacrifice news judgment and objectivity to show their regard for the Redskins. Aside from routinely extensive sports-section coverage, any item of unusual interest about the team, changes in personnel, or the league was likely to appear on the front page. When the venerated quarterback Sonny Jurgensen retired, the *Post* (the morning paper and larger of the two dailies) wallowed in self-pity. "It came sooner than he and many of his fans would have

FANS!

wished," the *Post* grieved in an editorial. "The solace for Jurgensen and his fans is that he erected a monument of achievement in this town. . . ." The *Post* had been smitten with Jurgensen's inarguable competence, but the contents of the piece suggested it was prompted by more than simple admiration for Jurgensen's professionalism. George Allen was chewed out for his callous treatment of the idol. Bill Kilmer, who would henceforth handle all the quarterbacking, was criticized in advance for the comparative dullness he was expected to bring to the Redskins' offense. And the readership was advised it owed thanks to a man who for two decades had made his living playing a game—at a pay rate exceeded by perhaps 1 percent of the American work force.

Not to be outdone in eulogizing Jurgensen, the *Star* headlined its editorial: "Still Loving Sonny." When several NFL teams launched a wildcat strike before the start of the next season, the *Star,* like the *Post,* kept readers abreast of labor news with several stories a day. In the waning days before the opening kickoff, the strike was settled; the *Star* ran its story under an eight-column front-page headline just beneath the masthead: "NFL Agreement: Pro Football Sunday." (The previous night on the late TV news the strike story was given top billing, ahead of fresh news on CIA outrages. On Sunday nights on all stations, come hell or high treason, the Redskins game was the lead story.) With Emersonian disdain for foolish consistency, the *Star* spoke in an editorial of the "magnificent inconsequentiality of the affair," and chided the players and owners for "taking themselves too seriously."

Of the two, in fact, the *Post* was far more inclined to use the editorial page to embrace, cheer, and commiserate with the Redskins. In 1974 the team reached the playoffs, but was knocked out short of the Super Bowl by Los Angeles. The *Post* opined on Super Sunday, ". . . this is the day that might have been. For, this afternoon, if things had gone the way they were supposed to go, the Redskins would be playing in New Orleans in the National Football League championship game . . . on that afternoon in Los Angeles, though, the magic wasn't there. . . . The four years of George Allen have been an exhilarating experience, but this season ended ignominiously and the shock of it has not yet gone away. Maybe next year . . ."

8

The Redskin Chronicles

When the World Football League, a makeshift outfit that lasted less than two seasons, folded in the fall of 1975, the *Post* denounced Commissioner Rozelle, who had issued an order making WFLers ineligible to join NFL teams until the end of the season. "In the short run, we admit, some of our interest is purely parochial," the paper proclaimed. "The commissioner's action appears to have denied the Washington Redskins the services of a running back they may need if this December in this city is going to be as interesting as it has been in the last four winters." This editorial appeared just below one on Gerald Ford's Sunday Massacre, the cabinet shake-up on which he'd held a press conference the previous night, a Monday. When WTOP-TV preempted a Redskins-rehash show for the conference, it received more than four hundred protesting phone calls. A radio station, WMAL, had avoided a similar reaction by cutting away from Ford after his first fifteen minutes to rejoin the regularly scheduled "Hathaway Huddle," another day-after football program.

In response to the community's across-the-board commitment to the Redskins, businessmen had made available a broader range of team-related merchandise than supporters of most other teams enjoyed. Beyond the ordinary run of souvenirs—helmets, uniforms, jackets, beer mugs, wastebaskets, ashtrays, lamps, wall plaques—a Redskins backer could find a fifteen-dollar music box that played the team fight song, "Hail to the Redskins." Someone who wanted to spend a little more and be a bit more conspicuous could tool around town in a four-wheel-drive Ford pickup truck, specially done in burgundy and gold, or an Oldsmobile station wagon similarly Redskinized. In suburban Bethesda a woman could visit a gynecologist who offered a Redskins waiting room, replete with photos of the squad. To fill yet another need, a Northern Virginia bank introduced the only NFL personal check in the country. "With all the choices you've got," the bank pointed out in newspaper ads, "there's really very little that says anything about you or the things you like. Which is the reason we wanted to introduce the first Washington Redskins checks . . . It says you're a fan. It says you support our very own home team . . . Get the first personal check that's not impersonal."

FANS!

For the dreary days of late winter, a travel agency announced a "special pro football pigskin cruise," with passengers to be accompanied by Sonny Jurgensen, Ron McDole, Len Hauss, "five other football greats," and Hank Stram, coach of the Kansas City Chiefs. Plans called for a seven-day cruise on the *Queen Elizabeth II,* to places like St. Thomas and San Juan. Among the activities would be seminars with the players aboard and showings of "official pro football films." The idea had sprung up in San Francisco, where the Pacific & Orient line had offered only the company of Hugh McElhenny, an old-time 49er, and discovered it could sell out a whole cruise ship. Some seven hundred customers spent a week in darkened rooms watching movies of years-old NFL games—while their luxurious craft cut through the subtropical waters of Baja California. If something like that could sell in San Francisco, to a population that was notably blasé about its football team, it was fail-safe in Washington.

Redskins glamour was central to other promotions. One fall households in the metropolitan area received "personalized" form letters from George Allen, suggesting the purchase of vacation property at a Virginia development. Sales increased in the weeks after the mailing, the owner said later. But, while some fans were willing to answer George's call, it became apparent that others would forego the pleasure of a resort home out of loyalty to another Redskin. "We've had people say that they might buy a lot here, but because of what Allen did to their friend Sonny Jurgensen, it's 'See you later,'" the developer told the *Star.*

A nursery owner reported that nothing could have been better for business than hiring Allen and eight players to spend an afternoon on the premises. "Talk about something attracting attention! We had three state police, two paid security men, and the county threw in five or six deputies. We have a four-lane highway out here that we completely stopped. Our parking lot holds 150 cars. The shopping center across the street holds another 450-500 cars, and we filled that up too. The crowd approached 20,000."

The big season, 1972-1973, when the Redskins went to the Super Bowl (only to lose to Miami), spawned any number of commercial opportunities. With fan sales resistance at an all-time low, a handful of players even cashed in on a post-season basketball game, billed as a "confrontation between the Miami Dolphins and the Washington Redskins." Some 2,200 spectators paid five dollars each to watch a game of roughly junior-high-school quality, punctuated every few minutes by the hawking of bumper stickers, pennants, and a phonograph record, "Titletown," cut by one of the Redskins. But that entrepreneurial coup was nothing compared to the opening a few months earlier of a shop selling nothing but souvenirs of the Redskins and some other pro sports teams. Two years later the remembrance of it still drove one of the proprietors into a froth.

"We were selling excitement," he said, "the association with the Redskins. To show how this thing took hold, we opened in December of 1972, which was a few weeks before the Super Bowl. With the combination of the Redskins winning and Christmas, we had to have special police to keep the people out . . . We ordered five thousand extra playoff programs, the same as the one that would be sold at the game. This had never been done before. We publicized the fact that we would have these books, and so much activity was created it was unbelievable. At 7:30 A.M. the line started forming—UPI had a picture showing the line out of sight around the block. The tractor-trailer truck with the programs had gotten there earlier, and it couldn't unload come nine o'clock. The police wouldn't let him unload! It was like food to hungry people—as fast as they could get them off the truck they were grabbed. 'I'll take five!' . . . 'I want twenty!' They were three dollars apiece. They cleaned us out like locusts . . . There was an ashtray in the store we were *using*. Somebody threw the ashes out and said, 'I'll take it.' The same thing happened with a trash can. I said, 'But, lady, it's *dirty*.'"

The previous year a crowd of about four thousand had stood in the rain at Dulles Airport to see the Redskins off to a mid-season game in Kansas City. Several city officials, including the chairman and the vice chairman of the city council, led a chorus of "Hail to the Redskins." Everyone was primed for the victory that would put the team in first place. The hopes weren't fulfilled—Kansas City prevailed, 27-20. But Sunday night, as the Redskins flew homeward, some eight to twelve thousand Washingtonians began heading to the airport. Traffic was backed up for ten miles on the Dulles access road. In the crush at the terminal a number of women fainted, and two heart attacks were later reported. Ambulances couldn't get close enough to retrieve the fallen. Back on the access road a young man got fed up with sitting in the bumper-to-bumper traffic. As he gunned onto the shoulder of the road, he ran into a bridge abutment that deflected his car down a steep bank, killing him.

This was evidence consistent with the thesis of Paul Gardner, an Englishman who wrote about this country's utter abandonment to sport in *Nice Guys Finish Last* (not to be confused with Leo Durocher's autobiography of the same title). Gardner found delightful irony in what had become of a nation founded by such joyless colonists. "If the first thing the Pilgrim fathers had done on landing had been to organize a game of bowls, or even of cricket, it would, no doubt, have been terribly English of them, but they did no such thing. They disapproved of leisure activities altogether." Some 350 years later the descendants of those ascetics found nothing remarkable in the delay of a televised presidential speech during the Cambodia-Kent State crisis to accommodate a National Basketball Association playoff game or, a few years earlier, the playing of the regular pro football schedule two days after the assassination of John Kennedy. Gardner wrote, "There were precious few enterprises that could have got away with that without a storm of public wrath breaking about their heads, but pro football was one of them."

At least Americans were consistent about the extent to which they'd let their lives be controlled by ballgames. If the murder of a president could be regarded as a trifle next to the playing of football, so could ordinary social events.

That's why Elmer Kiraly and Loretta Agostine of Pittsburgh made special arrangements when they realized the time of their wedding conflicted with a Steelers game. They arranged to have television sets installed at the church and the ceremony performed at halftime, so that no guest racked with indecision need choose between the wedding and Pittsburgh-San Francisco. In a similar foul-up Tommy Puckett and Julie Gaskin of Lexington, Kentucky, carelessly scheduled their nuptials for the afternoon when Kentucky and Syracuse universities were to meet in the national basketball semifinals. When the conflict was discovered, guests were sent postcards with a photo of a basketball player, a new hour for the wedding, and the message: "UK is No. 1, Puckett-Gaskin wedding No. 2. See you at the church and the tipoff, too."

In summer 1968 a New York couple set a wedding date six months in the future and lived to regret it, as their friend Andrew Beyer, a *Washington Star* columnist, related: "John thought the Super Bowl would be played a week earlier, Toni wasn't thinking about football at all, and neither of them could have guessed that their hometown team, the New York Jets would be playing the Baltimore Colts in one of the epochal games of football history. When they realized that the wedding would be competing against Joe Namath, John called the church and changed the time of the ceremony from three to five in the afternoon. Two hundred friends and relatives had been invited to the wedding but, Toni said, 'Practically everybody called and said they'd be at the reception but they wouldn't be able to make the wedding. They couldn't believe that we would do such a thing, schedule our wedding on the superest of Sundays. The people who said they would come were almost all aunts and uncles and people who didn't like football.'

"'Of the guests we invited,' John said, 'there were about 170 no-shows.' Toni's peace of mind was wrecked when her bridesmaids started clustering around the television set in her small apartment so they could watch the pregame show . . . When Toni arrived at the Immaculate Conception Church in Queens a few minutes before five o'clock, she observed that the pews were virtually deserted, though she saw many guests still sitting in the parking lot, listening to the game on their car radios. At five the guests raced through the vestibule past her, talking excitedly about the Jets' imminent victory. John was worrying, because the wedding was scheduled to begin and there was no priest in sight. 'I was getting frantic,' he said, 'so my best man went out back of the church and saw the priest in his car, listening to the game. Finally, when the church bells started clanging, he ran in. . . .'" In commemoration John and Toni celebrate their anniversary not on the calendar date but on Super Sunday.

Even when hardship is involved, fans remain faithful to their priorities. In the days before the Civil War, with travel still arduous, it was nothing for tens of thousands of Americans to drop everything and travel hundreds of miles to watch a horse race, the importance of which usually was attached to the fact that it matched an animal belonging to a southerner against one owned by a northerner. Nowadays, with conveniences like television and air travel, things are easier for fans, but some still make sacrifices. During the summer of 1973 a former college economics teacher who had worked for the Department of Health, Education, and Welfare, gave up everything to follow the Atlanta Braves baseball team around the country. The Braves' star batsman, Henry Aaron, was closing in on Babe Ruth's lifetime home-run record, and the fan in question was willing to go unpaid, live in a van, and dine in heartburn emporia to take in every moment of the quest. This kind of behavior is a common phenomenon. The European wire services discovered a Scotsman who lived on welfare because following the national soccer team took up too much time for him to hold a steady job. The Scot claimed to have witnessed in person every match his team had played in fifteen years. Tiny Tim, the entertainer, revealed to an interviewer that he had dropped out of school at fifteen to follow the Brooklyn Dodgers. This intelligence quelled some of America's uneasiness about a grown man who tiptoed through the tulips, but it also chipped away the mystique, and Tiny Tim's career began declining soon after.

Greater sacrifices yet have been made in the name of sport. Known suicides (see Introduction) seem to be infrequent, but every now and then dispatches from Europe or Latin America tell of fans whose shame over the defeat of a national soccer team drove them to self-destruction. A college football victory was the cause of an incident described by John Kenneth Galbraith in a speech at Harvard: "Burned in my memory of those fiestas is the boast of a celebrant . . . that from the top floor of a dormitory he could dive headfirst down a stairwell, onto the cement floor, and survive. All cheered him on. He was wrong."

In fall 1974, while watching the Alabama-Auburn football game on television, Paul Harris was shot to death by a friend during an argument over whether an Alabama field goal was good. In summer 1969 Frank

Graddock of Queens, New York, sat down in front of the television to watch a big game between the Mets and the Chicago Cubs. His wife wanted to watch something else. During a tense moment in the ninth inning she turned the channel selector. Frank punched her in the head and back, returned to watching the game, and when it was over discovered he had fatally injured his wife. Back in the 1930s when the Dodgers were Brooklyn and vice versa, Robert Joyce gathered regularly with a group of fellow fans at Pat Diamond's Bar and Grill. Joyce was brooding about a defeat by the hated Giants one day and was in no mood for the teasing he took at the bar. "You lay off the Dodgers, you dirty bastards," he demanded. The friends persisted. Joyce rushed out, returned with a gun and shot two persons, killing one. When police took him into custody, he sobbed, "They shouldn't have taunted me about the Dodgers."

Vicarious involvement itself poses a danger, as cardiologists studying stress related to rooting have discovered in recent years. In 1973 Dr. Charles B. Corbin reported (in *Physician and Sportsmedicine* magazine) a link between spectating and increased heart rates. There had been many instances of heart attack at the college games his study concentrated on, and some priests on the faculty of Providence College had been barred by their doctors from attending basketball games and ordered to turn off their radios if the score got close. "Several investigators," Corbin wrote, "have documented increased heart rates in spectators both in anticipation of the game and during the game itself." He concluded that the vicarious participant "must personally maintain a fairly high level of fitness to prevent distortion of the balance of the sympathetic and the parasympathetic divisions of the nervous system . . . to maintain his own good health." Two years later Dr. Harold Karpman, a Los Angeles cardiologist, speculated that "emotional stress in spectators may well be as great or greater than the physical effort put out by the athletes they watch. . .and their hearts are extraordinarily less capable of coping with tenseness than players."

On the other hand, apparently the stimulation can have a positive effect. The medical community of Kaposvar, Hungary, was astounded on August 31, 1975. Janos Pek lay in his hospital bed, listening to the opening game of the soccer season on the radio. When the announcer described the tripping of a forward on Pek's team, he sat up and shouted, "Penalty!" Nervous trauma had rendered him mute in 1964, and this was the first word he had spoken in eleven years.

The principle of fan-team symbiosis was illustrated by the life of a middle-aged Nebraska man whose relationship with a football team got a lot of publicity in the early 1970s. Charlie Winkler was renowned for organizing every aspect of his life so as better to worship the University of Nebraska Cornhuskers. An average of four times a week Winkler drove the 210-mile round trip between his Grand Island home and the stadium in Lincoln. He made a point of attending all games, home and away, varsity and freshman, with serious illness the only acceptable excuse for absence. He once drove five hundred miles in a day to take in both freshman and varsity games. He attended all intra-squad scrimmages. On occasion he drove to the stadium when it was empty, just to sit there and dream dreams of football. In his car he kept a supply of tape recordings of bygone games.

Winkler held six season tickets and spent about $2,000 a year following the team. He wrote letters to high school players, encouraging them to enroll at Nebraska, and on his honeymoon stopped off at Sturgis, South Dakota, to try to recruit a player.

Winkler styled himself the No. 1 fan in the nation. "When the team comes running on the field and the band strikes up 'Dear Old Nebraska U' the tears damn near scald my cheeks. It's life's ultimate experience," he said. Of course, he had a plan for the perfect death. He would suffer a heart attack during a game, be rolled over by companions to see the Big Red score one last touchdown, and then expire in bliss. At the next game a helicopter would hover above the field, scattering his ashes over the sacred turf.

Is He Jewish?

The origins of the concept are obscure and unquestionably ancient. As far as Western civilization is concerned, it was on the playing fields of Greece that glory was first discovered to be transferable from the laurel-draped jock to his neighbors. The notion survives, virtually unchallenged, as the foundation stone of almost every kind of spectator sport now flourishing: The linking of the participant's destiny with the fan's on the basis of common city, homeland, educational institution, race, religion, or place of national origin.

In the Olympic Games of yore a champion was crowned with a wreath. That was nice, but it was just a start. Once the hero returned to his hometown it was impossible for him to pick up the check for the rest of his life. Typically, he'd be escorted back into the native environs through a hole cut through the city wall in his honor. He'd get a lifetime meal ticket, sometimes a free home as well. He'd be slipped bundles of cash. A street might be named after him (just as now there is a street in Green Bay, Wisconsin, not to mention a food-fuel-toilet stop on the New Jersey Turnpike, named for Vince Lombardi). If he were a real superstar, poets sat around interminably making up odes to him. None of this was considered excessive compensation for enabling Spartans to feel superior to Athenians or vice versa.

Those were uncomplicated days. Given the relative homogeneity of city-state culture, a jock represented—besides his geographical brethren—his ethnic group, his religion, his race. After all, there was only one of each. Consciousness about sexism being what it was, *gender* never even entered into the question.

So it's safe to assume that ancient Greece never saw a spectacle like the one that held the United States spellbound in summer 1975. Foolish Pleasure, a colt, had emerged as the best of his generation in the "classic" spring races for thoroughbred horses. Ruffian, a filly, was also undefeated, but she had raced only against other fillies. Horsemen, always interested, as a practical matter, in whether a good female horse can outrun a good male horse, hoped to see a match arranged. The TV people envisioned something broader; they put up a fortune the owners of the two animals couldn't resist and billed the race as a "battle of the sexes." The whole country agreed that that was the way to look at it. Soberly, commentators declared that Ruffian "shoulders the hopes of millions of females. . . ."

After the race—Ruffian broke a leg in the first half mile, after which she had to be humanely destroyed—Dick Young, sports columnist for the *New York Daily News*, wrote, "She taught a great lesson. Before Ruffian, I never fully comprehended how much women were ticked off at men for this men's world that they believe they live in. Being an American woman is an ethnic thing, I now realize. Our women feel repressed . . . when the tragedy happened, so many pretty faces turned zombie in the late hours at Belmont, only then did I realize how deeply they felt about this thing. . . ." Young told of a phone call from a woman whose husband had disparaged her grief: "I asked her if she would have been so saddened had it been the colt that had died, and she said no. I said isn't that a sad commentary, and she said no. She said she would tell me something really sad. 'It is a terribly sad thing,' she said, 'that women must get their victories from a horse.'"

To say such a thing was to deny that Billie Jean King had ever existed. Two years before most of the public had even heard the name Ruffian, King had given American women a newfound sense of self-esteem. She had agreed to play tennis against middle-aged Bobby Riggs to avenge for her sex Riggs' defeat of Margaret Court the year before and to make about $250,000. The first match had been born strictly as a real-estate promotion. Riggs, who had been a champion twenty-five years earlier and still thought he could beat a woman of any age, challenged King (who declined) and Court (who accepted) to a winner-take-all match at a resort development near San Diego. Stimulated by the burgeoning feminist movement, interest swelled until the match became, in Bud Collins's words, "the ultimate male-female combat since Perseus had it out with Medusa." No self-respecting newspaper failed to cover the last week of the tension-filled buildup. A gigantic TV audience was assured. Then, anticlimactically, Riggs beat the pants off Court.

That did it, as far as Billie Jean was concerned. She arranged to meet Riggs in the Houston Astrodome in September 1973. Not only was the Astrodome packed (it was the largest live audience in tennis history), but except for the Super Bowl and the World Series no televised sports event had ever captivated such a huge percentage of the population. Newsmagazines did the obligatory cover stories. Even Riggs was awed by what had become of his gimmick: "I said to myself, this isn't tennis—it's something bigger." This time womanhood was not to be denied. King, in peak condition and at the top of her game, ran Riggs off the court, to the exultation and tearful gratitude of millions of sisters. "It helped women to stand taller," she said. "Our expectations were very low, but I think they have gone way, way up." *Newsweek* called her "symbol, spokeswoman . . . cult heroine." Also, as Robert Lipsyte put it in *SportsWorld*, "the Joan of Ace . . . was beseiged by toothpaste, deodorant, suntan oil and hair curler manufacturers, when it was implied that she had hung a pair of balls on every American woman who wanted them. . . ."

While gender identification in American sports was still in its infancy, religion had long since been standard basis for rooting affiliation. Citizens of Dallas couldn't have been too surprised at what they saw in their newspapers on a late December Sunday morning in 1974. The First Baptist Church of Dallas took out full-page ads in the major dailies. So did the Park City Baptist Church. The Baptist Foundation of Texas confined itself to a quarter-page.

Considering their timing the ads could have been Yuletide greetings. Considering their size they could have been announcements of the Second Coming. They were neither. Baylor University, a Baptist-affiliated school in Waco, was competing in the Cotton Bowl game, and the ads were declarations of Baptist solidarity with the gridiron crusaders. It had been years, after all, since Baptists had had a football team to be proud of.

The First Baptist not only boasted in print, it also dangled a lure in front of potential congregants: Guest pulpiteer that Sunday of Sundays would be none other than Grant Teaff, head football coach of Baylor. One of Waco's Baptist churches had a pastor who conducted services in the Baylor school colors; at the Columbus Avenue Baptist Church the Rev. Marshall Edwards also began his Sunday football-season sermons with comments on the previous day's game. After the victory that put Baylor in the Cotton Bowl, Edwards preached what, according to a reporter, "the congregation thought was his best football sermon." Sample: "On January first we will go to the Cotton Bowl and play the Nittany Lions [Penn State]. This will be the first time in history that the Lions will be thrown to the Christians."

"IS HE JEWISH?" That's the teaser on an ad that often shows up in the classified pages of sports publications. "Find out in the *Jewish Sports Review*, surprising and concise bi-monthly." How much is a reader entitled to know for $4.50 a year? A little bit more than whether he is or isn't. An issue picked at random contains a nostalgia piece about the second game of the 1966 World Series, "when the greatest Jewish lefthander [Sandy Koufax] and the greatest Jewish righthander [Jim Palmer, who wasn't full-blooded] opposed each other on the mound." An editorial urges Jews considering football to become linemen: "As a rule, Jews are not fast. Name a stand-out Jewish sprinter. Name the last Jewish base-stealer. You can't. My point is made." A track-and-field roundup reports that Brian Mondschein of Washington State ran the 400-meter high hurdles at the AAU national meet in 51.1 seconds, "among the best Jewish times ever." A column called "Abie's Irish Moniker" deplores the difficulty of identifying jocks of Hebrew heritage when so many lack telltale names.

The irony there is that a Jewish name in sports can be a blessing. As a general principle religious affinity sells tickets, and a Jew who makes good is also regarded as a novelty. The athletic community acts amazed, as if the imagined shtetls of America, with their ranks of frail scholars, had miraculously spewed forth a genetic freak: a strapping, coordinated Son of Israel. Hence *Sport* magazine gurgled over Ron Blomberg, a baseball player, as "A Jewish Yankee from Georgia . . . son of Goldie and Sol. . . ."

The New York Yankees had been looking for someone like Blomberg for a long, long time, and he was keen enough to grasp the role. "The greatest Jewish Yankee in history," he called himself. It had been an article of faith in the industry that the discovery of a bonafide jock descended from the Israelites (in time Puerto Rican origins came to be almost as desirable) would guarantee a booming box office in New York. Blomberg, in fact, was intended to be a savior for the Yankees, who signed him in 1966, when the dynasty that had won so many pennants was collapsing, taking with it ticket sales. Incidental benefits fell regularly to the Jewish Yankee: Dozens of co-religionists sent *mezuzahs* in the mail; better yet, offers to do commercials came in from Hebrew National Salami, Vita Herring, and the like. Obviously advertisers were willing to tread a fine line of stereotyping, but the association of Semitic delicacies with Blomberg apparently gave no public offense, where a fried-chicken testimonial by Henry Aaron might have provoked objections.

Because the prize ring's violent and coarse ambiance emphasizes the anomaly of a potential accountant or urologist gone wrong, Jewish boxers have always been able to capitalize on their bloodlines. Often this inspires chicanery. "What's a nice Jewish boy like Mike Rossman doing in the Garden beating up Irish Mike Morgan from Minneapolis?" Maury Allen of the *New York Post* wrote, adding later, "Ethnic excitement is always a part of boxing." True enough. But in this case the excitement was counterfeit. Rossman, who competed in trunks embroidered with a Star of David and was billed as the Jewish Bomber, was not exactly purebred. In fact, he was not exactly Rossman. He had been born Mike DePiano, to a father of Italian extraction; that being a mundane lineage in the fight game, he took his mother's maiden name, Rossman, upon choosing his profession. According to the Associated

Press, he was "being hyped as the next great Jewish fighter . . . a fitting successor to Benny Leonard and Barney Ross." Whether or not he ever became worthy of that mantle, his cut of the gate receipts would always be that much larger thanks to the emblem on his trunks. Stanley Ketchel, a legendary middleweight of old, wore the Star of David, too; he wasn't Jewish, but why go out of his way to destroy the illusions of innocent ticket buyers? On the weekly fight cards in Miami Beach there is usually at least one lad with a star on his trunks and a Jewish surname, even if his birth certificate calls him Kelly or Rodriguez. A March 1975 story in *Sports Illustrated,* headlined "This Cohen is the Real McCoy," told of a promoter's worry that a boxer he was plugging as "the last of the good Jewish fighters" might actually be an Arab. The article reported a heavyweight from San Diego, Ski Goldstein, who fought in New York in 1964 and was "discovered the next day to be no more Jewish than Cardinal Spellman," and a Puerto Rican named Marcos "turned to Marcus, Sydney." As for the disputed Max Cohen, the promoter had him checked out, and was relieved to be cabled " . . . dossier stands scrutiny. Certain Cohen is genuine Cohen."

Semi-Jewish Mike Rossman's punching bag that night in the Garden, Irish Mike Morgan, was no less a representative of venerated boxing tradition. To this day "Irish" automatically precedes the name of every boxer with an Irish surname, e.g., Irish Jerry Quarry, who was born in California and probably would not recognize the Auld Sod if he fell face first on it, but nonetheless wears a shamrock on his trunks. In Southern California the Mexican-American population is catered to. Welterweight champion José Napoles used to be escorted into the ring by men wearing sombreros and carrying Mexican flags.

Eventually the drawbacks of this approach outweighed its advantages; riots became fairly regular. In New York bouts involving Puerto Ricans were particularly touchy. At the old Madison Square Garden in 1965 Flash Elorde of the Philippines won a decision over Frankie Narvaez of Puerto Rico. Narvaez enthusiasts smashed bottles, broke up wooden chairs, and shoved the arena's organ over the side of a retaining wall. Ethnic rioting became so predictable that the Garden abandoned its weekly boxing cards. "I've got a great fight," Teddy

Is He Jewish?

Brenner, the matchmaker, said at one point. "Frankie Benitez of Puerto Rico against Villomar Fernandez of the Dominican Republic. But I don't care to put it on. It's too explosive."

There was a time when it was dangerous, for the same reason, to match a black fighter against a white. Only two events, Tony Gilmore asserts in *Bad Nigger—The National Impact of Jack Johnson*, ever triggered spontaneous nationwide racial conflict in America. One was the assassination of Martin Luther King. The other was the defeat of Jim Jeffries by Jack Johnson in 1910. Disturbances touched off by the bout left 19 dead, 251 injured, and more than 5,000 accused of disorderly conduct.

Sixty-five years later it was still profitable, if not as risky, to play the black-white angle in the ring, and the man who did it with the greatest intensity was neither a matchmaker nor a promoter. He was a participant, Muhammad Ali. Ali called one opponent, Joe Bugner, "the great white hope . . . I represent all the big black fighters there ever was . . . I can't let an Englishman beat the baddest brother in the world." When asked why he'd been signed up to fight Ali, Chuck Wepner, a heavyweight patsy, replied, "Ali wanted to fight somebody white who was ranked. Well, I'm ranked Number 8, and I'm about as white as you can get."

When he used up the supply of white heavyweights, Ali resorted to bleaching black opponents. Joe Frazier, whose skin was actually darker than Ali's, became, like Wepner, a "white hope . . . Uncle Tom . . . I am blacker than he is." Wilfrid Sheed wrote of their first bout, "One more flourish before Ali got in the ring. He appointed himself once again the Black Man—and made it stick. This time, as in some Genet play, Ali made us see color as purely a state of mind. He appointed Frazier white for the night, and presto, Frazier changed color."*

The irony was that Ali had ceased to be a symbol of black oppression, and in some eyes had become a racist himself. Before his

---

*Taking advantage of residual hatred for the colonialists Zaire had so recently expelled. Ali repeatedly told the public there that George Foreman "represents the white man of America . . . Foreman, in fact, is a Belgian." A lot of Zairians were shocked when the man who climbed into the corner opposite Ali's that night in Kinshasa wasn't white.

third fight with Frazier he tagged his longtime antagonist "the gorilla." Frazier pointed out that since this was a term used by whites to ridicule blacks, it spoke no better for Ali than for himself. But the champion kept regaling his training-session audiences with witticisms on the gorilla theme. As Nik Cohn described it in *New York*, Ali hunched down in the middle of the ring with an arm dangling low, his feet splayed, and one finger mashing his nose while his mouth flapped in a guttural sound. "Thus equipped, in the classic image of the coon, the mindless nigger minstrel, the champion shambled back across the ring until he stood right above his audience. The white crowd cheered him, and Ali accepted their tribute. . . ."

Sport *was* one of the first occupations in which American blacks were begrudged near-equal opportunity. Hence, many symbolic blacks have been athletes. In *I Know Why the Caged Bird Sings* Maya Angelou described the mood among the rural blacks of her childhood southern home when Joe Louis was fighting. People congregated at the general store, at a farm, wherever there was a radio. "Even the old Christian ladies who taught their children and tried themselves to practice turning the other cheek, would buy soft drinks, and if the Brown Bomber's victory was a particularly bloody one, they would order Peanut Patties and Baby Ruths also. . . ." When Louis is knocked down: "My race groaned. It was our people falling. It was another lynching, yet another black man hanging on a tree. One more woman ambushed and raped. A black boy whipped and maimed. It was hounds on the trail of a man running through slimey swamps. It was a white woman slapping her maid for being forgetful . . . This might be the end of the world. If Joe lost we were back in slavery and beyond help. It would all be true, the accusations that we were lower types of human beings. Only a little higher than the apes. True, that we were stupid and ugly and lazy and dirty and unlucky and worst of all that God himself hates us." Louis recovers, wins, retains the heavyweight championship: "Champion of the world. A black boy. Some black mother's son. He was the strongest man in the world. People drank Coca-Colas like ambrosia and ate candy bars like Christmas."

Only Joe Louis can say how acutely he was conscious of what he meant to other black Americans, but he would have to have been extraordinarily well insulated to avoid dwelling on it. Members of the white media were free with advice. "If Joe Louis forgets his resolve to be an ambassador of goodwill for his race . . . he'll never make the grade," a newspaper lectured. Bill Corum, one of the era's beloved sports columnists, wrote, "behave yourself. Be an example to your race as well as a champion. . . ."

Example or not, there was no doubt about his being an inspiration. Earl Brown wrote in the *Amsterdam News*, "He is the current natural pride of his people, a heavyweight champion every Negro hopes and prays for. His huge picture in fighting togs adorns every ham hock, fish fry and liquor joint in the community. The Depression, getting on home relief and singing the black blues because they didn't hit the number have been forgotten at least until after the great event by the Harlemites." In 1940 a black sociologist, E. Franklin Frazier, studied the precise role Louis was filling: "Joe Louis enables many lower class youths to inflict vicariously the aggression which they would like to carry out against whites for the discrimination and insults they have suffered." Frazier found that black children wished to be like Louis more than anyone else in the world. Charles S. Johnson, a historian, also learned that black children in the South had to be careful not to celebrate Louis's exploits too exuberantly, lest they bring down on themselves the frustrated wrath of whites.

When Jackie Robinson broke organized baseball's color line in 1947 by joining the Brooklyn Dodgers, he was thrust into a similar situation. Like Louis, whether he wanted it that way or not, he was a source of hope and pride to an entire oppressed race. His conduct would reflect upon—perhaps even change the attitudes of whites toward— millions of people who had nothing more in common with him than skin color. Branch Rickey, the administrator who opened the door for Robinson, instructed black spectators on how to behave at the ball park. "Not merely Robinson, but all black society is on trial," he said.

But where Louis had stood alone, with nothing for an identifying badge but his black skin and a white opponent in the opposite corner to heighten the symbolism, Robinson had *Brooklyn* written across the front of his shirt and eight men working in unison with him. Ostensibly the nine men were striving not just for their own gain but on behalf of a city, and the difference this eventually would make in the way the public identified with Robinson and other blacks was enormous. The measure of it could be reckoned thirty years later, when Ray Scott, black coach of a predominantly black basketball team, described to the *Washington Post* the response of a white, middle-class audience to an all-black lineup rallying to win a game in the name of Cleveland, Ohio: "There were nineteen thousand people there, and they were cheering like it was the original [lily white] Celtics. I had to look around and make sure we were really in suburbia."

What could account for the willingness to put aside so strong an emotion as race hatred? Was it necessary to go back to a hole in the wall of a Greek city-state to find an answer? Maybe the explanation lay in the nineteenth-century development of America's soul-game, baseball. In *The Old Ball Game* Tristram Coffin argued that town-versus-town baseball games had replaced town-versus-town melees. "Most of the games . . . ended up in brawls," but still they were "semi-civilized replacements for village-to-village wars."* This is an aspect of the game that has never left it. Coffin's example was the 1967 American League pennant race, when work came to a near standstill in four large cities so that everyone could pay attention to baseball. "During the final two games . . . a number of classes were suspended at such an unlikely place as Wellesley College so that girls who barely knew where Carl Yastrzemski would run after hitting the ball could take part in this modern village-to-village crisis."

Something similar must have motivated everyone in the Philadelphia metropolitan area one day in May 1974. By police estimates there

---

*After willingly maiming and being maimed in the name of a Texas high school and of the University of Texas, Gary Shaw reflected in *Meat on the Hoof* on the purpose to which he'd been put. On high school football in Denton: "There was a real feeling of community responsibility when you played for the high school team. You were defending your town against the aliens who were about to attack." The same analogy appears in Martin Ralbovsky's *Lords of the Locker Room* in the words of George Kirk, assistant football coach at Baylor: "The community expects a boy who's able to play to play . . . It's like the feudal times and each town is a kingdom at war with the other."

Is He Jewish?

were 2 million people in the downtown streets. "Little girls squealed and screamed, old men danced and sang, young boys stripped and streaked, several matrons keeled over and fainted, dozens of children were lost and police barriers finally collapsed," the *New York Times* reported. Along the parade route people were packed fifteen deep for three miles. The air was filled with confetti, toilet paper, and the sounds of sirens, horns, and firecrackers. It was, by a wide margin, the largest gathering of any kind in the history of Philadelphia. All because a hockey team had won the championship of its league.

As in Boston in 1967 (and other cities in other years) the celebration was over the success of a privately owned, profit-making business that— strictly for commercial reasons—called itself by the name of the city in which it was based. The Philadelphia Flyers weren't native sons any more than the Red Sox. Contemporary baseball players were drawn at random from all over the United States and Latin America. Employees of National Hockey League franchises were recruited (with rare exceptions) from Canada; they were imported to ply a trade to which the natives were unsuited. Nor was the condition of Flyerhood necessarily permanent. At any moment a Flyer could be transformed into a New York Ranger or a California Golden Seal, at the whim of an executive. Besides, a player's presence reflected not a desire to represent Philadelphia (or even the Flyers) but a contrivance called the "draft," by which pro sports teams apportion available players to avoid costly competition.

None of these things gave Philadelphians a moment's pause. Mercenaries they might be, but these eighteen-or-so puck-chasers from north of the border had wrought some gigantic metaphysical change in the city where they worked. Radios and TVs blared; newspapers used their biggest headline type to herald it across their front pages. "MIRACLE FLYERS . . . ," the papers said. Publications all over the country congratulated the city on what *Time* magazine called "the tangible proof that Philadelphia is at long last a winner." No more Philly jokes. The insults of a nation—the very epithets of W.C. Fields—had been repealed. Who dared mock a city where the Stanley Cup reposed?

The day of the Flyers' triumphal march was not an official holiday, but it might as well have been one. In some cases principals declared school closed, or teachers escorted their classes to the parade. Most of the schools just emptied, of both pupils and teachers, spontaneously. Thousands of commuters were left stranded in the suburbs because trains were filled with people on their way to the celebration. The police department committed a thousand men—who had to be shuttled around in eleven buses to stay abreast of the action—as its "official thanks" to the team for "bringing the city a major sports championship." (Invariably the spirit is catchy. In January 1975 a Pittsburgh judge issued an order for the Steelers to win the Super Bowl and dispatched a sheriff to New Orleans to deliver it. When the Steelers complied, the city fathers arranged to block traffic on downtown streets so a proper revel could be held. Police Superintendent Robert Colville said, "The mood should be festive. All our police are being instructed to carry this attitude throughout the celebration. We are as pleased as any other fan at the Steelers' success." After a certain number of beer bottles had been heaved at cops, however, it was necessary for the force to suppress its rapture and use dogs to break up the victory mob.)

At Independence Mall Kate Smith, the Flyers' good-luck piece, sang "God Bless America." Mayor Frank Rizzo earned some political points by presenting sculpted hockey players to each Flyer and forfeited a few by stumbling over Coach Fred Shero's name. The Flyers' public-address announcer told the crowd, "All of us here are better people because of them." (Phil Esposito of the Boston Bruins once described the effects of such a moment: "And suddenly I felt like the Pope. There was this mob below us, and I started blessing them. That's how big winning the Stanley Cup makes you feel.") Afterward it cost the city $50,000 to clean the streets, two and a half times the expense of sweeping up after the Mummers' Parade.

The public viewing of the Stanley Cup, two days later, had none of the undignified overtones of the parade. Those who came were respectfully silent in the presence of the trophy, and some wept openly. A middle-aged woman was seen blessing herself with rosaries as she passed what one observer called "the bier-like red velvet setting inside the . . . bank where the cup was on view amid a cascade of flowers." A guard at the bier said, "This reminds me of the time Franklin Roosevelt's body passed through Philly. The people are just as reverent."

Fans take very seriously the allegation that they are the real owners of pro teams in their cities, and the actual stockholders consider it imperative to nurture this belief: When ticket sales lag, the public is reminded that our (my) team needs our (your) support. Edward Bennett Williams, president of the Washington Redskins (and noted criminal lawyer), once testified at a House hearing that management had spent millions to give the seat of federal government something it could be proud of. (He did not mention whether revenues had offset the outlay.) "We really and truly believe and try to live by the creed that we hold our franchises in trust for the people in the cities in which we live," Williams said.

The only problem with the concept is that sometimes the beneficiaries take a dislike to the way their trust is being handled. In March 1955 when the Montreal Canadiens star Maurice Richard came to blows with a referee in the only act of violence considered wrongful in the sport, the league commissioner, Clarence Campbell, held hearings, then stunned hockey followers by suspending Richard not only for the rest of the season but also for the playoffs. Montreal fans, who had come to consider themselves proprietors of the team, were furious. Fifty-five of them phoned Campbell's office to threaten his life. The commissioner was warned to stay away from the Forum, where a game was to be played on St. Patrick's night. Rowdy pickets had surrounded the arena when Campbell, accompanied by his secretary, defiantly walked in. When he reached his seat spectators nearby began pelting him with rotten fruit. As the attackers closed to arm's length a tear-gas bomb suddenly went off inside the Forum, and the crowd dispersed. The fire chief ordered the building evacuated, and the game was forfeited to the visiting Detroit Red Wings. While the spectators spilled out among the protesters in front of the arena, Campbell and his party escaped through the rear. Then the rampage began: Bricks were thrown at windows, street kiosks burned down, and stores looted as bands of vandals spread through the city.

FANS!

Such figurative owners can be just as dangerous when they're happy. They terrified Bobby Thompson by applying for dividends immediately after his last-ditch home run had given the New York Giants the National League pennant in 1951. Thompson, quoted in *The Miracle at Coogan's Bluff,* recalled, "There was just this fantastic mob scene at home plate, and then it kind of turned into a riot. The next clear thing I remember was people trying to rip pieces of my uniform off. I thought, hey, I could get killed . . . So I took off for the clubhouse. Never ran so fast, I guess, weaving my way through all those people, all of them trying to get a piece of me." . . .

A fan who had been there said, "People were actually foaming at the mouth . . . Nobody cared whether they got hurt or not . . . No one wanted to leave, we stayed and stayed and stayed . . . Even after all the players had gone, there were still thousands there. They wouldn't leave. Even today I can't describe it properly. You had to be there to understand it. I was there, but even then I'm not sure I understood it."

Author Thomas Kiernan seemed tacitly to approve of the fact that events of such cosmic proportions defy comprehension. As if presenting his qualifications to write the sacred tract, he likened a boy's first visit to the ballpark to "a youngster's First Communion or Bar Mitzvah," explaining: "Devotion to the New York Giants had been almost as much part and parcel of my family's tradition for three generations as their belief in a righteous and redeeming God. Being the only male issue, I was naturally commissioned to carry on the tradition and pass it on to my own sons."*

Kiernan's symbolic trust becomes a practical aspect of everyday life in Massilon, Ohio. Within minutes after bearing a male child, a Massilon woman is presented with a football, a gift of the Massilon Mens' High School Football Booster Club. But the concept of the town's wives as brood mares is not the only thing that distinguishes "the

---

*The perpetuation of this faith would be a shaky proposition if it weren't for the belief that nine empty uniforms comprise a spiritual container whose meaning is constant, although the flesh filling the uniforms changes ceaselessly. The fact that the preternatural events of 1951 occurred largely because Leo Durocher, the Giants' manager, had shuffled new players onto the roster wholesale didn't inhibit Kiernan's iconology.

high school football capital of the world [a designation challenged by several other places, most notably the triangle of territory in Texas described by Beaumont, Port Arthur, and Orange]."

The population of Massilon is 32,539. The football stadium seats 21,345. The high school team's payroll includes a team dentist, a team chiropodist, and a team historian. Among the three adult booster clubs is the Sideliners, whose function, according to their press brochure, is "to be an adult group of buddies for the football players during the season. Each member of the Sideliners adopts a player for a buddy. He listens to any complaints a player may have or suggestions; he greets him before and after games, sits down and eats with him, takes him to a movie the night before a game." The many specialized coaches tool around in donated cars, and all the finest equipment is provided by townspeople.

(In *Nice Guys Finish Last* Paul Gardner marveled at the 1920s research—still valid apparently—of Helen and Robert Lynd, who found that in Indiana towns the most important "agency of group cohesion" was the high school basketball team. Gardner: "The idea of adults, including civic and business leaders, becoming starry-eyed over the performance of a high school sports team is not one that readily recommends itself to reason; but there it is. . . .")

Bart Starr, coach of the Green Bay Packers, had no doubt he'd find the same spirit of cooperation and sacrifice when he asked resident businessmen to create temporary jobs for his players so that they wouldn't disperse after the 1975 football season. In a letter printed in the final game's program he explained: "The competitive level of professional football demands that our players remain in top condition year around. In order to prepare a team for the demands of the 1976 schedule, we are seeking to keep as many of our players employed in this area in the off-season as possible. The closer the community and the players are off the field, the sooner the Packers will again bear the fruits of this unique relationship."

In a city as loyal to its pro franchise as Green Bay this wasn't asking much. Besides, if anyone's request was to be fulfilled unquestioningly it was Bart Starr's. Several years earlier, when he was still quarterbacking the Packers, a Methodist church school had polled its pupils to find the person they respected most in the world. Starr wound up in a tie for first place with Jesus Christ. Together they easily outpolled presidents, royalty, and humanitarians. Jesus' name was on the ballot, as well as those of all the losers. Bart's votes were write-ins.

Starr's acceptance of the coaching post had been greeted in the town as the dawn of a renaissance. After the departure of Vince Lombardi came the dark age of Green Bay football. A succession of pretenders failed to restore the Packers to glory, and were treated accordingly by the populace. Starr's immediate predecessor, Dan Devine, took the brunt of the mounting frustration generated by championshipless years: There were obscene phone calls in the night. His family was abused verbally at games. One of his daughters was spat on while riding the school bus. His dog was shot. "To hear the Green Bay citizenry tell it," Tom Dowling wrote in *Sport* magazine, "the farmer who shot Devine's dog was not only in the right, but was performing a rare act of civic duty. *Why, everybody shoots loose dogs here.* It seems useless to remind anyone that had the same farmer shot a straying dog belonging to Vince Lombardi, the poor man would have been flayed by local vigilantes."

This much was certain: No one in Green Bay would touch a hair on Bart Starr's dog's head. Rejoicing accompanied Starr's long-awaited ascension. In his inaugural speech he showed a sensitivity for the magnitude of the job; he quoted Winston Churchill: "To every man there comes in his lifetime that special moment when he is figuratively tapped on the shoulder and offered that chance to do a very special thing, unique to him and fitted to his talents. What a tragedy if that moment finds him unprepared or unequal to that work."

Behind all the consternation and hope was a fundamental assumption: Pro football just shouldn't be played better anywhere than in Green Bay. Where hockey was concerned, Canada was Green Bay many times magnified. In fall 1972 Team Canada, a group of stars drawn from the pro leagues, played an eight-game series against the Russian national team. Beforehand, Ken Dryden, the Canadian goalie, wrote in his diary, "Judging from the attitude of the people I have encountered the past few days, if we don't win this series 8-0 it will be a black mark for Canada. The newspapers, the television, the radio, the people in the street all say it has to be eight straight. Anyone who dares suggest that Canada might lose a game to the Russians becomes an instant outcast. We must not only win eight straight, but by big scores. Millions of Canadians are convinced that the Russians are villains, interlopers with the gall and the audacity to challenge us at our own game."

In the first game—in the Montreal Forum, the holy house of hockey—the Russians won by the mortifying score of 7-3. Stan Fischler wrote, "Canadians were humiliated as never before. To them the defeat was taken as a national castration." He wasn't alone in his imagery. Another writer said it was "as if the male population of this land suddenly had been sterilized by some diabolical secret plan." Things got worse before they got better. Team Canada won only one of the four games in Canada, tied another, and lost the first in Moscow before coming back to win the final three—the last game in the final minute by a single goal—apparently averting a national disaster. Irving Layton, a poet, heaved a sigh of relief: "I refrain from asking what would have happened if Team Canada had lost. Mass suicides across the country . . ."

Soccer is, of course, to many lands as hockey is to Canada. When a defeat by Poland eliminated Italy from the 1974 World Cup matches, despair swept the country. Economic and political troubles had been mounting. Now a rare source of national pride had been destroyed. Italy went into mourning. Black armbands and flags with black cloth pinned to them were seen everywhere. Brazil reacted similarly when its team also fell short of the championship that year. Black-draped coffins were carried through the streets. In Rio de Janeiro a cordon of police was needed to protect the coach's home from destruction by a mob.

Considering the importance attached to the World Cup by participating countries, what happened in Honduras and El Salvador in 1969 wasn't surprising. They weren't on the best of terms to begin with. Large numbers of semiskilled farmers from El Salvador had been migrating to neighboring Honduras, and taking jobs from unskilled locals. By 1969 there were 300,000 Salvadorians across the border, and in April Honduras began to enforce a law limiting land ownership to its native born, starting redistribution procedures in the area nearest El Salvador.

Two months later the playoff series for a World Cup berth began. Pro forma rioting followed the first game, won by Honduras on home soil; Hondurans assaulted every hapless Salvadorian trying to escape the stadium. El Salvador's fans got revenge on both counts when the series moved to their turf. Beginning to sense trouble, authorities rescheduled the third game on neutral ground, in Mexico City. But it was too late to cool tempers in high places. Less than a week after the second game the nations broke off diplomatic relations.

Two weeks later El Salvador's tanks rolled across the border, eventually penetrating forty-five miles into Honduras. Bombs rained down from Salvadorian planes onto Honduran ports and military installations. Several days of heavy fighting were followed by a month of intermittent hostilities, with each side accusing the other of atrocities and genocide. Counting civilians, casualties were estimated in the thousands.

The conflict that went down in history as the Soccer War came as no great shock to followers of international sport. In the soccer community there was even pride in having the Soccer War in the history books. In a commercial for closed-circuit telecasts of the 1974 World Cup in the United States, the narrator gushed, "You think the Super Bowl is big? Soccer excites the passions beyond belief . . ." The amazing thing was that it hadn't happened more often, that Belgium had failed to invade France in July 1975, for example.

"It was a day of national thanksgiving for this country's chauvinists," a dispatch from Paris began. "The Tour de France bicycle race was finally won by a Frenchman." As it happened, one of the chauvinists had made the victory possible. Sick of seeing a- Belgian, Eddie Merckx, win the race (as he had in five of the six previous years), the patriot took decisive action against the foreign menace: As Merckx pedaled past, the Frenchman dashed into the road and delivered a series of rabbit punches that knocked Merckx off his bike. The cyclist, who had been leading as usual, had to withdraw the next day because of kidney pain from the attack.

As for the preserver of France's honor, he answered a charge of aggravated assault by saying his actions hadn't been premeditated: "I was overwhelmed by something bigger than me." This made sense to his countrymen; one newspaper called the incident a *crime de passion*. Had Merckx won his sixth Tour he'd have surpassed every French cyclist in history—too great a disgrace to expect France to bear. As for the native winner, Bernard Thevenet, he was about to reap all the rewards a grateful homeland could bestow. He would become famous and wealthy, and if he chose to go into politics he would be welcomed like a retired general.

And elsewhere around the world? In Italy a contract bridge team was idolized. Brazil erected a statue of Maria Bueno and issued a commemorative stamp after she won the Forest Hills tennis tournament in 1959. As of 1974 the whole population of Sweden habitually stayed up until 3:00 A.M. to listen to radio broadcasts of Bjorn Borg's matches in the Western Hemisphere. When Franz Klammer, an Austrian skier, returned from the 1972 Olympics in Japan, a crowd of 200,000 greeted him at the Vienna airport. Hanni Wenzel, a skier from Liechtenstein, was picked up by the Crown Prince's helicopter after winning a slalom race at St. Moritz and ferried home to a torchlight parade by her countrymen in Vaduz.

If athletic history tells us anything, it's that fawning nations and nationalized jocks alike consider these demonstrations perfectly normal. Evidence of contemplation is sketchy. But occasionally a competitor stops to ponder the alchemy by which the muscle and coordination of an individual is turned into the spiritual gristle of a people. When Fanny Blankers-Koen returned to Amsterdam after winning four gold medals in the 1948 Olympics at London, she was received by tens of thousands of Dutchmen who lined the streets as she and her family rode by in an open coach drawn by four white horses. "All I've done is run fast," she said. "I don't quite see why people should make so much fuss about that."

. . .A School the Team Can Be Proud of

Let the football team become frankly professional. Cast off all deception. Get the best professional coach. Pay him well and let him have the best men the town and the alumni will pay for. Let the teams struggle in perfectly honest warfare, known for what it is, and with no masquerade of amateurism or academic ideals.

—the president of Stanford University, 1905

The university should hire professional teams to represent it . . . Arizona State would probably never have been known if it hadn't had a great football team. It's fine as a PR function. But it's hypocrisy to pretend it's part of the educational process in the sense of being part of the university.

—Arizona superintendent of public instruction, 1974

Few American institutions of higher learning would have passed up the chance to enroll a nineteen-year-old named Moses Malone in 1974. More than three hundred actively pursued him, although his scholastic potential seemed limited. He had struggled to keep a C average in a rural Virginia high school whose standards weren't particularly exacting, and many who came in contact with him found he had difficulty with standard English. In the enlightened spirit of progressive education those liabilities could be overlooked. Malone stood 6 feet 11 inches, and played better basketball than any other high school pupil in the United States.

Therefore colleges and universities all over the country spared no effort or expense to gain Malone's respect—and his person in their freshman class. Coaches traveled thousands of miles to Petersburg, a once-obscure town whose post office began stamping outgoing mail "Greetings from Petersburg, home of Moses Malone." The University of New Mexico's representative, John Whisenant, took a motel room and stayed three months, explaining it was cheaper than commuting. Recruiters in the Atlantic Coast Conference region, stretching from Maryland to South Carolina, popped in and out of town like route salesmen.

As the spring wore on it was hard to tell if Moses was enjoying the attention. Some reports said he often hid under his bed for hours at a time to make callers think he wasn't home. But sometimes he looked happy, as in the two-page photo layout in *Sports Illustrated* showing him alongside the red Chrysler Imperial that had miraculously become the property of an amateur athlete whose mother, his sole support, worked as a meat wrapper in a supermarket. Naturally there were whisperings about the car, as well as rumors of cash winding up in the hands of one or another of Malone's relatives. According to another story, Oral Roberts, the faith healer-evangelist, had promised that in return for Malone's signature on an Oral Roberts University scholarship, Malone's mother would be cured of her bleeding ulcer. Roberts responded, "In my heart I know there is no truth contained in this particular report."*

In *Sports Illustrated* Malone told of being "dragged" to twenty-four campuses, fawned over by each college president, "who talked to me like he wanted to be my father," and fixed up with dates. "Then when I got home those girls called me long distance and pretended they were in love with me. What kind of stuff is that?"

It was typical college recruiting stuff. Most schools that aspire to be high in the football or basketball rankings regard sex as a reliable tool. A

---

*In *Athletes for Sale* Kenneth Denlinger and Leonard Shapiro reported that when Dana Lewis, a star player, wanted to transfer to the University of Tulsa, his mother was contacted by an Oral Roberts vice president. "He said he'd just talked with the Lord and that He'd said it was His will that I stay at Oral Roberts," Lewis said. A coach at another school disclosed, "Oral told me it was God's will that Dale Brown be the next head coach . . . I told him I had . . . prayed to God myself. I said God told me to stay at LSU."

few institutions even use it to attract athletes in a minor sport. Sandy Mayer, a tennis player courted by Rice University, told Joseph Durso, author of *The Sports Factory*, he was taken to a Rice basketball game, shown the cheerleaders and asked, "Which one would you take if you could have your choice?" He chose and was told, "She's yours." Many college women apparently count it an honor to seduce on behalf of the alma mater, judging by the number that volunteer. Florida State has a corps of Gator Getters; Sweet Carolines is the collective name for the bait at North Carolina State. High school stars at the University of Louisville are greeted by Gibson Girls, named for football coach Vince Gibson, who instituted such a practice when at Kansas State, where he personally screened applicants and chose fifty a year. The practice seems not to cause concern. When a front-page photo in Louisville newspapers showed a football prospect at the local racetrack with a woman furnished by the University of Kentucky athletic department, resulting criticism focused not on the procuring service but on the vaguely disreputable practice of entertaining a recruit off-campus.

In any case, none of these blandishments had much effect on Malone. He signed up with the University of Maryland's coach, Lefty Driesell, who said he'd offered nothing more than Mother's comforting presence just two and half hours down the highway. Driesell, known as a master recruiter, was relentless in the quest, ultimately spending $20,000 of his institution's money. When the news became public, the National Collegiate Athletic Association announced it would investigate.

This was no surprise—what would have shocked cognoscenti was the assumption that any deal with Malone *was* kosher. The recruiting scandal, after all, is as trite a tradition as the pep-rally bonfire, and never had a recruit been lusted after like Moses.

As early as 1905 *Colliers* turned up evidence of doctored admissions credits, cash payoffs, and the use of out-and-out hired players. At the University of Minnesota two athletes who didn't even have a fictitious connection with the school had been paid to play in a football game. A pitcher who had transferred from Northwestern to Chicago a year earlier admitted, "You know what I'm after. It's the mazuma."

In 1929 the Carnegie Foundation reported on an investigation that paralleled *Colliers'*. When the report was published the coach of the New York University football team gathered his men around him and tried to soften the blow. "I've already read it," he said, "and you're going to be shocked when you see how little you're getting paid." The Carnegie Report could have been issued in 1975 with nothing but the dates changed: In the first half of the 1970s alone, the University of Minnesota, a huge institution, was found to have committed ninety-nine infractions, including cash payoffs and the provision of plane tickets and other gifts by alumni. Medium-sized Long Beach State University, among other things, was loose with academic requirements. (A linebacker named Charley Lewis who did not attend the school not only received credit for a full slate of courses at Long Beach, but was given straight A's.) At tiny Federal City College in Washington, D.C., credentials had been falsified and tests taken by surrogates for members of the school's excellent soccer team who were quicker with their feet than their minds.

Athletes for Sale quoted one high school basketball player who visited colleges and shopped for a scholarship: "I could count on fifty dollars and clothes if I pushed on just about every visit." Another said he was offered fifty dollars a week, a car, and a four-hundred-dollar-a-week summer job. In *The Sports Factory* Matt Snell, who became an Ohio State fullback, said, "I had offers of everything from girls to wardrobes to freezers stocked with food. . . . If you were a pretty good player you could get an alumnus to take a ticket off your hands for three hundred dollars." Wilt Chamberlain told in his autobiography of an informal arrangement under which alumni dropped by after games to hand him wads of bills; he estimated the four-year take at "fifteen or twenty thousand."

Barry Switzer, whose University of Oklahoma football team had been put on probation by the NCAA because of violations, came up with an idea for curtailing corruption in 1974. He suggested that character-molders like himself at major institutions submit to lie-detector tests. Doug Dickey of the University of Florida responded, "I'd hate to say we are in a profession where we've got to take lie-detector tests," but 75 percent of the coaches surveyed by the Associated Press thought it might be just the thing to help them all stop sinning. The Southwest Conference, in which competition was particularly intense, liked the idea so well it instituted a "polygraph rule," requiring athletes, coaches, parents, and alumni to submit if an infraction was suspected. As a result the best Texas prospects signed up to play in other regions, and conference members began lobbying for repeal of the rule.

This didn't mean schools in other parts of the country could afford to be smug. When Jack Rohan resigned in 1973 as Columbia University's basketball coach, he said the recruiting situation was the reason. "Everyone cheats, no one gets caught, and the penalties are light enough to make the risk worthwhile. It's gotten out of hand. It's impossible to document . . . I leave with a great deal of sadness. Also with a warning that you get the NCAE to come down hard on cheaters. Otherwise we'll have a major scandal again."

No one was listening. The coaches were out making sure they weren't outbid on next year's crop, flying around the country in planes provided by alumni—the fleet at the University of Alabama was known as Bear Bryant's Air Force*—with treasure provided by alumni, and sometimes even with alumni themselves, if the old grads could be useful. Lew Alcindor (now Kareem Abdul-Jabbar) was courted for UCLA in that way by Dr. Ralph Bunche. Robert F. Kennedy suggested to a New York football whiz, Richie Szaro, that he enroll at Harvard. West Point used an astronaut, Frank Borman, as a solicitor. While governor of Louisiana, John McKeithen did the job himself, carrying on a tradition begun when Huey Long's most conspicuously performed duty was orchestrating the activities of the Louisiana State football team and firing coaches whenever he found it necessary. McKeithen once said, "I must have entertained two dozen boys at the governor's mansion with milk and cookies." Kentucky could rely on one of the nation's biggest

---

*"In Alabama," according to a popular aphorism, "an atheist is a person who doesn't believe in Bear Bryant." Twice state legislators voted special exceptions to the law against naming state buildings after living persons, so that Bryant could be memorialized—on the stadium and the jock dormitory—in his own lifetime. When David Mathews was named Secretary of Health, Education, and Welfare in 1975, the *Washington Post* requested a wirephoto of the president of the University of Alabama. The picture sent was that of Bear Bryant.

celebrities, a chestnut colt. Joe Hall, the basketball coach, explained, "Secretariat is a Kentuckian all the way. We use Secretariat's name in recruiting. He's an attraction." If anyone was aware that Secretariat had raced for the Meadow Stable of Doswell, Virginia, he kept it quiet.

Most coaches count no sacrifice too great to capture a prospect. When Dan Devine switched from pro football to Notre Dame he acknowledged he'd begun wearing his hair longer than he would have preferred. "But when you get to be fifty you listen to what your teenage daughter suggests, because you've got to recruit eighteen-year-old boys." Lefty Driesell brings down the house at banquets with a vignette concerning a player whose mother kept pet snakes. He pantomimes a terrified Lefty in the living room, trembling on the inside but grinning obsequiously on the outside, while stroking the reptiles wrapped around his arms for him to admire and sputtering, "Yes, Ma'am, these are the *nicest* snakes I've *ever* seen."

In the end all of Driesell's graciousness couldn't keep Moses Malone charmed. The American Basketball Association coveted him as much as Lefty and his vanquished brethren had, and lucrative as some college deals might be, the pros could offer much, much more. It became clear in fall 1974—when Malone was due to report to Maryland—that he was undecided as to whether to play for educational or commercial purposes. The Utah Stars' pursuit could not be conducted as openly as Maryland's; after all, it violated the sanctity of university property. "We had an outpost on a hill overlooking Malone's house," the Stars' coach disclosed in *Athletes for Sale.* "We'd drive up there, park the car, check the layout to see who was around, and then we'd go down . . . Once we had to crawl through the backyard and were attacked by a big dog . . ."

Driesell did his best to monitor the pros' encroachment and twice sped to Petersburg in the middle of the night to help Malone avoid a rash decision. Meanwhile, fans everywhere took sides. Some argued he should get an education, have a degree to fall back on. Others disputed the value of a sheepskin for a fellow of Malone's intellectual interests and pointed out that a big pile of money was also something to fall back on.

When Malone, after much introspection, came out in favor of the latter view, syndicated columnist George Will applauded him: "Moses Malone . . . is skilled at putting a round ball through a hoop that is suspended from a height 3 feet and 1 inch above his head. This skill is revered by American institutions of higher learning . . . Even without the benefit of a Maryland education he figured out that Maryland could expect to get a lot more out of him than he could get out of Maryland. Maryland could expect massive ticket sales, lucrative television contracts, and a reputation as 'the UCLA of the East,' which reputation Maryland covets more than a reputation as, say, 'the Oxford of the New World' . . . all universities conspire to hold down athletes' wages. The formal name of this conspiracy is the National Collegiate Athletic Association. The NCAA is so devoted to the principle of amateurism that it doesn't want athletes to sully themselves by making real money from the NCAA members' multi-million dollar athletic programs."

This was not exactly the way the NCAA liked to think of it, but a dispassionate observer could hardly avoid the same conclusion. At the University of Michigan every football game drew more than ninety thousand paying customers, and admissions for all sports events accounted for more than $2 million a year. The athletic department there was set up as a legal entity separate from the university, with power to borrow and invest money autonomously. For the athletic director, Don Canham, a big part of the job was managing the investment fund. Canham, whose watchword was that the modern athletic director has to "hustle like a whore on Main Street," was renowned for the businesslike way in which he merchandised his product. He was a resourceful fund-raiser. On his arrival the athletic department was receiving alumni gifts of less than $50,000 a year; he soon raised the figure to more than $300,000. (That was impressive but not exceptional—the University of North Carolina, for instance, took in about $1 million a year in athletic donations.)

Canham was most famous for his advertising campaigns, particularly ticket brochures, which admirers compared to resort-area, real-estate literature. The glossy eight-page color folders, mailed to 1.2 million homes, contained not only a push on season tickets but ads for all sorts of Michigan memorabilia, from doormats to playing cards to ashtrays to lamps. It occurred to Canham that he could peddle business opportunities as well as school spirit, so he created magazine ads headlined "How to Mix Business with Pleasure . . . Try Michigan Football." As the ads put it, "winning football . . . is part of it. But for you, your friends, *customers* . . . there's much more . . . It's a unique way to entertain." Some twenty-five major colleges sent representatives to Michigan over a three-year period to learn, at the master's feet, the way to operate educational athletics. (The University of Maryland, for one, apparently took the "whore on Main Street" analogy to heart. One year the season-ticket pitch was built around Miss Maryland USA, who did commercials from the locker room and the ballfield, panting that Maryland jocks turned her on.)

Alumni are expected to be thankful for the chance to contribute to the acquisition and maintenance of gristle. Solicitors typically appeal to the alumni's pride and understanding, holding out the opportunity to rub elbows with the most important members of the community. For instance, when the William and Mary Educational Foundation was formed (a semantic subterfuge—the purpose was to enrich the athletic department), a mailing to twelve hundred carefully chosen fat cats enticed them with the prospect of meetings with the football coaches. Potential heavy contributors were tantalized with a pregame lunch with the head coach himself.

"The Fast Breakers need you," reads an "invitation to help Maryland basketball." Why? Because "Maryland cage supporters are pledged to helping Lefty Driesell make Maryland the UCLA of the East . . . Become a Fast Breaker and help the Terrapins accomplish Lefty's lofty goals." At the University of St. Louis, which had suffered fourteen consecutive losing basketball seasons, the task force charged with parting alumni from a remedial $200,000 simply asked, "Why be second class? We can be first class." No organization was more original than the booster club at Arkansas State University, which encouraged cash-short ranchers to make their contribution in meat—"an outstanding opportunity for farmers and ranchers to become involved," according to the athletic director, who promised choice stadium seats in return for choice beef.

A School the Team Can Be Proud of

It is axiomatic that alumni and local business people contribute more to a winning team than a losing one (though it then seems illogical for givers to take pride in the team's success rather than in their own ability to hand over enough money to make the success possible). Woody Hayes, who would later become famous at Ohio State, discovered the principle while coaching at his alma mater, Denison. His team was undefeated in 1947, the first time that had happened at Denison in fifty-eight years. To Hayes's astonishment $100,000 came rolling in almost immediately and practically unsolicited. The undefeated season eventually accounted for a fund of $900,000. Similarly, when the Virginia Military Institute "revitalized a stagnant program" and had a good football season, donations to athletics rose from $50,000 to $250,000.*

Once winning becomes habitual, advanced methods of extortion are employed. In 1974 the University of Oklahoma's athletic director proposed auctioning off the best seats in the football stadium, with bidding to start at $1,000. This was a variation on a successful Atlantic Coast Conference theme. With demand for seats to their annual basketball tournament spectacularly disproportionate to supply, athletic directors of the seven schools—each of which received the same number of tickets to distribute—could impose conditions. For the sake of appearances a few tickets were bestowed by lottery on the student body; the rest were peddled for whatever the market would bear. In 1976, for instance, each school sold twenty-two hundred tickets. Maryland allocated 100 to students and made the rest available on this fee schedule: contributors of $1,000 or more to the Maryland Educational Foundation (jock fund) could buy four and contributors of $500, two. To buy four from the University of North Carolina's allotment it was necessary to be a Super Ram who had not only given

*There is also an indisputable link between football-basketball records and donations for general university purposes, a reason cited by administrators for beefing up teams. A graphic example of the connection: Ohio State's aberrational football season in 1966. The team lost more games than it won. Donations to the school declined by $500,000. Even at Brown University, which could take pride in more than two centuries of academic excellence and had every reason to be inured to athletic ineptitude, contributions jumped markedly in 1975, when for the first time in generations the football team was respectable.

$1,000 for the year but a cumulative $2,200. At North Carolina State the cumulative requirement was $3,600.

This was a major advance in streamlining college sport. Games were being played for the enjoyment of people who paid the athletic department to obtain the jocks who played the games. Along with the student jock, the student spectator had been eliminated.

Coaches, whose jobs hang in the balance, understand better than anyone the need to conduct business as if the academic world is an annoyance that can't be eliminated but must be neutralized. Hired in 1974 to teach football at the University of Virginia, Thomas Jefferson's seat of genteel scholarship, Sonny Randle immediately announced: "We've stopped recruiting young men who want to come here to be students first and athletes second." The following year a math professor at North Carolina State was ordered arrested by the football coach when he refused to stop jogging on the running track while the team practiced. The coach, Lou Holtz, wasn't denying the right of a faculty member to use school facilities—he just felt there was a possibility the teacher was spying on behalf of State's next opponent.

And then there was Ohio State's Woody Hayes, who made his colleagues look like eggheads. On the rare occasions when he felt it necessary to stand up for OSU's emphasis on football, he defended it with great conviction: "Football is the most wholesome thing we have on our campus anymore." He even found it contributed to mental health. While his research showed about 25 percent of the student body at large in need of psychological counseling, "in all my years here I've sent only two of my players to a psychiatrist." One had been an exhibitionist and the other "got all caught up in religion."

The quotes are from Robert Vare's *Buckeye*, an exhaustive study of the preeminence of Hayes and his team on the OSU campus. In the tumultuous stadium of Hayes's psyche, life was football and football was life. He was a student of history who admired Napoleon for "dying a winner" and found his own offensive tactics indistinguishable from those of William Tecumseh Sherman's, to his great delight. In the Battle of Salamis, he told Vare, ". . .the Greeks beat the tail off the Persians. Only it wasn't for the national championship; it was for the world championship." On Watergate, Hayes reasoned, "The way I see it, Nixon had to cover up to win the election. Hell, I'd have done the same damn thing if any of my coaches had done something and I found out about it. My first reaction would have been: 'Well, shoot, we've done something wrong, but we can't make it right by letting the whole goddammed world know about it.'"

No man in Ohio was more famous or had more political clout. Shortly after inheriting the remainder of Richard Nixon's presidency, Gerald Ford arrived in Columbus to give a speech at OSU. He was awaited at the bottom of Air Force One's ramp by the governor of Ohio, the mayor of Columbus, and the university president. "And here," Vare wrote, "was the President . . . his political and cultural priorities in perfect order, bypassing these bemused officials and heading straight for the most important handshake of them all, that of the coach of the Ohio State football team, Woody Hayes." In a survey OSU students were asked to identify the university president, the chairman of their major department, and the football coach. About half knew the president's name. Only a few could name department heads. But just one freshman woman was ignorant of Hayes's identity.

Despite the force of Hayes's personality and philosophy, the campus was never completely free from debate on the relative importance of football. Admittedly there *was* liberalization during the Hayes years: Through faculty pressure the main library, closed on football Saturdays during the 1950s, was opened the following decade. But the faculty council unwittingly committed a grave heresy when it voted against letting the team go to the 1961 Rose Bowl, on the theory that the trip would interfere with academic work and cost the university money. A riot broke out in Columbus. Some ten thousand protesters attacked the Faculty Club with bricks and bottles. There were hangings in effigy and placards endorsing "Roses for the Bucks; Poison for the Faculty." The mob surged through the streets toward the state capitol, destroying property and lighting bonfires. The highway patrol was called in and the campus officially closed.

The editors of the Columbus *Dispatch* were disappointed, too. They published on the front page the names and addresses of faculty council members and speculated (the balloting had been secret) as to who had voted against the game. For weeks afterward teachers who had opposed the Rose Bowl, as well as those wrongly accused, got obscene mail and phone calls. The *Dispatch,* in a full-page editorial, said, "The disappointment comes as the finale of one of the finest football seasons here in the Columbus community, which has fostered college football as one of the finest traditions of academic life. . . ."

In succeeding years Hayes was to contribute to the tradition by heaving movie projectors at walls, tearing up sideline markers at games, punching spectators who came too close after defeats, smashing a camera into the face of an unwelcome photographer at practice, and using his TV show to denounce officials because their honest judgment had been "just as grossly unfair as it can be." In 1974 the student newspaper finally realized things had gotten out of hand and editorialized: "Football to the rest of the nation has become OSU. The *raison d'être,* academia, gets lost in the shadow of the goalposts. The football machine overshadows all other aspects of this university."

Hayes replied that it *should be* thus: "What else brings enthusiasm to the university and the city besides football? Otherwise you live on the blahs; you can't get up and cheer in math class."

True enough, Jack Fullen, a faculty leader who'd been engulfed in the 1961 Rose Bowl furor, said in an interview with Robert Vare, "Some positive goods do come out of football . . . My question is—is it worth the price? Is it worth it to have the distortion of values? I used to sit on the scholarship committee, and time and again we'd scrape around to try and get some money for a bright young law prospect or a physicist. But there was never any trouble getting money for an athlete. We have unlimited funds for recruiting top football players. Wouldn't we be better off recruiting top professors and students? Who knows how many scholars have stayed away from Ohio State because of our image as a full-blown football machine? I think we have been hurt by that image. I know we have."

But maybe it was no longer possible to be hurt by that image. Maybe in the average mind there was no distinction between college and football. An ABC interviewer-in-the-grandstand was told at the

A School the Team Can Be Proud of

University of Missouri, "We just live for football . . . Nothing else is important, classes or anything else. We just live for Friday when we start to party and get ready for the game." Commentators all over the country were gratified to see what happened when the University of California team improved in the 1970s. The longhairs started holding football rallies instead of protest demonstrations, igniting bonfires in homage instead of revolt. Normality, observers exulted: The leaders of tomorrow funneling their energies into the worship of hired brawn. "Perhaps there is also a dawning recognition," the *Wall Street Journal* somehow convinced itself, "that social progress will be fostered by sound ideas, argued articulately, rather than by pep rallies in the name of some vague concept of revolution." At Notre Dame, whose academic pretensions are no more modest than Berkeley's, a professor told Roger Kahn that there was no way to keep football from disrupting the atmosphere. "I try not to let it. . .but before a football Saturday there is a cicada-like nuance in my classroom. The air begins to vibrate. It is disruptive, yes."

Notre Dame, of course, is a special case, being the only American university with a nationwide nonalumni constituency. Many Catholics who attended no college identify with this foremost jock factory of their denomination; others are simply captivated by the Hollywood legends of Knute Rockne and George Gipp and the Four Horsemen. The extra-large cheering (and jeering) section make life difficult for the individual responsible for keeping the flame of football glory burning bright. Ara Parseghian, whose teams had won nearly all their games, gave up the head coaching job because it was endangering his health. Friends disclosed they had begun to fear for his life. By the end of his stint he was taking two tranquilizers, two blood pressure pills, and two sleeping pills a day, and had been inquiring about the serious illness Frank Leahy had developed while on the job a generation earlier.

"The pressures at Notre Dame are incredible," Parseghian said on resigning. "I don't think other coaches understand what it is about this place . . . There's no margin for error at Notre Dame. Every year we have to win, or contend for, the national championship. You simply cannot lose, and that's tremendous pressure . . . It's not just a state affiliation like Illinois or Iowa or even Ohio State or Michigan. It's sort of a national thing. Whatever happens, good or bad, the nation takes one position or another on it."

This warning did not dissuade others from seeking the job. The one who got it, Dan Devine, couldn't see how things could be much worse than they had in Green Bay. He was surprised at first to find a far more scholarly atmosphere than he expected at Notre Dame: Players actually were not excused from exams to attend practice. "There are millions of people who wouldn't have believed that," the dumbfounded coach said.

His hopes were dashed a few months later when Notre Dame lost a game. With the mid-season record at five wins and one defeat, rumors of Devine's imminent firing began to circulate. South Bend was rife with speculation. Devine complained, "My concentration is disrupted, and I can't prepare properly for Southern California this week." His veracity was borne out when Southern Cal romped all over the Fighting Irish. By then Devine had to acknowledge, "Everything that anyone has ever said about Notre Dame is true. I never realized what it would be like."

Satisfying followers of UCLA basketball proved just as impossible when Gene Bartow succeeded John Wooden, whose exaltation could be measured only by the grandeur in which he departed. Bob Hope, Mayor Tom Bradley of Los Angeles, and other dignitaries gathered at a testimonial and spent the evening, in the words of an observer, "expressing gratitude for being given the honor of honoring Wooden," who received a wristwatch and a Mercedes sedan. He was also given cuff links with ten diamonds each, representing the NCAA championships his teams had won; those victories were the totems that would henceforth make Gene Bartow's life miserable. After his first few months people noticed he was looking haggard and worn. His team had lost three of its first seventeen games. Bartow had lost fifteen pounds and was complaining of stomach trouble. He had stopped opening his mail, reading newspapers, listening to sports news on radio and TV. "I knew this job would have pressures, but never like this," he said. "It comes from all sides."

It doesn't take a place as big as UCLA, Notre Dame, or Ohio State for things like that to happen. Coaches everywhere have been

A School the Team Can Be Proud of

browbeaten and fired for being less than perfect; academic standards have been almost universally shunted aside; recruiting rules have been laughed at; in February 1974 one team, Morehead State (Kentucky), even made its followers happy by deliberately losing a game. Morehead's opponent was Illinois State, an independent. Since the game was to be held a tiring eleven-hour bus ride from Morehead, Coach Bill Harrell left his six best players at home. That way they'd be fresh for the important games a few days later—against Murray State and Austin Peay for the Ohio Valley Conference championship and a berth in the NCAA national tournament. Illinois State was not pleased by its resulting 39-point victory, which its athletic director called "a real hoax on the spectators and a real slam at the integrity of athletics in general." Everyone at Morehead, however, seemed to think they had properly served the highest principle of sport: landing on top of the heap. The six stars agreed that staying home had been for the best. Students polled on campus approved. Harrell argued he'd done the right thing and said he was coerced into it by the administration anyway. "Everyone who knows how much pressure there is on us understands," he said. "We felt like after we cleared it with our athletic director, we were doing exactly what we should be doing: rest up to win games. I had been told by my superiors that this is my year to win the Ohio Valley Conference. Our president told me we have to win the championship to go to the NCAA tourney. After we tied for the championship two years ago and lost a playoff, he said he didn't expect us to win every year, just every other year." Only one small flaw in the strategy emerged the next week—when Austin Peay won the pivotal game and the conference championship.

"Sports Is Like a Hurricane"

The athletic aesthetic is a tricky thing. Roy Blount, a journalist and writer of football books, once rhapsodized that "football is like improvisational theater . . . football is like sculpture . . . football is like music . . . football is like poetry." Olga Korbut, the pixie-cute Russian gymnast who made a big splash in the 1972 Olympics, took one look at the object of Blount's love and said, "What a mess these people are doing on the ground." What to say, except *de gustibus* . . . But differences of taste notwithstanding, this much is worth pointing out: For every sport that plays to an audience, there are some who perceive it as beautiful and regard it with deadly seriousness.

Bud Collins, on watching Evonne Goolagong play tennis: "The belief is in an experience—of beholding grace and athleticism and joy in a performance and of going away feeling better for it."

Stan Fischler, on hockey: "I love hockey as much as I revere a work by Rembrandt. I would be terribly depressed if some graffiti artist defaced that Rembrandt. Nowadays I have the feeling that my game of hockey has been defaced by the cretins who are running and playing the sport. I passionately hope that hockey, as I and many others once loved it, can be salvaged before it's too late."

Leonard Koppett, on the very condition of fandom: "Every sports' fan has his own personal golden age . . . a glorious period that coincides with the first full flowering of fan interest. It can happen to one fan at the age of nine, to another at the age of sixteen, but it becomes indelible at whatever point it hits and it is the true beginning of history for that particular fan. . . . "

FANS!

Except for Korbut, those quoted are sportswriters, and with all respect, none of them approaches the levels outsiders attain when it comes to taking child-play seriously or finding truth, beauty, and metaphor in every graceful stride and leap.

There may be times, as Freud insisted, when a cigar is only a cigar, but in the eyes of some beholders a baseball bat or a tennis racket is never just a literal cudgel. Syndicated columnist Joseph Kraft, rushing in where political pundits should fear to tread, interpreted the finesse that produced Arthur Ashe's triumph in the 1975 Wimbledon tennis tournament as a comment on the government's inclination to rely on brute force. After an analysis of Ashe's strategy that, to grant its due, was worthy of a fair-to-middling sportswriter, Kraft expounded on "the honor that comes from the head, not the heart. The Ashe way to victory is not the way this country traditionally favors. The usual American way is to go over the top with unstoppable power. That is how Ohio State wins football games. That is how General Eisenhower won battles . . . [Ashe] has proved that enlightenment is not a snare and planning not a delusion; that thought is not at war with resolution; that conscience does not make cowards. . . . " And so forth.

If Kraft could discover figurative depths in a tennis match (Ashe's conception wasn't all that lofty—he knew that trying to use sheer power against the harder-hitting Jimmy Connors was a sure way to lose), so could other profound thinkers intellectualize and inflate the meaning of jocks and their games. *Wall Street Journal* readers may have been surprised one morning that same year when they turned to the editorials and found, in space normally reserved for condescending fiscal advice to the administration or jabs at congressional Democrats, the publication's formal declaration that no one had ever played golf better than Jack Nicklaus. Had he not just won the Masters tournament for the fifth time? The *Journal* reasoned thus:

> *There is something satisfying about being able to identify the greatest anything of all time, but the opportunity to do so is exceedingly rare . . . But then there is Jack William Nicklaus. The Golden Bear [Nicklaus's nickname—and commercial trademark] has so clearly established himself as the quintessential golfer that if*

minority views exist on the issue they have been driven into
embarrassed silence . . . In no other human endeavor we can think
of must professionals compete against a living, breathing, absolute
standard. Imagine a young playwright shooting for the top in the
time of Aristophanes or Shakespeare . . . Mount Everest is the
highest mountain. And Jack Nicklaus is the greatest golfer of all
time.

Serious periodicals sometimes toss in bits of fluff here and there to prove they're human, but a member of the editorial board confirmed that it was not for the sake of whimsy that the readership came to be instructed on this issue. "I ride the Erie Lackawanna commuter train from Morristown, New Jersey, every day to the financial district," the editor said. "Every day I open my *New York Times* and plunge into the day's news. But I noticed on Monday morning that without even looking at the front page I turned to the sports. I looked at the fellow sitting next to me, and he had done exactly the same thing. Then I looked down the line of financiers and bankers, all reading their *New York Times*, and with very few exceptions everyone was looking at the story about Nicklaus. I just knew that before I wrote anything else, I had to write a Jack Nicklaus editorial."

The Shakespeare of golf happened to be a thirty-five-year-old midwesterner of bland personality and no visible distinguishing characteristic save the ability to smite a little ball more precisely than his contemporaries. Nothing he did had a direct bearing on the lives of editorial writers and commuting tycoons (except stockholders in his enterprises). Yet on some Monday mornings his activities were compelling enough to divert the nation's financial elite from preparations for another week of raping the small investor.

Where, if at all, had the *Journal* been injudicious? For openers, minority views about Nicklaus's paramountcy not only existed, but had not been driven into any sort of silence, embarrassed or otherwise. Readers could make reasonable claims for Robert Tyre Jones, now moldering in the grave but decades earlier virtually unbeatable and winner of thirteen major championships by age twenty-eight (Nicklaus had nine at that age); or Ben Hogan, who lost good years to a devastating auto accident; or Sam Snead; or Walter Hagen; or Byron Nelson; or Homero Blancas, who once shot a 55. Besides, the tees at every tournament were thick with young studs who often dealt this athletic Aristophanes his comeuppance.

So? What's the big deal if golfers can't be measured as precisely as mountains? Well, live pro golfers can benefit more than dead playwrights from favorable—not to say, fawning—ink in big-circulation newspapers, particularly financial journals. "Imagine a young computer firm trying to be as good as IBM . . . The Pacific is the biggest ocean and Colonel Sanders is the finest fast-food franchise." In the *Wall Street Journal?* Not in this millenium. But was Nicklaus, who peddles equipment, clothing, automobiles, and other merchandise, less a corporate entity than IBM or the Colonel?

"He served the vital function of giving us somebody to cheer," Larry King wrote in *New Times* on Sonny Jurgensen's retirement from pro football. The vital function Sonny Jurgensen served was, of course, to lure people into stadiums at prices up to fifteen dollars apiece. He was paid more than $100,000 a year because his skills made him the focal point of a game that was consciously organized to appeal to appetites for speed and violence. It was an efficient and successful enterprise: Would-be ticket buyers overran the turnstiles. Networks clawed for broadcast rights; commercial sponsors were dying to be identified with this game. And players earned gigantic salaries with all sorts of extra benefits, while remaining, by and large, thoroughly contemptuous of people foolish enough to invest money and emotion in their performances. Yet here was Larry King, professional cynic, whose custom in his regular column was to skewer commercial contrivance and institutionalized nonsense wherever he found it, defending one of the most aloof and detached of these mercenaries against a "loser label," speaking of "Sunday miracles," and thanking Jurgensen for "the considerable favor of acting out our fantasies."

What the *Wall Street Journal* and Larry King have in common with each other and every drunk who blubbers barroom paeans to his favorite jock is an unshakable faith that sports are finer, nobler than real life. King's reference wasn't personal; "*our* fantasies," he wrote, those that belong to all of us, up to and including a president who walked around with gridiron terminology swirling in his head. In fact, Gerald Ford seemed typical of a people who, not taking religion too seriously, looked to mass-audience sport for something to believe in. In the president's case there was a distinct overlap: The Rev. Billy Zeoli became his "ambassador to Christ" largely because on first meeting the then Congressman Ford he talked sports. Having conducted pregame prayer for a number of National Football League teams, Zeoli was able to offer more than the usual chapter and verse. He became not only a White House prayer-breakfast regular (along with other NFL celebrities) but also a spiritual adviser who provided the president sustenance in the form of weekly prayer memoranda.

Ford was convinced of the social value—to both city and nation—of paid athletic performers. "There are few things more important to a country's growth and well-being than competitive athletics," he once wrote. Concerning football, on whose idiom he drew regularly in official utterances, he said, "There is obviously a deep American involvement in and a great social significance to the game."

Actually, the same could be said of many games. Many years before, General Douglas MacArthur had expressed a nearly identical thought: "Nothing is more synonymous of our national success than is our national success in athletics." Before the ascendancy in the television era of pro football, there was no question in many minds but that America was baseball and vice versa. To needle Japanese soldiers during shooting lulls in World War II, GIs would shout "Fuck Hirohito!" As the emperor was descended from the gods, the Japanese needed a suitably exalted counterpart to profane. Their reply: "Fuck Babe Ruth!"

As for the idea of football as the heart and soul of the United States, this theory too has its subscribers. "One cannot understand this great country and its people without understanding its football," Fred Emery, chief Washington correspondent of the *Times* of London, once wrote. "I hold it to be a vital key to part of the politics and social mores."*

Max Rafferty, state superintendent of public instruction in

---

*Jacques Barzun: "Whoever wants to know the heart and mind of America had better learn baseball. . . . "

California, called critics of college football "kooks, crumbums, commies, hairy loud-mouth beatniks." Rafferty continued, "Football is war without killing. [Players] are the custodians of the concepts of democracy. As football players they possess a clear, bright, fighting spirit which is America itself."

Even the widely misunderstood decision by the National Football League to play its regular schedule two days after the assassination of President John F. Kennedy bolsters this viewpoint. Many Americans suspected a reluctance to give up gate receipts and television revenue, but spokesmen for the league later explained that playing the games was intended as a measure to help keep the country from falling apart in the trying days before the funeral. Twelve years later, more certain than ever of its destined role, the NFL took part in the Bicentennial celebration by sponsoring an essay contest in which teenagers were to write about "the role and importance of the NFL in American history."

Still, there were detractors. David Israel, a columnist for the *Washington Star,* sought the opinion of historians, not students, and learned from Amherst College's Henry Steele Commager, "No football leagues have any historical importance whatsoever." C. Vann Woodward, Sterling Professor of History at Yale, added, "I would support the idea that it sounds presumptuous." There was something to be said for this view. As administrator of several baseball teams over four decades, Bill Veeck had given the subject at least as much thought as has Commager or Woodward, and *he* wasn't so sure the function of sport in society should be magnified. "By being interested in sports," Veeck said, "it guarantees that when you talk about it, you won't be rebuffed. The other person will know what you're talking about. Other than sports, the only other time people can freely converse is during disasters. I guess sports is like a hurricane."

Fantasyland

Counting tears shed at the original performance in packed, hushed Yankee Stadium, together with those jerked by subsequent motion-picture dramatizations, American sports history's all-time record lachrymose moment surely must be fatally ill Lou Gehrig's declaration that "I consider myself the luckiest man on the face of the earth." (With George Gipp's fictitious plea—for Knute Rockne to ask the boys to win one for him—probably running a respectable second.)

Gehrig probably stretched the truth. According to some, he considered Babe Ruth luckier. The Babe was the one treated like a god, though he wasn't that much better than Gehrig. It was just that he had all that color and drama about him, and there was only so much room at the top. But this may be putting too fine a point on it; Gehrig's real feelings aside, the immortal line was spoken and heard as a most appropriate one for a man in his place. True, he was dying—prematurely, at that—but he'd had the *big-league career*, worn the Yankee pinstripes, guaranteed himself everlasting life in the record book (he played in more consecutive games than anyone else), been acclaimed by the masses for his prowess on the diamond.

Hadn't the poet argued (see A. E. Housman's "To an Athlete Dying Young") that it's not such a bad idea for a jock to check out before the fame wears off? Hadn't Homer believed that once you made it big in sports, there wasn't much to look forward to? *The Odyssey:* "There is no greater glory for a man as long as he lives, than that which he wins by his own hands and feet."

FANS!

This remained a timeless and universal truth in twentieth-century America. In *The Old Ball Game* Tristram Coffin recalled walking across the Philadelphia ballfield with a University of Pennsylvania colleague after a game in which the sainted Sandy Koufax had pitched. The companion stopped at the mound, pantomimed a windup, and said, "If I had that guy's left arm, damned if I'd be teaching economics." The same longing has been expressed by distinguished men of government, entertainment, literature. Justice Lewis F. Powell, Jr. of the Supreme Court once confided that, given a choice, he'd have been a pro athlete. Richard Nixon, inured to unworthiness as a Whittier College benchwarmer, often said he'd have settled for being a sportswriter. Possibly nothing is so common to American men of letters as homage to and yearning for athletic glory. Melvin Maddocks characterized John Updike's description of Fenway Park where the Red Sox play, as "rather in the tone of a lover." Irwin Shaw, whose football fantasy unfolded in "The 80-yard Run," once said, "In that sense we're all sons of Hemingway. Mailer carries it to extremes with his boxing fantasies. Jim Jones has it too." And Fitzgerald. And Malamud. And Roth, who seems unable to compose a work that doesn't deal with the great American theme. It could hardly have been an accident that in the one Roth novel that scandalized the public, *Portnoy's Complaint,* there was a single lengthy passage so pure that *Sport* magazine didn't fear to reprint it verbatim: "To be a center fielder, and nothing more," he fantasized—scatology and self-abuse had no place in such a reverie.

The roster of heavyweight authors tagging along with Muhammad Ali to his fight in Zaire moved John Leonard of the *New York Times* to indignation: "Garry Wills? Wilfrid Sheed? Norman Mailer? George Plimpton? Not to mention Hunter S. Thompson and Budd Shulberg . . . That's enough talent to bake a *Bhagavad-Gita* . . . Is this any way for grown-up writers to behave? . . . American writers go on promulgating the mysteries of sinew, the craftiness of give-and-go, safety blitz, double fault, power play, pick-off motion and betting the point spread. Can one imagine Günter Grass, Albert Camus, Gabriel Garcia Marquez and Kobo Abe similarly engaged as pompom girls? . . . American writers care, morbidly, about the Red Sox and the Knicks . . .

Fantasyland

This is the culture of little boys who'd rather grow up to be Pete Rose [a baseball player] than Gustave Flaubert; whose cathedrals are paved with astroturf . . ."

"Athletes get frozen in time," Frank Deford wrote in *Sports Illustrated*. "They get attached to a certain year. People say, 'Oh, yeah, that was his year.' 'That was Walt Dropo's year.' 'That was Dick Kazmaier's year.' 'Wasn't that Tom Gola's year?' Nobody ever says this about other people. Nobody ever said that 1776 was Thomas Jefferson's year." Deford's observations were on the death of a jockey, Tony DeSpirito. DeSpirito had had a year; he'd set a riding record. And his death took on, where Deford and others were concerned, a special dimension.

That often happens with athletes. Babe Ruth's body had lain in state and was viewed by thousands. Fans of Stanley Ketchel, the prizefighter, thought of him as having been "assassinated" despite the fact that Ketchel, in John Lardner's celebrated words, was "shot in the back by the common-law husband of the lady who was cooking his breakfast." After Howie Morenz died of complications from a broken leg sustained in a 1937 hockey game, his body was borne back to the place of his glory. Mordecai Richler described in *Esquire* the scene at the Montreal Forum: "His body was laid out at center ice and the greats of hockey took turns as guards of honour around the bier day and night . . . 15,000 fans quiet and motionless in a tribute to a man—and hockey—that has never been matched." Like Morenz, Steve Prefontaine was eulogized in the arena. Schools were dismissed early in Coos Bay, Oregon, so that children could get to the stadium where their distance-runner townsman, killed in a car accident, lay dressed in his Olympic tunic under a timer that began ticking as his former coach began the eulogy and stopped at 12 minutes, 36.2 seconds—the clocking Prefontaine had hoped to achieve for three miles.

The mystique of life and death carries over to victory and defeat. George Allen, coach of the Redskins, put it succinctly to the press after a tough loss, "Losing is like death." Figurative language being as indispensable to a coach as his whistle and clipboard, it was first assumed that this was just Allen's hyperbole for disappointment. Not so.

He had actually worked out a system of jock thanatology. In a magazine article he elaborated: "If players are willing to accept a season in which they win half their games, they will win half their games and they will emerge half alive. A lot of players are half dead and don't know it. If they lose all their games and the fact does not kill them, they are already dead. Some players are dead. This is the way I feel." Even Allen's manner after games seemed attuned to the conceit. After victories he held forth above the crowd of reporters from a chair set on a large table. After defeats the chair was on the floor. Some observers half seriously suspected George meant to shorten the tumble that would signal the Grim Reaper's expected arrival. On such occasions Allen even managed to assume an ashen complexion and a rasping voice, as if to confirm that he *did* have one cleated foot in the grave.

With a substantial portion of the National Football League at least halfway across the River Styx, and so much emphasis on spiritual implications throughout the athletic community, it's no wonder so many happenings are ascribed to unseen powers. "The Bosox have the aura of baseball destiny about them," wrote a witness to Boston's 1975 American League pennant drive, "even their misfortunes are blessed." How else to account for the success of a team experts considered inferior to its opponents? Evidently, Providence looks after the underdog, as it seemed to some in 1969, when the New York Mets were thought to have no chance in the National League race. "It was, everyone said, a matter of destiny," wrote Paul Gardner, a detached Britisher, in *Nice Guys Finish Last.**

Neil Offen, author of *God Save the Players*, wrote, "When the Mets won it all in 1969, it was a transcendental event, much more than just

---

*When the Mets did win, the only thing to compare it to—the only thing more gloriously inexplicable—was the finish of the 1951 season when Bobby Thompson's home run in the last inning of the last playoff game won the pennant for the New York Giants.

Thomas Kiernan's book on the subject is titled with the phrase that came to describe that swing of a baseball bat: *The Miracle at Coogan's Bluff.* "Coogan's Bluff," he wrote, "is a sacred place . . . a miracle transpired . . . unfurled like a banner from heaven." And, in fact, Thompson's homer had all the consequences of an explicit friendly greeting from the Almighty: "Strong men wept and embraced perfect strangers, people danced in the streets and booze flowed like water. It was the armistice, Lindbergh's homecoming and the repeal of Prohibition all wrapped up in one crazy, unbelievable event."

baseball or sports. My mother, who has always said she'll understand baseball when they start to play it in Yiddish, was excited by that summer. She didn't know what was happening, exactly, but she knew it was something important and something good . . . the cosmic underdog was breaking through."

It could work the other way. When the basketball team in town failed in the 1975 finals the *Washington Post* editorialized: "The Bullets seemed fated from the beginning of the final round to lose the National Basketball Association championship . . . if they hadn't lost the way they did . . . the Fates would have found some other way for them to lose."

Attentive as they are to those responsibilities, the Fates don't spend all their time choreographing basketball playoffs and pennant races. Some working hours are devoted to planning the lives of unborn male children. "I sincerely believe that there is such a thing as a Dodger," Steve Garvey, a Dodger, told a reporter. "I don't think there's such a thing as a Padre or a Brave or a Met. I sincerely think that I was born to be a Dodger."

Garvey may have been influenced by the discovery of his faith-healing ability, a gift seemingly granted very few despite the spiritual bonds between so many fans and so many jocks. Steve Garvey may not have been a Babe Ruth, but he certainly was a hero by contemporary standards, and far better suited to the role than the dissolute Babe.* Clean-cut, respectable in thought and deed, he had been an Athlete-for-Nixon. Both he and his wife, Cyndy, had an abiding respect for their country's institutions: Shortly after Cyndy bore a daughter she saw the message, "Steve Garvey just had a baby girl, Krisha Lee," across the television screen in her hospital room during a World Series break. "I had told him on the phone that her name was Bliss Ann," Cyndy later told *Sports Illustrated.* The nurse argued that it was too late to change the original choice, already entered on hospital documents. "But they changed it," Cyndy said. "It had been on television, after all."

*Somewhere there may be a trivia buff with a list of the expiring young lives pulled back from the brink by the fulfilled promise of a personalized Ruthian home run; going by stories handed down, the teenage population of the 1930s would have been greatly reduced if not for the baseball-healing of the previous decade.

FANS!

The off-field highlight of Garvey's career was his Ruthian regeneration of a small fan's life. This is how he told it in 1975:

In 1971 I went to Orthopaedic Hospital in Los Angeles to visit a boy . . . who was suffering from cancer. The boy had just had an operation to remove the lower part of the leg, and he was in a bad way. It was a hollow feeling, seeing him there on the bed . . . The doctors said he had an 18 percent chance of living. He was heavily sedated.

I took his small hand in mine. His mother said, "Ricky, Steve Garvey's here."

And I started to feel a little squeeze from that ten-year-old's hand. He started opening his eyes. Although he couldn't talk, when he opened his eyes it also opened mine. I could feel the strength in that little boy's hand. I knew then that Steve Garvey had a place.

Last year in Dodger Stadium, Ricky walked from the dugout to first base with Steve Garvey on an annual night for crippled children. I don't really believe that I have any special powers. But Ricky that night gave me a medal with an inscription that said, "To Steve Garvey, thank you for giving me the will to live."

Whatever mystique attaches to ballplayers and their deeds, belongs by extension to their tools and garments and the very bricks and girders of the places in which they play. So it was natural that considerable interest should develop around Henry Aaron's 715th home run and the tangible item most closely related to it—a baseball. Perhaps in the context of American manhood, there is no greater achievement than to have hit more home runs than all others; to one writer Babe Ruth's decades-old mark of 714 "glowed in the consciousness of American sport like a pale ring around a planet." It mattered little that the incumbent god and his successor had played in different eras, under different conditions, against different pitchers, in different-sized ballparks, and had hit their home runs at different rates relative to times at bat; a cataclysmic point in American history was approaching. NBC television realized this and made plans to interrupt regular programming for homers 714 and 715. (As luck would have it, 715 came during a nationally telecast game.)

Fantasyland

More than 100 reporters, assigned by their publications to the Aaron beat, spent September 1973 and the first week of the 1974 season going everywhere the Atlanta Braves went. Complex as they were, the logistics of reporting the feat were nothing compared to preparations for tracing and recovering the ball whose flight would denote the great moment. That was one important baseball.

A ball must fly over a fence in order for a home run to be created. This is not true in the case of an ordinary run, an annoying circumstance for major-league baseball in 1975, when it chose to beat the drums a little by honoring its millionth run. The first, if anyone cared, had been scored by Wes Fisler of the Philadelphia Athletics on April 22, 1876. The millionth, if anyone still cared, might be scored by anyone on any of twenty-six teams; therein lay the need for a computer hookup—with Mel Allen and Ralph Branca doing the flacking at millionth-run central in New York—joining telephones in every stadium to electronic, digitally timed clocks accurate to a thousandth of a second, so that the correct run was sure to be identified even if two players appeared to be crossing home plate simultaneously in Kansas City and Anaheim. By and by, with the computers whirring ceaselessly, Bobby Watson of the Houston Astros touched his spikes to home plate with No. 1,000,000. Watson had scored on another player's home run, and since he had gotten to second base on his own merit the ball was only of incidental relevance. As for the millisecond of his crossing, significant or not, there was no way to package it. The only answer was to take Watson's shoes and ship *them* off to the Baseball Hall of Fame.

In the Aaron melodrama the ball was everything. Private collectors coveted it like a rare and curse-free gem. The first bid announced publicly was $5,000. An Ohioan doubled it. Hearing this, two Georgia men offered $11,111 and a pledge to keep the ball in Georgia. Next a Baltimorean raised the ante to $15,000. Finally, in the closing days of the chase, Sammy Davis, Jr. (the song and dance man) said he'd put up $25,000.

The baseball hierarchy had its own ideas, of course, as well as sophisticated plans to foil potential counterfeiters. Whenever Aaron came to bat, the game was stopped long enough to introduce balls from a special stock, marked with appropriately complex code numbers in indelible ink. If 715 should wind up in the hands of one of the pirates outfitted with baseball gloves, fishnets, and other receptacles (leftfield grandstands, where—Aaron being righthanded—the ball was likely to arrive, had been occupied by such mobs since well before No. 700 was struck), at least it could be ransomed without fear for its authenticity.

Aaron hit No. 714, tying the Babe, in Cincinnati on the first day of the 1974 season (NBC broke into a soap opera, "Another World," for the replay, and Western Union announced a record for telegrams sent to an individual) and failed to hit another before the home opener a few days later. All Atlanta was alive with anticipation. Disc jockeys were giving generous air time to two new hit songs, "Hammerin' Hank" and "Move Over, Babe, Here Comes Hank." About $2,000 worth of fireworks had been assembled on Capitol Avenue, behind the outfield, hooked up to a detonator. The packed stands were full of celebrities and baseball dignitaries. There were cannons to be fired and balloons to be released.

The shallow part of the outfield was painted with a large red, white, and blue map of the country: This was the site of the pregame "Henry Aaron, this is your life" ceremony, which began with Aaron's being escorted to the map under a gauntlet of crossed baseball bats held by teenaged girls in miniskirts and blouses with Aaron's uniform number (44) printed on them. Aaron's parents were led to the approximate location of Mobile, Alabama, where he was born. The scout who brought him to the major leagues stood on Milwaukee, the Braves' home at the time. A team executive stood on Bradenton, Florida, the training-camp site where Aaron made the starting lineup.

Aaron walked in the first inning. Next time up, in the fourth, he hit Al Downing's second pitch over the leftfield fence. According to Phil Musick, Aaron's official biographer, "Atlanta Stadium exploded, literally." George Plimpton, there to write *Hank Aaron: One for the Record,* retained his grasp of English usage but fared no better than Musick with his composure; he found "the notepaper shaking in my hand." This was a common symptom. A Japanese newspaperman wrote (in language disconcertingly reminiscent of John Hersey's quotes from

Hiroshima survivors), "I saw it. I know I have to be calm. But I find it impossible to keep my writing hand from continuing to shake." The reporter from *El Sol de México* ended his account with, "We lived through this historic moment, the most fabulous in the world. Thanks to God we witnessed this moment of history."

Plimpton tried to assess the impact of this home run: "It was a simple act by an unassuming man which touched an enormous circle of people, indeed an entire country. It provided an instant which people would remember for decades—exactly what they were doing at the time of the home run that beat Babe Ruth's great record of 714 home runs . . . whether they were watching it on a television set, or heard it on a car radio. . . ." (Interestingly enough, Thomas Kiernan ascribed the same sort of memorability to the Giants' 1951 "miracle" and claimed that it was the "single most commonly recalled event in the American experience" between the death of Franklin Roosevelt and the assassination of John Kennedy.) Home run 715 seemed to have as much effect on those who missed it as those who saw or heard it; having had the foresight to station a reporter-photographer team outside an Atlanta Stadium toilet, the *Atlanta Journal* got an exclusive on the tragedy of a man who went at the wrong moment, and in Florida a cab driver died after shooting himself because his wife forced him to turn off the TV (before the home run) and go to work.

As for the ball, its destiny was preordained. Luckily, in Atlanta the home-team bullpen lies between the leftfield fence and the retaining wall of the stands; the home run ball had dropped into the glove of relief pitcher Tommy House, who had already made up his mind to turn it over to his teammate without seeking a reward. So the transfer of the ball to its rightful owner was not besmirched by grubby commerce. Nor was there any question of Aaron's bartering the ball for material gain. He understood that it belonged to the ages. Without ado he handed it over to the proper authorities, to be taken to the one place sacred enough for its permanent repose. Henceforth, the holiest relic of American sport would be kept under lock and key at the Hall of Fame in Cooperstown, New York, like a thousand subordinate icons.

Another baseball, coincidentally, had been the rationale for the

FANS!

Hall's existence. In 1935 Abner Graves had found in his attic in Cooperstown an old ball that, it was inferred, must surely have belonged to his ancestor, Abner Doubleday. Doubleday was celebrated as the inventor of baseball. He wasn't, of course; the game had developed from ancient English pastimes, but Americans needed a clear-cut domestic origin to believe in. Now that Doubleday's personal baseball had been discovered, a special place was needed to preserve and revere it, "a shrine," as Paul Gardner put it, "where the faithful could come and view the sacred objects." With funds from the New York state legislature and private help the project was begun, and in 1939 (the supposed centennial of Abner Doubleday's brainstorm) the Hall of Fame was dedicated by President Roosevelt.

Before long other sports imitated baseball, validating Gardner's religious metaphor. Dr. John P. Koval, a De Paul University sociologist, described people drawn to football memorabilia as "pilgrims like those who flocked to touch the robes of Christ . . . I imagine people staring at an old football in a glass case . . . like bones of a saint or splinters from Christ's cross." Only a mystery of faith could explain the pleasure afforded by such visions, since the actual sight of a ball is only minimally fascinating. One envisions a stupefying scene in Cooperstown, the visitor following the guide from crypt to crypt, hearing " . . . the one Henry Aaron hit for his 715th . . . and this is the one Mickey Mantle hit for his 500th . . . and this is Roger Maris's 61st . . . and this is the one Bobby Thompson . . ." On the other hand, there is no accounting for what will hold the attention of a fan. The pro football Hall of Fame specializes in reassembling entire outfits worn by the greats. The uniforms of Jim Brown, Sammy Baugh, Lou Groza, and Sonny Jurgensen are on display there. So are warmup hoods worn by two members of the '25 Pottsville Maroons, along with the Anthracite Coal Trophy won by the Maroons that year; the hat worn by coach Potsy Clark of the Detroit Lions, famous for its battered appearance; a helmet worn by Tony Canadeo; the bronzed shoes of placekickers Ace Parker and Ben Agajanian; a piece of the goalpost from the 1958 championship game; along with the bass drum of the Baltimore Colts' marching band, and the wrist band on which the replacement for an injured Baltimore quarterback noted plays, so as not to forget the signals, in 1965. The golf collection, going more for glamour, contains a picture of young Franklin Roosevelt hitting a 5-iron shot; the golf seat the Duke of Windsor used while watching tournaments; a set of clubs President Ford used for one round; President Eisenhower's personal clubs—donated after his death by his wife, Mamie—inscribed with his signature encircled by five stars; and an excellent replica of Bobby Jones's actual Calamity Jane putter.

By no means is the accumulation of such mementoes restricted to these museums. Untold numbers of collectors trade constantly at conventions and in their own publications, the bulk of transactions being in the picture cards that came in cigarette packs in the old days and in bubblegum packs now; there was once a display of 200,000 cards at the Metropolitan Museum of Art in New York and a single specimen can be worth more than $1,000. But many collectors are after the same scorecards, statuettes, medallions, and garments that are staples of the halls of fame. When the renovation of Yankee Stadium began in 1974, the old seats were peddled to the public ("When Babe Ruth hit his 60th home run—this seat was there!") for $7.50 each plus five empty Winston crushproof boxes. In 1974, *Sports Illustrated* told the story of a Pittsburgh man with eight rooms full of such astonishing memorabilia that a city councilman had called for the establishment of a local museum so that the citizens might not lose "this treasure," and the chairman of the Smithsonian Institution lamented his inability "to convince my people in Washington that such an enormous collection exists in somebody's residence." For sheer extravagance it's likely no one ever outdid Joan Whitney Payson. Payson owned the New York Mets from their birth until her death; she had bought a team because her beloved New York Giants had moved to San Francisco, taking with them Willie Mays. When Mays grew too old to be of use to San Francisco, she bought his contract—not in the illusion that he could help the Mets, but to have him as a souvenir. The situation provoked so much derision that a few years later, when the Milwaukee Brewers purchased Henry Aaron from Atlanta, management hastened to assert, "We haven't bought a piece of nostalgia."

Shrines, like memorabilia, are in the eye of the beholder. Many consider the ballpark itself a holy place, its destruction an unspeakable desecration. It is altogether possible that more piteous cries have been wailed about the demolition of Brooklyn's Ebbets Field than any other torn-down American structure. No one lamented that playground more eloquently than Roger Kahn, who wrote, "I have been trying to find a single memory so vivid and so real that one can understand, with the shock of recognition, what the place called Ebbets Field once meant. It was my ballpark and before that it was my father's ballpark . . . It was the Elysium of boyhood . . . The wrecker's ball, crashing against Furillo's wall, destroying mortar, laying waste a monument. Steam shovels assaulting soil that had felt the spikes of Reese and Robinson. We thought, we had always thought, that Ebbets Field would stand for centuries."

It's a Living

I've got nothing good to say about my short stay in Japan playing baseball," Joe Pepitone wrote in 1974. Like many another washed-up big-leaguer, he had crossed the Pacific with justifiable hopes of prolonging his career in a land where a marginal American could still look slicker than most of the native talent. Naturally there were cultural adjustments to make, but working conditions were good and foreigners made to feel welcome. Or so American fans had been led to believe. In an essay published in the *New York Times* Pepitone disabused his countrymen of the illusion that Japanese baseball was a hospitable milieu for the Western jock.

True, "the fans loved Americans . . . give you the shirts off their backs." True, when Pepitone and wife deplaned in Tokyo they were given "about twenty dozen roses." True, he was provided with an interpreter, his $2,000-a-month apartment was paid for by the team, his salary was $70,000 a year. *But:* "It just wasn't major league. I had to carry my own bag. I never carried my own bag in the United States, and I wasn't about to start doing it in Japan."

That complaint could evoke only sympathy from any knowledgeable fan. None but the uninformed or sadistic could fail to agree that Pepitone had been subjected to an intolerable humiliation. He was conditioned to a certain way of life—he was a *star athlete.* "Membership in this golden company," wrote Pat Jordan, a former baseball player himself, "brings a host of privileges. For an athlete certain rules are suspended, amenities not required, life's unpleasantness diminished and his every deficiency muted in the eyes of non-athletes. In his presence, the conversation invariably revolves around the athlete, his talent and his sport. Even far removed from a stadium he remains the center of attention, the hub of a private universe that is satisfyingly simple. An athlete floats above the complex and the disagreeable, which become for him the unreal. His private world is the real world."

One of Babe Didrikson Zaharias's biographers quoted a friend who was with the golfer when she took a liking to a wristwatch in a store window: "She said she'd always wanted one, and the next thing I know, we're in the Rolex office. She said to the receptionist, 'I'm Babe Zaharias, and I want to see the boss.' Babe was invited into his office . . . They gave her a gold Rolex. They gave me a gold Rolex. They gave her another gold Rolex for George. In those days it was worth $1,000." Restaurant tabs are commonly picked up by owners who are thrilled to see celebrity jocks in their establishments. Speeding tickets turn into friendly "warnings" when cops discover the car pulled over is driven by a big-name athlete. Many women—"bimbos," as jocks call the women at their disposal—consider it an honor to be allowed to provide gratification.

The company of jocks is sought in the best social circles, college stars mixing with wealthy alumni, pros with team owners and their ultrarich associates, tennis players and golfers with the country-club society whose grounds are used for their tournaments. Since golf is a pastime of the old and distinguished, opportunities to make the right contacts are plentiful, and for someone of Arnold Palmer's stature even ceremonial rounds with presidents become a bore. On a swing through Washington for an exhibition in 1975 he told reporters he planned to play with friends at Burning Tree, home club of every president since Taft. Would Gerald Ford be in the foursome? "No," Palmer said, "and if he joins us, he'll be a fifth member of our group." Next, Palmer was off to Brussels for a round with King Leopold of Belgium.

Some aren't so cavalier about the fawning attention of the world's statesmen. For Muhammad Ali the thrill never seems to wear off. On his first visit to the White House, at Ford's invitation, he exulted, "My meetings with presidents of countries are completed now," and recited a list of other heads of state who had received him. In a *Playboy* interview, he said, "I was over in Ireland and had dinner with Jack Lynch, the prime minister. I wined and dined with King Faisal of Saudi Arabia." He told Roger Kahn, "In Egypt Nasser offered me his own daughter in marriage, and I coulda lived there by the Nile . . . the Italian government has expressed serious interest in rebuilding the Coliseum so I can fight Foreman there." While dining with Prime Minister Tun Abdul Razak of Malaysia, he announced proudly over a phone hookup to a New York press conference, "We are here in the White House in Malaysia . . . " (Robert Lipsyte, who accompanied Ali to England, found him constantly thanking "you lords and you common market everyday people.")

Lesser jocks are catered to by lesser politicians, a contact that has led some aging athletes to look to politics as a reasonably soft second career. Major-league baseball sent Wilmer (Vinegar Bend) Mizell to Congress, and pro football contributed Jack Kemp. Two old track-and-field heroes, Bob Mathias and Ralph Metcalfe, also were elected to the House. Bud Wilkinson, former University of Oklahoma football coach, ran for Senate in 1964 and, according to analysts, would have whipped Fred Harris had the Democrat not had Lyndon Johnson's landslide victory over Barry Goldwater going for him. When Sonny Jurgensen retired from pro football he said he'd already been approached to run for Congress by Virginia politicos who were certain the vastly popular quarterback would appeal overwhelmingly to the electorate.

The next best thing to politics is show business, which not surprisingly has a rich history of aggrandizement founded in sporting fame. According to Rex Lardner, as long ago as 1889 heavyweight boxing champ John L. Sullivan was getting more offers to appear on stage than he could possibly accept. From the shower of propositions that fell after his knockout of Jake Kilrain, Sullivan chose a role in which he played a blacksmith in a touring melodrama; he actually shaped horseshoes on stage. Succeeding titleholders followed Sullivan's example. James J. Corbett, even before becoming champ, appeared in a play called *Gentleman Jack* and later became a vaudevillian. Bob Fitzsimmons, like Sullivan, was cast as a blacksmith. Jim Jeffries played the lead in *The Man from the West*.

A generation later the biggest sports stars of the period, Jack

FANS!

Dempsey and Babe Ruth, capitalized on their fame in vaudeville. After the 1926 World Series Ruth went on a twelve-week tour at $8,333 a week, one of the highest salaries in the business. Johnny Weismuller cashed in on three Olympic swimming medals by becoming Tarzan on the screen. His act was followed—and improved on—by Sonja Henie, the Norwegian figure skater, who became the third-leading box-office draw in the movie industry in the 1930s and reportedly earned more than $1 million a year.*

In the 1940s Babe Zaharias worked up an elaborate vaudeville routine. Her amateur athletic status had been called into question because of an endorsement for Dodge cars, and after playing harmonica at a Chrysler auto-show exhibit she took her act on the road. She'd open by sashaying down the aisle singing, "I'm Fit as a Fiddle and Ready for Love." Then she'd blow a few selections on the harmonica (on which, by all accounts, she was a near-virtuoso), strip down to a running outfit to demonstrate her form over hurdles set up on the stage, and finish by driving plastic golf balls into the audience.

In recent years Maury Wills, Don Drysdale, Johnny Bench, Willie Davis of baseball, Rosey Grier of football, and Jerry Quarry of boxing have all taken a crack at nightclub singing, mostly with modest success. Heavyweight Joe Frazier followed suit at Las Vegas, only to fall into the orchestra pit and break his ankle. Mark Spitz, the swimmer who won seven gold medals in the 1972 Olympics, put together an act intended for the showroom of a Las Vegas casino and tried it out at a Los Angeles amusement park. The *Los Angeles Times'* reviewer opined, "Spitz dances briefly and is winded. Spitz sings, though it is impossible to distinguish his voice from the eight other singers shouting into the mikes beside him. After each introduction Spitz runs offstage. I can understand why."

The trick, of course, is to get to the point where the song-and-dance is unnecessary, where the name itself is a form of capital that keeps

*The *Sport* magazine roster of athletes, active and retired, with movie credits now includes: O. J. Simpson, Ken Norton, Timmy Brown, Keith Wilkes, Alex Karras, Fred Williamson, Jim Brown, Rosey Grier, Kareem Abdul-Jabbar, Don Meredith, Joe Kapp, Archie Moore, Fred Biletnikof, Dick Butkus, Larry Csonka.

multiplying spontaneously. One of the few jocks who ever reached that financial nirvana is a man named Edson Arantes do Nascimento, known everywhere on earth as Pele. There were few countries where this most famous soccer player in history could safely walk the streets without bodyguards. The enormity of this struck Pele in Los Angeles as he strolled with his wife along Hollywood Boulevard, and it suddenly occurred to him that he wasn't hemmed in by a swarm of frenzied worshippers. He lifted his wife in joy and shouted, "I'm free, I'm free!"

Such adulation has its rewards, of course: For example, the roughly $5 million (estimates and published reports ranged from $4.7 to $7 million) he was offered to play for the New York franchise of an American soccer league that was struggling financially for its existence. The announcement of his acceptance was worth a three-column headline on the front page of the *New York Times*. A Rumanian member of the New York Cosmos, approaching his new teammate for the first time, crossed himself and said, "I dreamed of someday just shaking your hand. But to play with you, this is a miracle." During an early game in Boston Pele was set upon by a pack of souvenir hunters; he'd have been stripped naked had he not learned long before to wear two pairs of shorts. Only seconds after the fans got to Pele, his personal bodyguard reached the star, throwing himself over Pele's body, as Secret Service agents are instructed to do if someone starts shooting at the president. Back in his homeland two songs he wrote hit the top of the Brazilian charts; even his own brand of coffee, Cafe Pele, became the best-selling coffee in the country. And in 1961, when it was feared that his contract might be bought by a team in another country, the Brazilian legislature declared him a national resource, making his export illegal.

He was called Brazil's most important ambassador. He acquired more sobriquets than Babe Ruth: at home *perola negra* (the black pearl), in France *la tulipe noire* (the black tulip), in Chile *el peligro* (the dangerous one), in Italy *il re* (the king). When Queen Elizabeth made an official visit to Brazil in 1968, she requested a meeting with Pele. After a game in England Prince Philip went to the field to shake Pele's hand rather than waiting, as customary, for the player to approach the royal box. His travels were state secrets, guarded by codes known only to top-security officials: "The Big Crocodile will go to Frankfurt. . . . " His presence interrupted political disputes in Algiers and Khartoum, and caused a two-day truce to be observed in the war between Nigeria and Biafra.

Pele was fabulously wealthy before joining the Cosmos. As of his retirement the previous year, he was the biggest individual taypayer in Brazil; the government's piece of his action averaged about $48,000 a month. Twice a year he met with the federal tax minister for readjustments. His annual income was estimated at $2 million, much of it generated by a company established in Brazil to administer his fortune and merchandise his trademark. He owned apartment buildings, valuable coastal real estate, and millions of dollars' worth of securities. He was paid $200,000 a year to drink Pepsi and a comparable amount to wear Adidas shoes. His home—with private soccer field and 40-seat movie theater—was valued between $600,000 and $1 million. The Santos team paid him a salary of $400,000 a year, plus $10,000 for each exhibition game (average: forty a year). On exhibition tours Pele collected as he went; once he was arrested in Salisbury, Rhodesia, by customs officials wanting to know why he was carrying a briefcase with $100,000 in cash. Even his "retirement" was lucrative. Pele made fortunes playing "farewell" tours to dozens of countries for several consecutive years, until even the most gullible worshipper grew skeptical of claims that *this was absolutely* the final, ultimate, last chance to see Pele play.

But the New York contract was bigger than anything Pele had ever seen before. Gerald Eskenazi wrote in the *New York Times* of a phone interview with Pele's manager, who said, ". . . we're sitting on the floor of the living room with an electronic calculator trying to figure out how much money he'll make. We're converting the dollars to *cruzeiros*. But we don't have enough digits on the calculator." The Cosmos' general manager, Clive Toye, denied rumors that part of the team's obligation was to pay Pele's income tax and put the value of the package at about $4.5 million for three years. Officials of the team, owned by Warner Communications Company, said the return was almost sure to exceed the investment. For one thing, the Cosmos could expect to gross an extra $100,000 a home game from spectators who never would have paid a cent to see Pele-less soccer. With fifteen home games a season, that amounted to $1.5 million, not including extra parking, hotdog, and beer receipts. The Cosmos, moreover, would henceforth share in gate receipts as visiting team, getting 50 percent of the gross above the opponent's pre-Pele average. Warner was to receive $250,000 a year for handling Pele's worldwide licensing and endorsements, and there would also be plenty of exhibition games, presumably including—in the not-too-distant future—more of those lucrative farewell tours. In all, by renting the most popular soccer player in the world, Warner expected to gain about $2 million a year.

In the history of jock worship only one man has accumulated more financial clout. By virtue of skill at golf and what is called (in the contemporary devaluation of the word) "charisma," Arnold Palmer is credited with the creation of an industry. Palmer's personality has supposedly made golf fans of millions who barely noticed the exploits of earlier competitors. Unlike Ben Hogan, who habitually wore a white linen cap, and Sam Snead, who favored straw and was bald anyway, Palmer went bareheaded and let the breeze muss his hair. When bearing down hard on the last few holes of a tournament, he had a crowd-pleasing habit of throwing his cigarette aside and hitching up his pants. He generously shared his emotions with the audience, spanning the range of facial expressions from anguish to ecstasy with the facile professionalism of a polished actor. He was friendly and extremely accessible to the media.

Early in his career Palmer won a few tournaments excitingly, by making a "charge" at the finish, a plot device that is more arresting to sports fans than to devotees of old cavalry movies. The expression "Palmer charge" became a cliché in good standing and outlived by at least two decades the few actual heroics that brought it into use. Palmer alone, people said, was the reason huge crowds began paying to watch golf tournaments, which enabled sponsors to pay exciting-sounding amounts of prize money ($100,000 to $200,000 a week became common during the Palmer years). This influenced television networks to broadcast more tournaments, which made even more money available to the touring players and increased outside opportunities by giving them more recognition than they'd ever had before. "His influence increased prize money from $600,000 in 1954, when he turned pro, to $7.2 million in 1972," Palmer's ghostwriter said in one of his autobiographies.

That didn't even begin to tell the story of Palmer as a redistributor of wealth. Besides the benefits to his colleagues from that prize-money explosion, there was a powerful urge planted in who-knew-how-many Americans to try to do what Arnie did. Millions took up golf for the first time. If, then, Palmer gets credit for all the additional golf clubs, balls, clothing and accessories sold, golf courses and clubhouses built, maintenance thereof, taxes thereon, whiskey drunk therein, and all jobs appurtenant thereto—his contributions to the game and the national economy would have to be reckoned in the billions.

Arnie didn't do badly by himself either. Estimates of his net worth hover around $20 million, and it may far exceed that amount. He reportedly received $8 to $12 million for selling off some of his conglomerate's assets to NBC. The conglomerate—Arnold Palmer Enterprises—had included a golf equipment firm, laundry franchises, clothing, and other concerns. Oddly enough, Palmer still had trouble believing he was really rich. Having grown up in a family that struggled through the Depression, "he keeps thinking of hard times," according to his book. Once, gazing contemplatively at his powerful forearms, he told his agent that no matter what happened, he'd always be able to dig ditches. Of course, if Palmer wanted to stop thinking of hard times, he could look out the window at the acreage he owns or the country club to which he also holds title. He could walk down the street to the airport where his personal jet is parked. (In Gates Learjet ads—the subdued, corporate sort that show up only in those publications with good demographics—Palmer was identified as "*businessman,* professional golfer, pilot . . .") He could fly the jet to Orlando, Florida, to his 27-hole private golf course, "a place to go to sharpen up for the winter tour . . . I have a condominium there . . . I also use it for taping television commercials. . . ."

If Palmer's huckstering activities were so hectic as to require his own private golf scenery, Joe Namath could have used an entire film studio. Namath's case was special; most athletes' income is directly attributable to their skill and the public's respect for it, but Namath has benefited from other people's propaganda. The strategist was David ("Sonny as in Money") Werblin, owner of the New York Jets in 1964, the year Namath finished playing football at the University of Alabama and was drafted by Werblin's American Football League team. This was during the premerger period, and Werblin wanted not only to win Namath from the older, more-respected National Football League but to do it in a way that would glamorize his team and, incidentally, the AFL. So he offered what, at the time, was an outrageously lavish sum: $400,000 over four years.

Then, instead of lamenting the horrifying inflation in the price of a good quarterback, he turned Namath, who already was a $400,000 wonder who had to be seen by anyone with a vague interest in football, into a sex symbol recognizable to everybody. This was accomplished by lodging Namath in a plush penthouse apartment, on what was then known as the swinging East Side, with llama-skin rugs and a ceiling mirror above the bed. Photographers were always welcome. While flacks distributed a steady supply of tales about Namath's appeal to and prowess with women, the principal abetted the operation with an autobiography loaded with smirking, giggly passages. Presto: an amiable bumpkin became Don Juan. "In another century," Mike Royko, the syndicated columnist, marveled, "somebody with his chronic droopy-eyed leer would have been pegged the village idiot. And I remember when a quarterback's most famous appendage was his arm." But, while the Roykos sneered, the Werblins and Namaths collected, the owner hauling in invigorated gate receipts and radio and TV contracts and the player accumulating ancillary rewards. On Madison Avenue Namath was recognized as a natural for any commercial in which sex might help push the product. No cleverness or complexity called for— just a few bosomy girls draped on Namath's physique, a few monosyllabic expressions of ecstasy, and America's favorite leer. The admen got more creative as they went along, progressing from shave cream to shirts to bedsheets to pantyhose, and as Namath's outside income increased, so did his football salary, until it approached $500,000 a year.

By that time baseball finally had someone comparable, at least in terms of financial excitement. It happened by accident. Owners had long since eliminated any competition for players, and even the biggest stars had to be content with about $150,000 for six months' work—but because of a contractual fluke the game's best pitcher became a free agent in fall 1974. A labor arbitrator ruled that the owner of the Oakland A's had defaulted on an agreement with Catfish Hunter.* In the 24-team auction that followed, no one could match the $3.5 million bid by the New York Yankees, by far the most ever paid a baseball player.

The transaction reaffirmed that a huge expenditure can do as much good for the payer as the payee. As the Yankee management knew, Hunter's bonanza would be the talk of the sports pages—hence, of the saloons and country clubs—for months after it was announced. Hunter's value as a drawing card was doubled. He was now a curiosity as well as a good pitcher, and season-ticket sales immediately began to rise accordingly. (He also became a figure of speech. When Revlon enthralled the business community by hiring a superstar executive named Michel C. Bergerac away from ITT for a package that added up to $5 million, the *New York Times* described Bergerac as "the Catfish Hunter of the boardroom.")

Meantime, without quite as much fanfare, dozens of basketball and hockey players were doing almost as nicely as Hunter, simply because two independent leagues were competing for the same supply of gristle. When the World Hockey Association was born, Bobby Hull, who had been making a living wage with the Chicago Black Hawks of the National Hockey League, was paid nearly $3 million to play in Winnipeg. The Philadelphia franchise gave Derek Sanderson of Boston $2.75 million; he played eight games for his new team, got into a dispute with management, and left with a $1-million settlement. In basketball

*This public identity, incidentally, was one of those outright fictions calculated to make ballplayers look more colorful than they really are. Hunter's name was Jim, which was what he was called by everyone who knew him personally. Charles Finley, the shrewd and shameless owner, had spun a tale in which Hunter, as a child, had run away from the farm and turned up after much familial anguish with a string of catfish.

salaries between $250,000 and $500,000 became commonplace; Commissioner Lawrence O'Brien of the National Basketball Association said the league's *average* pay in 1975 was $109,000. A few players remained naive enough to wonder at their blind luck. After signing a $3-million contract with the Philadelphia 76ers, George McGinnis said, "It's too much . . . There's no way I'm worth three million dollars to play basketball. I used to do it for nothing." Philosophically, McGinnis was in the minority. His contemporary, Marvin Barnes, was questioned on his plans at the end of a stint in the service of Providence College. "I won't play for less than a million dollars," Barnes said. "I'd rather go to work in a factory."

Sauerkraut

A revealing comment once slipped from Lanny Wadkins, who competes in golf tournaments for a living; he referred in an interview to the professional hazard bothering him most at the time: "crow's feet" around the eyes.

The little lines were a liability when it came to commercials. A man in Wadkins's position had to learn a good deal about makeup to offset the effects of daily toil in the sun. The hairdo needed expert attention, too, if he wished to maintain his value to the huckstering industry.

And why shouldn't he? If a golfer went into a tizzy over facial creases, it was only because endorsement contracts are the whole reason for trying to get famous in sports. Athletic skill is a ticket to prosperity, flackery a route to obscene riches. For telling the public what products to buy, some jocks earn many times their sports salaries. Sam Snead's agent said the golfer's outside income for 1974 was four times what he won in tournaments. Henry Aaron, Jack Nicklaus, Billie Jean King, Eddie Merckx (the Belgian bicycle-racing idol), to name a few, all derived their serious money from lending their names to commerce. And the byword of the ball-playing trade is that New York is the place to be; every team-sport jock with an ounce of sense contrives to be signed up by or traded to a franchise there because, as his agent has explained to him, 20 of the 21 biggest advertising agencies and 166 of the 500 biggest corporations in the United States have headquarters in New York.

The roots of the phenomenon cannot be traced with much precision. Possibly the fruits of victory in the ancient Olympics included paid testimonials for chariot manufacturers, but this cannot be stated as fact. Even limiting the inquiry to modern America, it is possible only to identify the approximate time (certainly not the original athlete and product) when the approval of a famous jock was first recognized as a selling point.

Sometime before 1890 baseball players started praising cigarettes for pay and allowing pictures of themselves to be distributed in the packages. A photo of James Corbett, who won the heavyweight boxing championship in 1892, was peddled in the same way. Corbett figured in another venture destined to become a sports-commerce classic: A plaster cast of his right fist was the model for a paperweight. In 1908 Johnny Hayes of New York won the Olympic marathon; his purported employer, Bloomingdale's department store, practically papered the walls with his photo and informed the public that Hayes had done his training on the store's roof.* The most striking possibility raised by a study of old-time commercialism is that America's most revered sports event, the World Series, owes its existence to the ready-made clothing business. Its genesis, in 1903, is attributed largely to the efforts of John T. Brush, a National League team owner who used the ballpark as a place to display ads and pass out promotional materials for his clothing company.

Despite such evidence of genius, commercial exploitation of sport grew slowly. There were limiting factors: The advertising industry itself was still primitive and its revolutionary media, radio and television, nonexistent. Local advertising meant that relatively small sums were involved. There was yet no sports figure whom the whole country had elevated to godhood. Sometimes even ethics presented an obstacle—a few ballplayers had not developed the keen, unfettered business acumen of their colleagues and clung to the antiquated idea that products they themselves didn't use shouldn't carry their endorsement. In 1909 Piedmont cigarettes ("The Cigarette of Quality") included Honus Wagner's photo—without first seeking permission—in its regular series of 350 big-leaguers. Wagner, who didn't use tobacco, forced the

*In *The Olympics* Richard Schaap called Hayes's job a fiction, similar to those created for present-day college athletes, arranged so he could draw a salary while training.

company to withdraw the issue (and the few Wagner cards that got into circulation are now worth—to members of a subculture known as sports collectors—more than $1,000 each).

Along came the Roaring Twenties, and with them Babe Ruth, a hero who loomed large enough to demand and get big money, whose exploits could be reported on radio and whose glamour was potent enough to sell anything his name was affixed to; Ruth put to rest the fallacy that the endorsed product need be something logically connected with the endorser or at least something he used and liked.

For the times Ruth's testimonial fees were staggering. Where Harry Hooper of the Red Sox, the Boston fans' favorite, was getting $50 to flog a patent medicine in 1920, the Babe was paid $10,000 to push Home Run cigarettes. Articles of clothing were named after him; the cap he favored became "the Babe Ruth cap for men and young men." Among the products linked to his name were clothing, chewing tobacco, pipes, beverages, baseball equipment, and golf clubs. At the height of his popularity, even the Baby Ruth candy bar (named for President Cleveland's daughter, the first child born in the White House), was often identified with him, with people requesting a "Babe Ruth." Ruth's agents suggested the candy-makers change the spelling and put their man on the payroll; considering the circumstances, this must have seemed a redundant expense and the company declined. In retaliation a George Herman Ruth Candy Company was formed and an authentically Ruthian confection produced, but the venture was headed off by an injunction obtained by the Baby Ruth people.

The Babe's greatest legacy may well be the universal application of athletic fame to huckstering, a principle reflected constantly in the media of today. The name of a baseball player, Carl Yastrzemski, on a label is presented as the logical reason to buy a loaf of bread. Larry Csonka, a football fullback, recommends a dance instruction studio. ("He's an Arthur Murray man!") Another footballer, Dick Butkus, speaks authoritatively on the merits of a freight concern.

And a racing car proclaims the existence of a certain brand of sauerkraut, as in 1975, when the Silver Floss Sauerkraut Company tied its destiny to the Indianapolis 500. The company assumed sponsorship of driver Roger McCluskey's car and plastered it with self-laudatory messages. To anyone unfamiliar with auto racing this might seem a nonsequitur and the link between a racing car and a can of pickled cabbage obscure. But the introduction of sauerkraut to the oval-racing scene conformed to promotional orthodoxy, which holds that a racing vehicle is ipso facto an advertising vehicle. As an adman connected with the Watkins Glen races once explained to the *New York Times,* the auto-racing crowd is, percentagewise, extraordinarily young, prosperous, and impressionable: "We look upon road racing as an important marketing vehicle for reaching an upscale audience . . . what we're selling is America's continuing love affair with competition on wheels . . . an opportunity to reach this kind of an audience with the kind of impact you can't get through any other medium." Hence, the speeding chariots sell everything from traveler's checks to soft drinks to wristwatches.

Likewise, speedboats push an eclectic range of products. Martini and Rossi, the vermouth people, have a hydroplane called *Dry Martini*; a Brazilian driver has *Drink Brazilian Coffee* painted on the side of his boat. Snowmobiles in the big cross-country race from Winnipeg to St. Paul carry ads for beer and the U.S. Navy, as well as for their own manufacturers. Cyclists in the big European races are pedaling billboards, covered from cap visor to fender with slogans for soft drinks and the like. And when Evel Knievel made his abortive attempt to vault the Snake River Canyon, his Sky Cycle and his helmet were decorated with decals for Nabisco candies, and Bobby Riggs was present in his Nabisco Sugar Daddy jumpsuit. (Riggs, having no vehicle save himself to decorate, had worn Sugar Daddy garments for his tennis matches with Margaret Court and Billie Jean King.)

While naming racing vehicles after things spectators can buy is standard, the practice is unheard of in the dignified milieu of international yacht racing. The only challenge of note was made by Alan Bond, an extremely upward-mobile Australian businessman, who competed for the America's Cup in 1974. Bond "gave in," as *Time* put it, "to his crassly commercial instincts" and decorated his boat with a promotion for Yanchep Sun City, his resort development on the west coast of Australia. "Mounting the challenge has cost him $9 million," *Time* added, "but he figures the money well spent. The major purpose of Bond's nautical campaign is to promote his projects. . . ." The New York Yacht Club nevertheless reacted stuffily and ordered him to purge his craft of the commercial message.

Against this backdrop a sauerkraut-mobile hardly stands out. Indianapolis and other tracks sported cars like Johnny Rutherford's *Gatorade Special*, decorated like an elongated jug of the celebrated juice, the *Alex Foods Tamale Wagon*, and the *Alloquasto Frostie Root Beer Pennsylvania Bicentennial McLaren Special.* By comparison the *Silver Floss Special* was a model of dignity (although when the public mistook it for the sporting offspring of a dental-products concern, the name was changed to *Silver Floss Sauerkraut Special*). Whether it was speeding around the Brickyard in the cause of dental floss or sauerkraut probably was irrelevant. The strategy was a smashing success. As the ads began to roll, Silver Floss's sales graph angled sharply upward. Figures for April 1975 more than doubled those of the previous year. Halfway through May, the month of the race, the total for May 1974 was surpassed.

Executives of the company rejoiced. "This tool of racing is fantastic," a spokesman told the media. "This is the second most popular sport in America, and we couldn't advertise on a racehorse. [As in yachting, the issue had not been worked out yet.] We took Roger McCluskey because he projected the calm purpose of maturity with the special energy of youth at forty-four."

In reciting McCluskey's sauerkraut-like qualities the Silver Floss man was simply paying homage to the convention of pretending the product and its endorser have something significant in common. Sample: "For Johnny Rutherford speed counts. Endurance counts more. He has a sharp eye for functional elegance. His watch is Rolex . . ." First National City associates itself with auto racing because it is "the world's fastest traveler's check."

Such rhetoric is unnecessary for makers of cars, motorcycles, minibikes, bicycles, and tires, all of which can be promoted as things the consumer *needs* no less than the heroes using them in competition. For the same reason, tennis and golf offer similar opportunities. The tennis boom of the 1970s brought a proliferation of rackets, shoes, and clothing, each item guaranteed by a member of the expanding roster of stars to improve the purchaser's game beyond all imagination. In *Carnival at Forest Hills,* Marty Bell noted how well pro tennis lent itself to mass marketing: Players, not belonging to teams, were free to dress as they pleased and could be ultraglamorous models for leading designers. With the eye of a fashion commentator, Bell described a prematch scene involving Arthur Ashe and John Newcombe:

> *Watching the two men warm up, an insider could see that Ashe and Newcombe were very important people just by the gear they wore and used. Arthur Ashe wore white shorts, a light-blue shirt and matching socks with a gold stripe around them. They came from his own line of tennis clothes and were made by Catalina.*
>
> *John Newcombe wore a pink shirt. On the front there was a white circle with a black mustache and a winking eye—his own trademark. His white shorts bore the same emblem. They were from a line of clothes that Newcombe was introducing this week at Forest Haven for Interwoven.*
>
> *Ashe played with a Head racket which he designed and endorsed. Newk played with the Rawlings Tiebreaker Racket which he designed and endorsed. . . .*

Along with a television phenomenon called "celebrity tennis"—an entertainment rooted in the belief on Broadcast Row that common folk would be enthralled at the sight of show-biz stars on the court—a new marketing wrinkle developed. Ads appeared urging readers to imitate celebrities imitating tennis players; thus Ashe and Newcombe were replaced in some of the warm-up suit ads by Lloyd Bridges and Mary Ann Mobley. In a further refinement of the basic jock-sell format, a pro tennis player and a pro cosmetics maker, both female, jointly presented advice on keeping the strokes sound, the lips glossy, and the cheeks peachy.

The drift away from the locker room may have been ill-advised. In the early 1970s American Telephone & Telegraph commissioned a research firm to study viewer response to commercials. "We have discovered," an AT&T man later told the press, "through various surveys that the sports star enjoys a tremendous recognition factor—superior to that of Hollywood movie stars and nameless models picked on looks." Furthermore, there was the question of "believability," the phone man added. The research firm administered an "arousal test" to twenty-five subjects, who were wired to a computer as they watched commercials flashing across a screen. The subjects were monitored for sweat and other signs of being turned on by the message or its deliverer. What the survey showed was that Bill Russell, of basketball fame, was not only more identifiable but more trusted by the public than stars of stage, screen, and television.

Russell had had the advantage of three highly visible jobs. After being regarded for over a decade as a near-Homeric hero in his role as center for the Boston Celtics, he coached that team successfully, became a commentator on network basketball telecasts, then went back to coaching. Moreover, jock-journalists, whose credo is "an image for everyone, and everyone in his image," had consistently fostered the notion that Russell was a man of high principle.

In the phone company test only Russell topped the 500 mark, outdistancing not only the Hollywood crowd but such athletic glamour pusses as Mark Spitz. AT&T concluded that Russell was the only one whose sincere admiration for direct long-distance dialing and lower weekend rates really shone through, and so he became the company's television image for many years to come. (In a classic exposition of the advertising mentality, Ma Bell's representative declared of Russell, "He's a very strange guy—he doesn't do anything unless he believes in it.")

A similar philosophy seemed to be guiding several advertisers who based their campaigns on Joe DiMaggio's testimonial a quarter-century after the end of his baseball career. A New York bank went so far as to use DiMaggio's photo in print ads with no identification. On television too DiMaggio has been, since 1974, one of the most ubiquitous presences, plugging something called Mr. Coffee, whose brew the Yankee Clipper calls "the finest," although he privately admits he is strictly a tea drinker.

The Mr. Coffee campaign was severely disillusioning to Russell

Baker, the *New York Times* satirist, who wrote, "the great people of the world simply [don't] hawk consumer goods on television," but it was specifically DiMaggio's pseudoaristocratic air that made him the right man for this lucrative job. The main consideration was his "class image," *class* being a word that recurs time and again in analyses of jocks' commercial aptness. Having done little huckstering while an active athlete, DiMaggio had set himself unmistakably above the money-grubbing. Now, like Sir Laurence Olivier for Polaroid, he was elevating the product to his level, rather than descending to its.*

Similarly, it was thought advisable to partake of the Olympic Games' prestige. This could not be done officially, however, until very recent times; the breakthrough came with the creation of a Department of Licensing and Concessions within the organizing committee for the 1976 summer games in Montreal. Ads were placed in publications like the *Wall Street Journal* inviting corporate folk to put in bids for commercial licenses and buy a little piece of Olympic goodwill. "The range of products which lend themselves to this licensing programme," the ads said, "are virtually limitless: T-shirts, track suits, sweat suits, sweatshirts, shells, flight bags, halter bags, posters, pennants, decals, flags, ties, neckwear, toys, glassware, medallions." Nothing had been forgotten. Between the lines loomed the implication that nobody who was anybody could afford to be without a merchandising license. In an interview Richard Gareau, the licensing department chief, said, "The international movement has not yet awakened to the tremendous commercial potential which is available to it through its publicity and goodwill. If we can make this work, I think we should score in a very big way."

The words had not been long out of his mouth when a three-page spread appeared in *Sports Illustrated,* the first page bearing a photo of Joe Namath in a Brut-green blazer and the message, "Fabergé is proud to announce that Joe Namath will be the spokesman for Brut during its TV sponsorship of the 1976 Olympic Games." The next page showed Brut's supporting jock lineup and declared: "We believe our association of Brut with the Olympic Games is a natural one. For it is a truly

*Contemporaneously, the "class" game was being played in reverse by another new product, Lite Beer. Mickey Mantle and Whitey Ford, also former Yankees and identified

international product, used by men in 120 countries of the world. Symbol of the closeness of men in a world made smaller . . ."

This was shortly after Fabergé had concluded its multimillion-dollar deal with Namath. Richard Barrie, executive vice president and chief operating official, had been quoted in *Newsweek:* "Namath is what most men wish they could be and most women want—he's No. 1 in sports, he's young, good-looking, rich . . . could remove the feminine stigma . . . and . . . masculinize cosmetics." Brut already had a stableful of jock flacks—among them Willie Mays, Mickey Mantle, Wilt Chamberlain, Jimmy Connors, and Muhammad Ali. "We didn't just buy another sports star to do some commercials for a lot of money," Barrie said. "We bought some excitement." This claim of transcending mere sporty magnetism was a vogue in the industry. In the spring of 1974, when Henry Aaron broke Babe Ruth's career home run record, Magnavox signed him to a million-dollar, long-term contract to sell television sets. The company man who announced the deal said, "Perhaps most importantly, Henry Aaron is the type of person with whom Magnavox would be proud to associate in its business activities had he never hit a home run." (But could anyone name a modestly educated, reticent black man with *no* career home runs who was paid to praise Magnavox products?)

Jocks and their agents were becoming increasingly conscious of the need to project the right aura. An "image coach" once displayed hockey player Dave Keon at a reception for more than 100 advertising and industry executives, whom he told, "This is . . . what we call the total package. The name Dave Keon generates excitement." An agent for Tom Seaver, the New York Mets' pitcher, placed ads in many publications emphasizing Seaver's solid-citizen appeal and not only his availability but that of "Tom's lovely wife, for those situations that call for young Mrs. America or husband-and-wife sales appeal." Steve Garvey's handlers, the William Morris agency, "shopped him as the all-American boy" so relentlessly that his Dodger teammates began to resent the reflected burden of righteousness.

---

in jock exposé stories as inveterate carousers, did commercials plugging the revolutionary suds, which were so unfilling the players could guzzle twice as much as in the old days.

FANS!

If anyone needed a reminder of the consequences of stepping out of line, it was provided by Mary Bacon, one of the first successful female jockeys. An attractive, glib blonde, she was in demand among advertisers. Then she blew it all with a declaration of political principle at a rally of the Ku Klux Klan in Walker, Louisiana. Guest-speaker Bacon gave a rousing address: "We are not just a bunch of illiterate southern nigger killers. We are good, white Christian people, hard-working people working for a white America . . . When one of your wives or one of your sisters gets raped by a nigger, maybe you'll get smart and join the Klan." The national media had no sooner picked up the story than Bacon reported losing endorsement contracts with Dutch Masters cigars and Revlon cosmetics. She even lost riding assignments at some of the thoroughbred tracks and turned up shortly afterward riding quarterhorses at Los Alamitos in Southern California, where her views on society presumably were no liability.

Where there once had been chaos, there was now order and system in the testimonial business. For much of it modern athletes owed a debt to Mark McCormack. Though there had been visionaries from the start, it wasn't until the age of mass communication that the concept of jock-marketing was taken to its logical conclusion, and beyond, by men like McCormack. His was a pioneer profession with an improvised description: specialist in athletic management and sports promotion. His organization had more than 250 employees in twelve offices around the world. *Sports Illustrated* said, "He is the most powerful man in professional sport," more potent even than the league commissioners. Feature stories marveled at his affluence: Before age forty-five he had acquired a palatial home in his native Cleveland, an apartment overlooking Central Park, a London townhouse, and a condominium in the Fiji Islands. His income was reported about $500,000 a year. He often collected as much as 50 percent of a client's earnings, with the average around 25 percent. Confiscatory as it sounds, many a jock was grateful for whatever share he or she was left with. At a time when he was one of the three most celebrated golfers in the world, Gary Player said, "The best thing that ever happened to me in my entire life was meeting

Mark McCormack. All the material success I've had I owe to him. He has gotten me the best contracts, the most lucrative deals. But for Mark, I'd have just been peanuts."

Laura Baugh came on the scene in the early 1970s, equipped with modest ability in top-level golf competition, a pretty face, and a first-rate feminine physique. When she put her financial destiny in McCormack's hands, she was still too young under the regulations to play on the women's pro tour in the United States. Less dynamic management might have let the property stagnate, but McCormack hustled it into a new marketing region, entering Baugh in a major Japanese tournament. "In Japan, as McCormack hoped," *Sports Illustrated* said, "the golf-mad, lens-happy Japanese could not focus often enough on the curvy blond prototype of western pulchritude."

Photos of Laura Baugh went on sale all over Japan. People stood in lines for hours to buy Laura Baugh calendars. Ultimately there were clocks, photo albums, cosmetics, school supplies, English-teaching cassettes, sports clothing, recordings, and golf accessories bearing Baugh's name or image. Domestically the golfer was featured in a televised toothpaste commercial, answering the question, "How's your love life?" Her financial life was just fine. She had earned more than $100,000 in six months, becoming the highest-paid female golfer though she had yet to play in an official American tournament and was not to achieve much competitively for years to come.

Skier Jean-Claude Killy was another McCormack property. As Killy's glow faded in the years after his Olympic triumphs, McCormack faced the challenge of brightening it up again. The promoter devised a television series of ski races in which Killy's weekly opponent was given a head start. Thus the hero would look glorious in victory and exonerable in defeat. For other clients McCormack developed "winner-take-all" tennis matches with purses so gigantic the networks found it easy to stir up excitement and peddle high-priced commercial time. (Halfhearted attempts were made to hoodwink the public into believing the winner would take home $250,000 or $500,000 and the loser nothing, but little investigative reporting was needed to determine that the loser's guarantee usually exceeded $100,000.) McCormack also instigated

FANS!

tennis and golf tournaments to give his jocks exposure. When Tony Jacklin was accepting congratulations at the victory ceremony for the 1969 U.S. Open golf tournament, McCormack pushed his way through the crowd to turn the champagne bottle's label away from the cameras; vintners, he said, would be free to make proposals later. McCormack was blunt in his attitude: "Fans do tend to be children. They try to pretend that the athlete of their fancy is out there doing what he excels at for some greater good or glory than a buck . . . the fault lies with the fan and not the athlete, who always knew he was playing for the dollars and not much else."

Beyond its intrinsic merit, this reasoning provides lots of latitude for insincerity. McCormack changed the equipment contracts of his client Arnold Palmer so that the endorsement of one club maker applied only to certain countries; new markets around the world were thus made available. Gary Player once represented seven equipment makers in different parts of the globe simultaneously. Occasionally, multiple endorsements raise problems. John Newcombe once complained that his game was hurt by the need to switch from a steel tennis racket to a wooden one when in a locale where he professed to favor the latter. Rod Laver became exasperated with a racket he was paid to praise; he used another brand—painted to look identical to the endorsed product.

Thanks to their widely acknowledged probity and rectitude, jocks are rarely taken to task in these matters. Now and then, however, someone in journalism or government takes issue with a particularly transparent pretense. In one instance Leonard Koppett searched in his *Sporting News* column for the logic by which a star of tennis or golf can be said to "represent" a resort. His example was Billie Jean King "of Hilton Head, South Carolina." King had not been born or raised there. She didn't live there at the time. She may not even have stopped there for a cup of coffee once a year, but still she was the resort's resident celebrity.

Occasionally the Federal Trade Commission has felt obligated to pay attention, too. In 1972 the agency investigated a commercial in which Lou Brock, baseball's best base stealer, sped around the basepaths and thanked a certain brand of candy for generating his swiftness. In what was regarded as a landmark decision, the FTC ruled that candy cannot be credited in advertising as the source of an individual's speed. The commission also obtained an order restraining Domino Sugar from advertising its product as the "official sugar" of the National Football League and major league baseball. An FTC spokesman pointed out that one refined sugar is essentially identical to the next, and that a compensatory arrangement accounted for the preference of the leagues in question.

Three years later the FTC announced a policy that would apply to athletes as well as other public figures. Henceforth they would be required to be "bona fide users" of what they endorsed. Reference was made to Joe Leonard, a racing driver who had been sponsored by Viceroy cigarettes. "I like Tareytons," he had confessed, "and I used to put Tareytons in the Viceroy packs. But Tareytons have a little white ring around them which gives it away. It was kind of a farce." How the FTC would police suspected cheaters wasn't clear, but there could be no doubt of the agency's resolute intentions. A spokesman said, "If Joe Namath says he eats Maypo for breakfast every morning, he has to eat Maypo. He really does have to. An athlete is no expert on after-shave lotion or cereal, and to use his identity as a hero to say something about a product he doesn't use is misleading."

It was left for *Time* magazine to exculpate the phonies: "Does anyone care? The hype of advertising works on such a different plane from conventional truth that it is a form of American dada. It is edifying, perhaps, but hardly necessary for it to be literally honest."

Wilt and Richard

Only rarely does an athlete have second thoughts about his advice to the public. After all, his role as counselor to consumer or voter is both a birthright and a commonplace, no more to be contemplated than his sturdy physique and muscular coordination. He recites his piece on behalf of whatever is to be sold, collects his compensation, and turns his attention elsewhere.

But now and then a jock learns the hard way not to be so indiscriminate. Poignant testimony is found in the autobiography of Wilt Chamberlain, nationally known for many years as a basketball center for the University of Kansas and a succession of professional teams.

A marvelous athlete, he was the first of the game-controlling seven-footers. He was the only player ever to score 100 points in a National Basketball Association game. He commanded one of the highest salaries in sports. He got additional attention by flaunting his sexual exploits, living lavishly, and building a million-dollar ultramodern house, scaled to his giant dimensions, in the hills north of Los Angeles.

He had no particular training or expertise as a political thinker. But in the presidential campaign of 1968 he tried to convince the electorate that if it liked him, it ought to like Richard Nixon.

Chamberlain had met Nixon by chance, on an airplane, several years earlier and had developed a genuine admiration for the former vice-president. "I remember being tremendously impressed with his intellect and his grasp of world problems and his willingness to see things in global, rather than just national, terms," he wrote, contrasting Nixon's attitude favorably with Lyndon Johnson's.

"Looking back on it," Chamberlain added, "I suspect I was also subconsciously influenced to back Richard by several things he and I had in common. Throughout his political career, he'd been called a 'loser'—the guy who couldn't win the big one. Me too. He'd been shafted by the press quite a bit. Me too. . . ."

And so, Chamberlain explained, he supported Nixon not for gain but out of a sense of kinship, for the good of the Republic and in the hope that his advice would come to bear on the direction in which the ship of state was steered: "I wanted to be on the inside, where I could see just what was going on and how major policy and personnel decisions were made . . . If Richard won, of course, I figured I'd have some input at the White House, a chance to talk to the top man about some social and poltical issues I felt very strongly about."

Chamberlain's views on various issues covered the far reaches of the political map, but most of his positions—for instance, on civil rights, marijuana, and prostitution—were leftward of the Democrats' platform that year. On deeper reflection he might have realized that the sort of president who would appoint John Mitchell as attorney general was not his boy.

He also failed to reckon on the likes of H.R. Haldeman, Nixon's chief of staff, and Haldeman's henchmen. "As it turned out," he related, "I was deceiving myself about having much input at the White House after Richard was elected. This was my first look at high level politics and I was pretty naive. I didn't realize how insulated the president of the United States is after he's elected. Richard sent me a card or letter every now and then, congratulating me on a championship or a great game, but I had about as much opportunity to influence him as I had to influence the Pope."

Throughout the courtship Nixon was hard pressed to stay one step ahead of Chamberlain's disillusionment. Since Chamberlain, being not only a basketball star but a black one, was presumed to have influence over those of the same ethnic affiliation, he was made Nixon's ambassador to the black convention delegates and alternates. When

Wilt and Richard

Spiro Agnew was chosen as the vice-presidential candidate, Chamberlain was deployed to talk the blacks out of a walkout, which would have embarrassed the GOP.

"I did my job," Chamberlain recalled, 'but I wasn't too happy about it. After the convention I went to see Richard. 'How can I sell Spiro to black people?' I asked him. 'Don't judge Spiro until you've talked to him,' Richard told me. 'He's done some good things for blacks. I'll set up a meeting for you in San Diego in a couple of days.' Well, I met with Spiro. I told him he should say 'black' not 'Negro,' and say it like he means it and isn't afraid of it. I also told him he should say 'law and order and justice,' not just 'law and order'—and mean it. We talked for quite a while, and he kept telling me how liberal he was and how much he'd done for blacks in Maryland and how much he agreed with everything I was saying. The next day, Spiro had a meeting with a group that had a lot of blacks in it. Do you know that dumb fuck must have said 'Negro' and 'law and order' 10,000 times? I'm sitting right there, looking at him, and sliding down in my chair every minute. I finally walked out. The next day, I told Richard, 'You gonna have some problems with Mr. Spiro.'"

Subsequently Chamberlain taped some interviews for use in predominantly black areas, but his enthusiasm for the campaign waned. And after the election he began to comprehend that the philosophical kinship he felt with Richard was largely illusory, particularly when Richard tried to stock the Supreme Court with one white supremacist after another.

Chamberlain had fallen into the trap that had snared Jackie Robinson, of whom Roger Kahn wrote, "Politically he was an infant. Successively Richard Nixon conned him and Nelson Rockefeller bent him to the expediencies of his will." Chamberlain had been naive enough to take his role seriously and might not have felt himself so exploited had he realized why he was wanted by Nixon, and approached the business of endorsement—political or otherwise—in the traditional spirit.

As long ago as 1920 athletes had learned to separate ideology from the practical matter of their celebrity value. Ty Cobb had been recruited to endorse James M. Cox for president after the Democratic convention. The Republicans sought to counter the move with an even bigger baseball name. There was only one. An agent was offered $4,000 for the support of Babe Ruth and an extra $1,000 to deliver Ruth to Marion, Ohio, as an ornament for Warren G. Harding's "front-porch" campaign. Ruth balked at first, saying, "Hell, no, I'm a Democrat." Then he regained his reason and asked, "How much are they offering?" They were offering enough to make him a Republican, although the deal later fell through when the scandal of the crooked 1919 World Series broke and the value of a ballplayer's testimonial declined.

As subsequent events suggested, such endorsements may be relatively worthless even in times when athletes aren't regarded by the public as swindlers. The active backing of Joe Louis, the most beloved man ever to hold the heavyweight boxing championship, was insufficient to get a series of presidential candidates over the hump.

Louis's first effort was made in 1940 on behalf of Wendell Willkie, partly because Jesse Owens, the second most revered black athlete of the period, had already joined the cause. Pressed to explain his affiliation, Louis said, "I'm in Willkie's corner because I think he will help my people." He also disclosed, "I was born Republican. My mother was Republican, a Republican and a Baptist." As if to confirm that his blessing wrought no miracles at the polls, Louis supported another losing Republican, Grant Reynolds, in a Harlem congressional race against Adam Clayton Powell. He backed Dewey against Truman, Stevenson against Eisenhower. He broke the streak just once, in 1960, when he stood behind John Kennedy; in 1968 he nearly fell to Nixon, but finally declared for Humphrey. Louis was as reliable a barometer as Maine, only in reverse.

Nevertheless, some jock endorsements are considered indispensable. In *Buckeye* Robert Vare asserted, "Coach (Woody) Hayes' endorsement is one of the most sought after political prizes in the state." Vare pictured biggies vying for the prize with varying degrees of success: "In 1960, when a group of students asked him to greet vice-presidential candidate Lyndon Johnson during a campaign on campus, he declined, solemnly explaining that the coach of the Ohio State football team ought to be above partisan politics. A month later, when Richard Nixon addressed a large rally at the state capital downtown, there at his side was Wayne Woodrow Hayes."

But enlisting Hayeses, Louises, Cobbs, and Ruths is a routine exercise that proceeds pro forma and is recognized by the masses as the expedient it is. There are other ways for a creative political figure to turn public affection for athletes to his advantage. These involve theatrics in which the jocks are merely props; the show of affection is unilateral but often more effective than reciprocal backslapping.

In one of its subtler forms this means embracing a whole sport, as did Dr. Henry Kissinger in the summer of 1975, when he threw out the first ball at the all-star baseball game.

The timing of the secretary of state's ballpark debut was interesting. It coincided with a spate of pundits' analyses that Kissinger, in the midst of his most serious troubles yet with Congress, had decided to take his case to the people. All was not rosy in the Middle East; détente with the Soviets was looking like no bargain. What Kissinger needed most was a warm feeling among the populace, confirmed by the pollsters' findings, that nobody was in his league when it came to tending to global peace.

For the man with the Teutonic accent and the Dr. Strangelove air, what better way to offset his liabilities than to demonstrate such enthusiasm for the "national pastime" that even the demands of shuttle diplomacy couldn't keep him away! He mingled on the field and took his box seat among the other honored dignitaries, Mickey Mantle and Stan Musial.

A wirephoto of the grinning secretary communing with ballplayers made front pages around the country. Shortly afterward, despite his cramped schedule, Kissinger found time for an Associated Press interview on the subject of his credentials as a fan; he pictured himself as a certified baseball nut who, as a lad, had kept a devout ear to the crystal set to follow the exploits of the Yankees.

He must have been pleased with the results. Come autumn, with the business of the planet no less pressing, he showed up at the World Series, this time getting photographed wearing a Red Sox cap and sharing a comradely guffaw with Boston's Carl Yastrzemski.

This was a practice more typical of local, elective politicians, who must let their constituents know where they stand. Before that same Series, in which Boston played Cincinnati, Sen. Edward Kennedy of Massachusetts introduced a resolution that "the Senate of the United States recognize the quality and excellence of both of these great teams, wishes both teams well and hopes that the home team will be victorious in each game." The resolution carried, presumably helping Kennedy's standing with the pro-Red Sox, anti-busing residents of Boston. Kennedy's colleagues had voted yea without realizing that Boston would be the home team for four of the seven games.

Tom Bradley, mayor of Los Angeles, had found the all-star game as useful as Kissinger. Players were voted onto the teams by the public; Bradley kept a ballot box in his office and had conducted a personal ballot-punching ceremony—from which the media were not excluded— on behalf of Dodgers who were nominated.

Bradley was a model of moderation compared to John Lindsay in 1969, who was being blamed for all of New York City's problems. The streets were full of garbage and potholes. Racial tensions were high, causing a long teachers' strike that fall. Luckily for His Honor, the Mets were in the running and, what's more, this circumstance was considered a *miracle* (a jock-jargon word meaning the team's quality had been seriously underestimated before the season). In *SportsWorld* Robert Lipsyte related how Mayor Lindsay played the opportunity:

> *He came to baseball late. But he stayed. He would course into the locker room behind a flying wedge of aides, remote, stone-faced. When the television camera's red light glowed, he would snap on a smile and stride up to congratulate the game's hero. The Mets were image-conscious, and none of them had ever turned a naked back on Lindsay, as I had once seen a Los Angeles Dodger do to the then Vice President, Hubert Humphrey.*
>
> *Lindsay was taller than most of the Mets and handsomer. He materialized on television as somehow having been involved in the pennant race . . . When pitcher Jerry Koosman poured champagne on the Mayor's classic head during a stagey televised locker-room party, he was also bestowing what was construed by the fans as an endorsement from the whole team.*

This is not to denigrate the thousands of other politicians, unmentioned here, who time and again have shown themselves to be deft at wrapping themselves in sweat clothes. But none could match the standard set by Richard Nixon, who refined self-jockification to a degree never before seen in high office. He not only surpassed all who came before or since in the prosaic task of accumulating jock endorsements, but actually created a whole new art: jock politics.

No awards dinner or hall-of-fame induction ceremony had been too small for Nixon. He was the one who had brought locker-room language to the people; his public pronouncements were replete with "end runs," "fourth-quarter finishes," "game plans," and other colorful phraseology. Nixon had even code-named himself "quarterback" for sensitive operations in which his identity was concealed.

Nixon's rise to power coincided with the heyday of pro football's Green Bay Packers, whose coach, Vince Lombardi, was known to millions upon millions of Americans as a symbol of unquenchable thirst for victory and unblinking-in-the-face-of-pain masculinity. Lombardi was author of the "winning isn't everything, it's the only thing" dictum. It would have taken a far less sporty man than RMN to overlook the possibilities.

Before the campaign he had seriously considered making Lombardi his running mate. (One of his earliest appointments was that of special advisor Bud Wilkinson, who in the 1950s, at the University of Oklahoma, had been the collegiate equivalent of Lombardi.) At a 1970 reception in Green Bay for the Packers' quarterback, Bart Starr, Nixon saw an opportunity to express esteem for both his own war policies and his secretary of defense, Melvin Laird. "I think it is only proper," Nixon told the gathering, "to speak of him in this room where all of us who follow football . . . know that the defense is essential if you are going to be able to win the game.

"I remember two Super Bowl games [Green Bay had won]. *I think* Bart will agree that the defense played as much of a role in winning those games as the offense . . .

"And I think, too, as we look at the United States of America today, we look at the defense of America which Mel Laird, a great son of Wisconsin, now has responsibility for.

"The defense is important. As Mel Laird has said, not because the

United States wants a war but because with that kind of defense we can discourage anyone who might want to engage an offense."

During his presidency, Nixon wrote or phoned the following (this compilation, which follows the list in Neil Offen's *God Save the Players*, is probably incomplete):

George Allen, coach of the Washington Redskins. Allen was a frequent White House visitor and was often in phone contact with Nixon. Even as the city of Washington, as well as the whole country, raged over the Saturday Night Massacre, Allen received his customary congratulatory call for a victory over the Cardinals. The next summer, just a few days before Nixon threw in the sponge, he received an important vote of confidence. "I don't think he should resign," George Allen said. "That's the type of determination and leadership and doggedness you have to have in a president."

Jack Nicklaus, pro golfer.

Ralph Houk, major-league baseball manager.

Bob Devaney, college football coach.

Henry Aaron, major-league home run champion.

Vince Lombardi, emperor of American football while in Green Bay and Allen's predecessor in Washington before his untimely death.

Marty Liquori, amateur trackman specializing in the mile run.

Harmon Killebrew, major-league baseball player.

Johnny Majors, college football coach.

John Wooden, college basketball coach.

Frank Gifford, television sports commentator and former pro football player.

Paul (Bear) Bryant, college football coach.

Orville Moody, pro golfer. As an ex-Army sergeant who had won the U.S. Open, Moody had particular political value. After Nixon's call Moody reported the president's obscure remarks: "He congratulated me and said something about this being not a win for the elite but a big blow for the middle class."

Reggie Jackson, major-league baseball player.

Hank Stram, pro football coach.

Len Dawson, pro football player.

Joan Whitney Payson, major-league baseball team owner.

Don Shula, pro football coach. One week before a Super Bowl game Shula's Miami Dolphins were to play, Nixon phoned at 1:00 A.M. "I thought it was some idiot calling at that time," Shula later said. "Then I found out it was the president of the United States." Nixon diagrammed a passing play for Miami's use against the Dallas Cowboys. It was tried and the pass was intercepted.

Arnold Palmer, pro golfer.

Darrell Royal, college football coach.

Ted Williams, major-league baseball manager and former player.

Bill Kilmer, pro football player.

Danny Murtaugh, major-league baseball manager.

Earl Weaver, major-league baseball manager.

Joseph Danzansky, Washington businessman seeking to buy a baseball franchise.

The Washington and Lee High School rowing team.

Congratulations after the fact were not enough; whenever possible, Nixon contrived to be at the scene of an event. He turned up one afternoon in 1972 at the Redskins' practice field, to the surprise of absolutely no one, but to the discomfiture of one lineman, Ray Schoenke, who was affiliated with George McGovern's campaign. Schoenke refused to pose for the pictures that were to go out on the wires showing the president surrounded by helmeted heroes.

Nixon made a little speech to the Redskins: "I've always said that in life as well as in sports, politics, and business, what really makes a team or a country is when it has lost one, it doesn't lose its spirit. I think this government has it. You're going to go on and win."

By this point some of the Redskins were feeling the strain of constant presidential vigilance. "He's really hurting us," Billy Kilmer said, expressing a wish that Allen instruct Nixon to lay off the pregame rhetoric and adding that Nixon-suggested plays always backfired.

Larry Csonka, then fullback for the Miami Dolphins, said, "President Nixon may identify with football players, but I don't identify with him and I haven't met a player yet who does. The man upsets me with his role as superjock. Here he is, the one man in the world who has at his fingertips all the information and influence to make a lot of people's lives better. But what's he doing calling football players on the telephone and giving pep talks to teams? . . . It makes people think football is more important than it really is."

This, as Nixon knew, was an impossibility in the minds of many Americans. It was doubtful anyway that his intention was to increase public esteem for football; surely it was to do the same for Richard Nixon. Besides, to many observers Nixon seemed comfortable, in both official and informal situations, only when he could steer the conversation to his best subject.

In April 1974, when he flew to Xenia, Ohio, recently wiped out by a tornado, he talked baseball with the residents. Luckily Henry Aaron had hit his 715th home run the day before, so the President of the United States had something to discuss with the disaster victims.

Football was Nixon's totem of normalcy. When Washington's Mall was occupied by 250,000 antiwar demonstrators one Saturday in November 1969, Nixon, in Paul Gardner's words, "reassured the silent majority by letting it be known he would spend the afternoon watching the Purdue-Ohio State game." The invasion of Cambodia the next year brought droves of outraged students to town. Nixon thought to make political hay by walking, fearless, among his young adversaries one night at the Lincoln Memorial. He engaged a band of dissidents and asked what campus they had come from. Syracuse University, they replied, "Syracuse" Nixon said, perking up. "The Orangemen." With that, he was off on an encomium to Coach Ben Schwarzwalder and his perennially formidable eleven.

If the old "talk football" trick wasn't much help with the college vote, it was nevertheless more often an asset than a liability. Once Nixon, who kept a football on his desk, was to receive the nation's oldest living military officer—a retired admiral living in San Diego—at his San Clemente digs. The ceremony was what is known in White House newspeak as a "photo opportunity," with photographers and reporters crammed into the office so that the next day the country knows for certain that the president is still alive and doing something.

This particular session offered the opportunity for embarrassment. The admiral was a very old 104 and showed few signs of sensory perception. It was clear immediately he would be unable to take part in the conversation. For the quarterback of the White House team, no sweat. He first made pointed note of the old boy's Alabama birth and his crimson blazer. Now, crimson, as every knowledgeable politician should know, is the color of the University of Alabama. And the University of Alabama fields uniformly excellent football teams. Having made the connection, Nixon cut back nimbly into a description of an Orange Bowl game just a few years earlier involving the Crimson Tide. He was able to go into meticulous detail, nicely filling the alloted time.

That Nixon's major contribution to his profession would endure became apparent as soon as Gerald Ford inherited the big coaching job in the Oval Office. Ford immediately emulated what seemed to him the previous administration's crowning public-relations achievements— one of his first acts after taking office was to phone a pro golfer to congratulate him on winning a minor tournament.

Right away he began attending sports banquets and playing whenever possible in pro-am golf competitions. Before long his counselors were cautioning against an excessive show of zeal for recreation in times of economic crisis and post-Watergate malaise; they urged him to adopt a more sober demeanor. In response, the All-American boy from Michigan redoubled his assaults on par.

In the fall of his first year the networks were considering dropping

FANS!

the Army-Navy football game from the TV schedule. Ford announced he would attend, and ABC was compelled to leave the game on the tube. The new president even imitated his exiled patron's football-figurative language, speaking often of the "game plan" for some governmental exercise and describing the United States' withdrawal from South Vietnam as "quitting the game on the last play of the last quarter." Ford continued to call golf champions and to suggest playing dates with them; in one instance his reward for turning up on the circuit was a photo that went nationwide in the newspapers and appeared above the lead story in *Newsweek*. It showed the president emoting, as convincingly as any pro, after a missed putt. He invited tennis player Arthur Ashe to the White House after Ashe's 1975 Wimbledon victory. On Bob Gibson day in St. Louis, he sent a telegram to Busch Stadium praising Gibson's "overall pitching excellence which is unsurpassed in our time." And after the 1975 World Series he spoke to Sparky Anderson, manager of the Cincinnati Reds, and three players, telling all of them the quality of the games had been "good for baseball."

When opportunities arose the president played the racial angle. He called to congratulate Frank Robinson on becoming the first black manager in the major leagues. He stopped by a Washington hotel to hug the wife and the grandmother-in-law of Lee Elder, first black golfer to qualify for the Masters Tournament, and to tell Elder, "I like what you're doing."

Jerry-the-jock's enthusiasm seemed so genuine and spontaneous that it came as a shock when Jack Anderson disclosed the contents of a memo in which the president had assigned a staffer to keep abreast of potential congratulatees. Ford was to be provided with the name, phone number, and biographical data of at least one champion a week. One of the first subjects was Al Kaline of the Detroit Tigers, who got his 3,000th big-league base hit (regarded as a major milestone in baseball) about a month after Ford took office. The president rang up the Tigers' locker room and gushed to Kaline on the greatness of his accomplishment and the sentimental aptness of its having occurred in Kaline's native Baltimore. Kaline, of course, had no way of knowing that every word that came over the line from the White House was being read from a typewritten script.

Jesus Christ (Pro Football) Superstar

Cassius Clay, born and raised a Christian, became Muhammad Ali, a Muslim, upon ascending to the heavyweight boxing championship. More than once after winning a bout he disclosed that Allah, not Ali, had been responsible for the knockout.

As remarkable as this information may have sounded, it was not inconsistent with explanations for other athletic happenings. For one thing, Ali was not alone in surrendering to the urge to promote his theological views to his sporting audience. Many jocks regard the privilege of preaching as a natural extension of their authority to sell merchandise and politicians. At a time when it is commonly heard that sports have become a religion, it isn't surprising to find superstars supplied with more piety than they can use, who can't resist sharing it with their own worshippers.

The process is lubricated by a widely held belief—among not only laymen but professionals—that God can get awfully concerned about the outcome of a ballgame. Some decades back it seemed entirely appropriate for a Brooklyn minister to hold a public service to pray for a pennant for the Dodgers. As a matter of fact, Dodger-loving clergymen have been more receptive than most to the proposition that the Big Box-Seat Holder in the Sky is one of their kind: A priest once went so far as to ask the borough's residents to pray for Gil Hodges to get a hit in the 1952 World Series. (Hodges fared no better than Job in trying to break out of the slump, leaving yet more of God's children to wonder why He permits suffering.)

FANS!

But if Brooklyn is the Mecca, so to speak, of athletically oriented theologians, it is hardly the only place where spiritual leaders and their flocks pray for victories. The phenomenon is not even restricted to this country or to Western religions.

In some African nations, for instance, witchcraft is regularly practiced on behalf of jocks. In Kenya, according to a survey, 95 percent of the pro soccer teams employ witch doctors and soothsayers. Widespread faith in their efficacy has led to problems (there was a near-riot at one game over a pigeon that was hovering near one team's goal; at another, fans complained that their team's defeat had been caused by a dead cat outside the stadium), but none so serious that a team with any regard for its prospects would abandon the rites.

When Baltimore and Boston were to meet for the 1975 American League baseball championship, a Baltimore radio station sent one of its disc jockeys to Nairobi to find a witch doctor who would cast a spell on the Red Sox. He took with him a Baltimore uniform, to wear while being blessed, and a photo of the Boston team, to be hexed. In retaliation, the Red Sox asked a Salem woman who represented herself as a witch to return the curse. She declined, on the ground that it was beneath her dignity.

Occupants of many church pulpits are less inhibited. Football games, for example, seem to have transcendent meaning in the Bible Belt. (After the semifinal game for the 1974 World Football League championship a Florida Blazer told the TV audience his prayers for victory had been answered, and another member of the team declared, "We're God's disciples. We're God's disciples, and we came here with a mission.") This is particularly true in southern and southwestern college towns, where football victories are among the most passionately desired blessings.

Invocations at University of Alabama games given by the Rev. Hugh W. Agricola, rector of the Episcopal Church of the Advent of Birmingham, often include the wish that "Bear's [Bryant] will be done" or that Alabama be given the strength to destroy its foe. Agricola's regard for the Crimson Tide was so warm that his prayer before a pro game in Birmingham included a call upon the Lord to imbue the combatants with the fire and skill "to make this a contest worthy of this football capital." Before the Baylor-Oklahoma State game of 1974, the Rev. Marshall Edwards of the Columbus Avenue Baptist Church, addressed the Deity with these words: "I am so tired of pompous prayers that I told my wife I was going to pray for what I wanted to pray for . . . I find it difficult to pray objectively because I like to think your favorite colors are green and gold."

Players themselves dispute the prudence, if not the value, of the victory prayer. This is especially true in pro football, whose doomsday atmosphere and (in most cases) Sunday play generate more religious activities than other sports. The Detroit Lions' chaplain, Lloyd Livingston, once pointed out that his spiritual charges realize how easily their devotions could be neutralized: "There are probably Christians on both sides who are praying to win."

Peter Gent, a wide receiver for the Dallas Cowboys who became a writer, noticed a certain verbal circumspection at pregame chapel sessions, lest the Lord take offense at an outright appeal for victory on a silver platter: "They always made a point of pointing out that they were not really praying to win. Otherwise God would have been pissed off."

Misunderstandings can occur so easily. All Roger Staubach did, after quarterbacking the Dallas Cowboys to the Super Bowl title in 1972, was thank God for the championship on national television. People jumped to conclusions, according to Staubach. The speech "created the wrong impression," he contended in his autobiographical *First Down, Lifetime to Go*. "I mean, I wouldn't have blasphemed God if we had lost."

In living contradiction to those of little faith stands Bill Glass, who became a fulltime evangelist after retiring as a star pro defensive lineman. Glass expatiated, in the following passage from *Get in the Game*, on his discovery of the power of prayer in his college days. The scene is a tête-à-tête with a fellow Christian and football enthusiast who was exhorting Glass to new athletic heights:

> *"You've been playing fairly good football so far, and all your coaches are relatively pleased. But honestly Bill, you've just been mediocre. So, if you play inspired football your senior year,*

amazing things can happen . . . Let's pray specifically that you may become an All-American, and that as an All-American, you may use whatever glory this honor brings you to the glory of God."

During this prayer meeting we had a peculiar awareness of God's presence. With these challenging thoughts and convictions before us, we rose to our feet with the realization that something big might happen. . . .

To be named to the All-American team was my secret goal for my entire senior year. I had been praying and working for this victory . . . Making the All-American team has always been a source of strength to me because I feel it was a direct answer to prayer. I had never had this kind of ability and had never played this quality of football. I was shocked and pleased and thankful to God.

Of course, the assertion that God might have helped a bit and the inference that He was doing His own work through the athlete in question are separated by a fine line. It takes someone surer of himself than Bill Glass to cross it. Muhammad Ali has done it often.

Under the predawn monsoon skies of Kinshasa, Zaire, in October 1974, Ali stunned prizefighting cognoscenti around the world by knocking out George Foreman and recovering the heavyweight championship. Immediately after the fight he divulged, "That wasn't me out there tonight. That was Allah." Amplifying on the theme, he asserted, "I proved Allah is God and Muhammad is his messenger," which is standard Muslim doctrine except that the Muhammad referred to is a different one altogether.

Ali's religious and pugilistic activities had been intermingled since the prefight buildup for his 1966 meeting with Floyd Patterson, "trumpeted," in Robert Lipsyte's phrase, "as the crescent and the cross." Unlike most of Ali's subsequent opponents, Patterson, a Catholic (who also was black), was a willing foil who, whenever prompted, expounded on his intention of bringing the fistic title back to Christendom, where it belonged. "The image of a black Muslim as the world heavyweight champion disgraces the sport and the nation," he said at one point. "Cassius Clay must be beaten and the black Muslim scourge removed from boxing." (Patterson's choice of words was remarkably reminiscent of the cries of white Americans after the first black scourge, non-Muslim Jack Johnson, won the title in 1908.) On this particular occasion Ali showed more restraint than was later his wont. "It wouldn't be fair for a man of his abilities—such a puny light man who can't take a punch—to stand up for all the Catholics in the world," he said. "Besides, I don't want no religious wars."

"To me this is holy war," the same man said nine years later, before taking on Foreman. "Therefore all the powers of the heavens are against him. I predict I will have no problem. The same powers that got me victory over the draft, the same powers that got me past Ken Norton and Joe Frazier will get me past George Foreman."

Ali continued the theme the following summer when he went to Malaysia to defend the championship against Joe Bugner, an Englishman whose denomination was never specified but who presumably was a Christian. Upon arriving in Kuala Lumpur, Ali told twenty thousand admirers massed at the airport, "When I go into the ring I go with Allah and when Bugner fights me he fights Allah. So there's nothing he can say, there's nothing you can say, there's nothing no government, no president can say when I am backed by the Lord of all the world." In all likelihood, Ali's purpose was only to solidify rooting support among the predominantly Moslem population and perhaps to sell a few extra tickets to the bout. Ignorant of social conditions in the Asian nation, the Greatest, as he styled himself, didn't realize he was scaring the wits out of local authorities.

They had already seen enough religious-racial friction between Moslem Malays and Chinese, whose enmity had led to rioting in Kuala Lumpur in 1969. Now, given Ali's unilateral declaration of holy war, there were genuine fears of a riot by Moslems should the champion be defeated. "When Ali speaks of the bout as being a holy war and says 'Allah protects me with his divine shield,' he makes it sound as if the honor of Islam is at stake," the *Washington Post* reported. "American reporters put it down to the old Ali razzamatazz and laugh. But the large-circulation local newspapers dare not print a word of it, and the police fear that unsophisticated Muslims might get too carried away emotionally."

FANS!

Word was passed to Ali's manager, Angelo Dundee: The 1969 riots had been terribly violent; nearly three hundred had been killed. The alarmed Dundee reportedly told his fighter, "Cut the holy war shit—they already had one here."

Bugner did his part by trying to negate the spiritual implications. "I'm not fighting Allah," he said, "because I could turn around and say Allah was fighting God. I respect Allah, I respect Buddha, I respect everybody, but I'm going to give Ali a thrashing."

The efforts came too late; the damage was done. Thousands of Malaysian Muslims were daily facing Mecca and praying for an Ali victory. The chief minister of the state of Sabah was quoted publicly: "Every Muslim will pray to Allah for his [Ali's] success. May he come out of the ring triumphant as the champion and the standard bearer of Islam. . ." A security official told the *Post*, "If Ali loses, there is a strong possibility of rioting in the streets. Some of our people here are very simple and they take their religion seriously. To them, nobody talks about a holy war unless they mean it, and Muslims might become too upset if he should lose."

Police leaves in Kuala Lumpur had to be canceled. Some pessimists in the city went so far as to stockpile food. But as the oddsmakers had predicted, Bugner turned out to be no match for Allah and lost a unanimous decision.

The Muhammad Ali Fisticuffs Show and Revival moved on, this time to the Philippines for a third meeting with Ali's archrival, Joe Frazier. Before the whole troupe departed for Manila a press conference was held in promoter Don King's New York office. There, Drew (Bundini) Brown, one of Ali's most prominent sycophants, turned to Frazier and said, "You can't beat us. You can't beat God."

Whether Bundini referred to Ali or Allah was left unclear, in keeping with the jumbled, slightly-out-of-focus theology that usually emanated from the Ali camp. The chief priest himself frequently discoursed on his role not only as Allah's messenger but as a debunker of Christian superstition. With little or no provocation Ali would recite his favorite part of Black Muslim doctrine, namely that white men, devils created by a mad scientist, would someday soon face judgment at the hands of black men who never smiled, who were currently awaiting the apocalyptic moment in floating space platforms. In *The Muhammad Ali Book*, Wilfrid Sheed relates a session with grammar school children. "When you die," Ali informed them, "you rot, you don't fly no place." He disabused the youngsters of belief in Christ's ascension—"How they get him up there?"—and then took on the Immaculate Conception, saying *he* wouldn't swallow a story like that from *his* pregnant daughter: "I know what kind of spook gave *you* the baby. That was one of the brothers who gave you it."

Underlying all this instruction was the premise that Allah had empowered his servant to cuff lesser men around the prize ring with elan so that his preachments might carry authority. "Allah knows if I win, I'll keep doin' His preachin' for Him," the boxer said. "That's why I win all the time. I'm usin' my fame to talk about this man." He spoke of being "on a divine mission."

He told Robert Lipsyte, "We're all like little ants. God sees all these little ants, millions of them, and he can't answer all their prayers and bless every one of them. But he sees one ant with a little influence that the other ants will follow. Then he might give that ant some special powers.

"I'm like a little ant. Lots of other little ants know me, follow me. So God gives me some extra power."

And, in carrying his vision of himself to its logical conclusion, Ali described himself to George Plimpton as "a prophet."

Other evangelically inclined jocks have turned to the missionary pulpit. Bill Glass, doing business as his own evangelistic association, began touring the country conducting "crusades" in various cities. He followed the well-established Fellowship of Christian Athletes, whose mission is "to confront athletes and coaches—and through them the youth of the nation—with the challenge and adventure of following Christ." Athletes in Action, though smaller than the fellowship, has been even more energetic, organizing pickup teams of pro stars to spread the Word athletically from school to school.

In *The Gingerbread Man*, the story of his career as a sports promoter, Pat Williams told of having Paul Anderson, a weightlifting champion of the 1960s, give a show before a baseball game. "It was unbelievable," Williams marveled, "but each stunt topped the last." Anderson drove nails through two-inch planks with his bare hands, lifted 85-pound dumbbells with his pinkies, hoisted a 250-pound barbell over his head eight times and, as a finale, sat the eight heaviest ballplayers on a wooden platform, crouched beneath it until it rested on his shoulders, and lifted it off the ground. Then, eschewing electronic amplification, he addressed the crowd in a voice made resonant by other powers: "I've lifted more weight than anyone in the history of mankind. I once lifted over six thousand pounds in a backlift. I've been declared a wonder of nature from the United States to Russia. I've been written up in *Ripley's Believe It or Not*. I've stood on the center platform at the Olympic Games. They call me the strongest man in the world. But I want you to know, ladies and gentlemen, that all of these things are secondary in my life. I, Paul Anderson, the strongest man who ever walked the face of the earth, couldn't get through a minute of the day without Jesus Christ. The greatest thing in my life is being a Christian. If I can't make it without Christ, how about the rest of you?"

Anderson's performance went over so well that Williams soon featured baseball coach Bobby Richardson, who had been a star second baseman for the New York Yankees. "When you receive Christ by faith," Richardson promised the fans, "God will pardon all your sins, past and present . . . Christ will never leave you nor forsake you. You never have to be afraid again."

Halfway around the globe, the same function was being fulfilled by one of the most famous swimmers in the world. As the Associated Press reported it in July 1975, Shane Gould, an Australian who had won several Olympic gold medals, had "found a new path to glory." After hobnobbing with "prime ministers and ambassadors" and raking in endorsement cash, Gould announced, "I've totally rejected all that or at least not totally accepted it. Neil [her fiance] and I want a Christian lifestyle . . . There are a lot of lost people in the world. We want to share with them what we believe in." Gould declared she would honor her contractual obligations to endorse swimsuits, accessories, breakfast foods, and whatever, but vowed to refuse new offers. Meantime she was headed directly for work at the New World Christian Youth Center, specializing in redeeming surfers and members of motorcycle gangs.

Every one of the aforementioned apostles considered athletic fame a legitimate source of religious authority. "I believe I can become what God intended me to be more fully in pro football than anywhere else," Bill Glass once said. "I believe He wants me to share my faith with people everywhere. What better platform could there be than that of the NFL? I know pro football has given me entry into the lives of thousands of people." On a Los Angeles crusade Glass said, "Athletes may try to renounce their influence on others, but they can't," and urged his former playing-field associates to join in advancing the cause.

Gerald Ford agreed heartily. He referred to the jock evangelists in a *Sports Illustrated* article written while he was vice-president, as "the vanguard of our young leadership. I know that in terms of spiritual awareness they are way out front."

It was partly with a view to keeping them there that an organization called Sport World Chaplaincy, Inc., was founded. The Rev. Ira Eshleman, construction magnate turned preacher, founder and president of Bibletown in Boca Raton, Florida, started Sport World both to fill the spiritual needs of jocks themselves and because "these heroes were in a position to influence and assist millions of people, especially youngsters who might never listen to a teacher, pastor, policeman or parent."

According to Sport World literature, one outstanding middle linebacker, Jeff Siemon of the Minnesota Vikings, continued to play football only because "the game . . . provides him a platform to speak about his belief in Christ . . . in his own words 'that's what makes football all worthwhile.'"

The corollary notion is that nothing converts like success. As Bill Glass put it, "People are more interested in what an effective defensive end has to say than an unsuccessful one."

Glass was not just whistling "Rock of Ages," according to Roger Staubach, who wrote, "When the Cowboys played Miami in the Super Bowl, I had promised that it would be for God's honor and glory, whether we won or lost. Of course the glory was better for God and me since we won, because the victory gave me a greater platform from which to speak." Terry Bradshaw, Staubach's Pittsburgh counterpart, both as a passer and proselytizer, agreed: "You know that for a fact. When you speak in a church, they bill you as the quarterback for the Steelers."

Some athletes, notably Peter Gent, are rankled by the ostentatious devoutness of his Dallas Cowboys colleagues. The team has more than its share of prayer meetings and evangelists. "They go around doing part-time gospel work, using their influence as athletes, when few have any credentials as far as theology," said Gent, who saw Pattonesque contradictions in the use of prayer before battle. He fictionalized a typical locker-room scene in his novel, *North Dallas Forty*:

> *The prayer thanked the Good Lord for giving us the chance to play football in the United States of America, and asked his protection, reminded him that none of us care about winning or about ourselves (a little reverse psychology on the old Master Workman). I almost laughed at the mention of our sound minds and bodies. Finally the Monsignor . . . invited us to join in the Lord's Prayer. . .*
>
> *". . . the kingdom and the power and the glory forever. Aaamen."*
>
> *The supplicants rose to their feet and broke into a long, animal roar, preparing for battle, as the Monsignor had so eloquently put it.*
>
> *"Let's kill those cocksuckers!" Tony Douglas screamed, leaping up from his knees. He caught himself and glanced sideways at the Monsignor, who was standing near him. "Sorry, Monsignor."*
>
> *"That's all right, Tony," the Monsignor replied. "I know how you feel."*

Bill Glass confirms that Gent, in all his wrath, did not exaggerate. In his autobiography, Glass told of a teammate who took charge of locker-room oratory each Sunday; the player profaned that day's opponents floridly and at length, then dropped to his knees and led his fellows in fervent prayer.

"Football, okay, it's a violent game," concedes Mike McCoy, a

Green Bay Packer whose custom is to write *Revelations 3:20* alongside his autograph. But, McCoy adds, "living is violent. It's all right if you stay within the framework of the rules of the game, and not violate your Christian beliefs. That to me is not a conflict."

Nor to the clergymen who align themselves with a particular team or ride the circuit ministering at large to jocks. The Baltimore Colts have been told by their priest after Sunday mass to "go out and clobber the other team in a Christian manner." In fact, the merger of football and Christianity has done much to enhance Jesus' image, beef him up, make him appear *macho* in a way that never occurred to the rest of his followers.

No less an authority than Ira Eshleman says the mild, peaceful Jesus so often portrayed is a misconception. When at the pulpit, Eshleman likes to tell his flock, "The pictures I see on the walls of Jesus Christ are sickening. They should picture a man at his best physically as opposed to a weakling."

The Reverend Tom Skinner, according to a religion journalist, shows the Washington Redskins the "Locker-room Jesus, the man with hair on his chest and sweat on his brow and dirt under his fingernails. The man who needs deodorant."

But when it comes to taking a fundamentalist deity and stuffing him into shoulder pads and a helmet, no one has matched the efforts of Norman Evans, a Miami Dolphins lineman and author of *On God's Squad*. "If He would play for the Dolphins," Evans wrote, "I guarantee you Christ would be the toughest guy who ever played this game . . . Jesus was a real man, all right. If He were alive today I would picture him as a six foot, six inch, 260-pound defensive tackle who would always make the big plays and would be hard to keep out of the backfield for offensive linemen like myself. Anytime you were up against Him, you'd know you were in for a long afternoon. He would be aggressive and a tremendous competitor . . . I have no doubt he could play in the National Football League. This game is 90 percent desire, and his desire was perhaps his greatest attribute. Yes, He would make it with the Miami Dolphins today, and He would be a star in this league."

Pantheon — One Leg at a Time*

The idea staggered me," F. Scott Fitzgerald wrote in *The Great Gatsby* through his narrator Nick Carraway. "I remembered, of course, that the World Series had been fixed in 1919, but if I thought of it at all I would have thought of it as something that merely *happened*, the end of some inevitable chain. It never occurred to me that one man could start to play with the faith of fifty million people."

Fitzgerald, with his infallible instinct for his countrymen's values, was right on the money. *Eight Men Out*, Eliot Asinof's study of the fix, disclosed that even the gambler who instigated the scheme originally had misgivings. Joseph (Sport) Sullivan was "troubled by the idea at first . . . It was a very special American event. To tamper with it seemed treacherous, almost like sacrilege."

As later events showed, Sullivan and his colleagues were able to suppress their reverence for national institutions. Many months after the fact the sordid story leaked out in bits and pieces from the grand jury room to which the involved White Sox players were being summoned one by one. The Cincinnati Reds, it became increasingly certain, *had* won the Series by virtue of a betting coup in which Chicago players were paid to lose.

Jaws hung agape from coast to coast. Condemnatory resolutions were passed by legislatures and youth groups. Asinof analyzed ". . . the scandal was a betrayal of more than a set of ball games, even more than

*Underdog athletes' hackneyed phrase to remind each other their opponents are only human: "They put their pants on one leg at a time."

of the sport itself. It was a crushing blow at American pride . . . baseball was a manifestation of the greatest of America at play. It was our national game; its stars were national heroes, revered by kids and adults alike, in all classes of society. In the public mind the image was pure and patriotic . . . there is no way to gauge the extent of the damage on the American psyche."

But why such emotional havoc? How was it that competitive impurities in a few exhibitions of athletic prowess could lay waste the psyche of an entire people?

"The trouble was," Asinof answered, "Americans expected higher morals from ballplayers than they expected from . . . anyone else."

This has been so since sport became a form of mass entertainment. The audience, disposed to imagine the intermingling of proficiency and virtue, won't settle for one without the other. Accordingly, a mythology formed concerning the attributes of a big-league jock. He was chaste, at least. Better he should be asexual. When Joe DiMaggio married Marilyn Monroe his New York Yankees teammates were asked by fretting commentators whether the union would be *good for baseball.* (Yogi Berra's legendary reply: "I don't know if it's good for baseball, but it beats the hell out of rooming with Phil Rizzuto.") The hero shrank from alcoholic beverages and tobacco. Henry Aaron, appearing on a TV talk show in 1975, asked for an ashtray in which to stash his cigarette at air time, explaining, "I'd like to kind of hide it from any kids who might be watching." Similarly Commissioner of Baseball Bowie Kuhn ordered the World Series winners' locker-room champagne kept corked until the TV cameras had departed. The jock of myth wouldn't *dream* of touching drugs. He kept his hair cut short and (after the turn of the century) his face clean-shaven. Above all, he practiced conventional Western religion—the more ostentatiously the better—and pledged absolute, unquestioning allegiance to his government. He did these things because of a sense of duty to all his fans, but especially the young ones. The essence of the issue was contained in a short statement made some fifty years after the Series scandal by a man named Mickey Cohen. "Cassius Clay," he told an interviewer, "is a rotten example for kids."

The complainant was the sort of celebrity who had acquired a permanent modifier for use in periodicals: "*Gangster* Mickey Cohen. . . ." He had done eleven years in federal prisons, closing out his latest debt to society—a tax evasion rap—in 1972. As much as the subject of his gripe, Cohen was in the public domain. Yet it could have been anyone—star-quality felon or otherwise—voicing a conviction that made perfect sense to all right-thinking Americans: A man like Mickey Cohen answers to no one for his actions, at least not before talking to his lawyer, but a Muhammad Ali, a man whose occupation was punching people in public, a *champion*, should weigh his actions against the illusions of small boys.

Just as in 1920 Americans were using jocks as human mirrors in which to see reflected themselves, with their collective qualities of nobility, morality, and patriotism. To reflect a different image was a terrible mistake.

That was already clear in 1908 when Jack Johnson became the first black man to hold the heavyweight boxing championship. Johnson offended public sensibilities in a much more fundamental way than Ali would half a century later. He'd had the temerity to win the title, an unspeakable presumption for a man of his hue in the first decade of the twentieth century. But he didn't stop at merely being the wrong color. He was white America's archetypal "uppity nigger." He sinned by living high, boozing, and tearing around in fancy cars. He blasphemed by openly courting white women.

As *The Oxford Companion to World Sports and Games* so Britishly puts it, "His exuberant personality brought him much criticism." While boxing promoters scrambled to find the white man who could beat Johnson (and in the process turned race loyalty to their profit with a White Hope Championship tournament), politicians and police hounded the champion. Johnson's marriage to a white woman is considered the historical impetus for passage of the Mann Act (forbidding transport of a woman across a state line for "immoral purposes"), a federal statute ostensibly aimed at prostitution.

Johnson's lifestyle also prompted Seaborn A. Roddenberry, a Georgia congressman, to introduce a resolution in 1912 to ban intermarriage, with the observation that "No brutality, no infamy, no degradation in all the years of southern slavery, possessed such villainous character and such atrocious qualities as the state laws which allow the marriage of the Negro Jack Johnson to a woman of the caucasian strain."

Johnson's defeat of Jim Jeffries in 1910 set off riots throughout the United States. In the aftermath of the bout, Congress passed a law forbidding interstate commerce in the marketing of fight films. The measure cost Johnson a fortune over the years. With the establishment unified against him, he suffered financially, went into European exile, and some years later succumbed in Havana to a White Hope named Jess Willard. To the further delight of his antagonists he was ultimately nabbed on a Mann Act charge and spent eight months in prison.

Johnson's specter survived his ring skills by decades. Twenty years passed before another black man was allowed to fight for the heavyweight title, and the latter's decorum in public was finely circumscribed by his predecessor's image.

It was imperative for Joe Louis to seem the humble, grateful, passionless colored man of the only sort entitled to the adulation of the masses. Gerald Astor, a Louis biographer, quotes a boxing moralist: "You know why he'll be remembered long after a guy like Jack Johnson is forgotten? Because he knew his place—nobody could point a finger at him with white women."

Interracial sex being the main bugaboo ("Above all," Louis's manager had told him, in dispensing instruction on a black champion's conduct, "you must never have your picture taken with white women") Louis was scrupulously surreptitious in his carnal adventures and avoided, throughout his career, the virulent hatred that destroyed Johnson.

If Louis represented great progress toward conformity with public expectations, Muhammad Ali was a throwback to Johnson. He displayed a spirit too inflexible for saying or doing the politic thing; he acted as if he owed the caucasian strain nothing. His problems began when, a day after taking the heavyweight title from Sonny Liston in 1964, he announced his affiliation with the Black Muslims (an Islamic black separatist group) and the renunciation of his given name, Cassius

Clay. These changes would have caused controversy even were the country at peace, patriotic fervor dormant, draft calls minimal.

The idea of an influential jock espousing such a threatening cause—at that time Black Muslims still officially regarded whites as "devils"—never sat well with the sports-conscious public. Thousands would never refer to Ali by his chosen name and preferred to think of him as either a dupe of the insidious Elijah Muhammad or a dangerous militant, a man who had no claim to the admiration a heavyweight champion ordinarily got. What complicated the situation was Lyndon Johnson's great need during the mid-1960s for American boys to fight a war in Asia.

As usual, attention focused on the presumably ablest-bodied, i.e., the top jocks. Also as usual, many of them—especially in football and basketball—had chronic injuries that disqualified them, or were able, through the influence of team owners, to enlist in reserve units. Few saw active duty; the only pro athlete wounded in the Vietnam war was Rocky Bleier of the Pittsburgh Steelers.

Ali contended that he was exempt as a Muslim minister. For a time that question was academic; Ali's pre-induction intelligence test score was in the 16th percentile, well below the passing grade of the 30th. He was classified 1-Y—unfit to be a soldier.

Rumors were spread that strings had been pulled on Ali's behalf, and millions wanted to believe it was true. How, it was asked, could this glib fixture of the TV talk shows, who practiced psychology so cunningly on boxing opponents, be too stupid for the U.S. Army? The answer may have had something to do with the cultural bias of standardized tests and the sort of education available to blacks in the public schools of Louisville, Kentucky; it was a fact that Ali could barely read. It soon came not to matter anyway.

When it seemed reaction to Ali's exemption could grow no more strident, the draft board lowered its standards enough to qualify all who scored in the 15th percentile or higher. Ali was reclassified 1-A. He chose the occasion to firm his position. "I ain't got no quarrel with them Vietcongs," he declared, provoking a fresh wave of recriminations.

In April 1967 he was ordered to report to his draft jurisdiction in Houston for induction. Despite his unequivocally stated intention of refusing induction and fighting the case in court, it was widely speculated that, faced with conviction and the loss of his considerable earning power, Ali would take the graceful way out by becoming an athletic ornament for the armed forces. That was what Joe Louis had done in World War II, giving exhibitions and pep talks to the troops. So had many other jocks, some of far less stature. The free ride was available even to such marginal figures as Bobby Riggs, a tennis champion of modest renown during the forties, who later admitted, "My most important duty on Guam was to keep a 4:00 P.M. tennis date with the admiral and his aides."

At any rate there clearly was no danger Ali would turn up in the Mekong Delta toting a rifle and floating like a butterfly through the rice paddies. Howard Cosell, the sportscaster, wrote that Army sources said that if Ali had submitted to the draft, he would have been required only to spend thirty days entertaining troops overseas before being allowed to return home to fight Floyd Patterson. In the end Ali rejected this option; he stood in place when his fellow draftees took the symbolic step forward.

No sooner had the news of Ali's refusal been made public than the New York State Boxing Commission, under the chairmanship of Edwin Dooley, revoked both Ali's license and his championship. Cosell wrote:

> *Mr. Dooley, a former congressman, was doing the popular thing. But there had been no arraignment, no grand jury hearing, no indictment, no trial, no conviction, no appeal to a higher court . . . In other words, due process of law had not even been initiated, let alone exhausted. Under the Fifth Amendment, no person may be deprived of life, liberty or property without due process of law. Yet every state in the Union adopted the action of the New York Commission. Now here was Ali: unable to fight anywhere in America; stripped of his right to leave the country, hence unable to fight overseas either.*

Three years later a federal district court upheld Ali's claim that his constitutional rights had been abridged by the boxing commission. Meanwhile, the government was winning the draft refusal case; Ali was convicted and the conviction was sustained by the circuit court of appeals. In May 1971 the decision was reversed by the Supreme Court, which found Ali's religious claims valid.

This was vindication but not reparation. Ali had suffered great loss, of both income and irreplaceable prime physical years. His situation had been such a liability that, according to Cosell, someone in the federal government pressured the American Broadcasting Company to remove Ali from his role as commentator for an amateur boxing telecast. When Ali's boxing license was restored in October 1970 he set out to regain the championship, starting with a bout against Jerry Quarry in Atlanta. True to the tradition of Seaborn A. Roddenberry, Gov. Lester Maddox of Georgia declared the day of the fight a "Day of Mourning."

Ali's experience could be taken as evidence that blackness is still a predominant offense against society's idealization of its jocks. But for the athlete unwilling to conform politically, it has been no advantage to be white.

In his first season as a pro basketball player Bill Walton publicly denounced the United States government and the FBI, which had brought his name into the Patty Hearst-Symbionese Liberation Army case. Even before the flap Walton, a vegetarian who talked and dressed like a "hippie," had been regarded by sports fans as a misfit. For a time he shared a house with Jack Scott, one of the early sports sociologists and himself a bogeyman to orthodox thinkers. When Scott, too, was linked with the underground elements that had helped hide Hearst, he and Walton held a well-attended news conference in San Francisco. Walton reproached the FBI for its methods and urged "the people of the world to stand with us in our rejection of the United States government."

His comments evoked a bitter response, much of it on the level attained by Furman Bisher, columnist for an Atlanta newspaper and *The Sporting News*. Bisher lumped Walton with a "rebel cult" characterized by "much hair, anti-soap-and-water, and a wardrobe that appears designed for sewer cleaning." Those who were above attacking Walton for his choice of attire suggested instead that the unshorn basketball star was not only unpatriotic but somehow immoral in continuing to accept compensation from the Portland Trail Blazers while criticizing the government. The management of the franchise hastily dissociated itself from Walton's views. In the course of the disclaimer, Larry Weinberg, president of the Trail Blazers, pronounced the United States "the freest and most democratic nation in the world," but he neglected to explain why his employee shouldn't feel free to take advantage of that.

Walton was beginning to learn about the unwritten clause in the First Amendment that exempts heroes of the playing field from freedom of speech. In an interview with the *Oregon Journal* he tried to clarify his position: "I'm not a wild-eyed, crazed maniac. I have come to what I believe are responsible conclusions. I can't stress enough that it's not the American people or the Constitution of this country that I think should be rejected. It's the trend, the practices and the actions of recent governments. . . ."

To which *The Sporting News* replied in an editorial, "Scarcely a week had passed before this cage star-political leftist-social critic had backed off . . . Some observers suggested [he was] inspired by fear he'd blown his chances to collect fully on his rich cage contract. But anti-capitalist Walton wouldn't worry about that, would he?"

Intellectually, the denunciations were on a par with the thinking of then Vice-President Spiro Agnew, who several years earlier had reviled Jack Scott and Dave Meggysey, a pro football player turned writer, for disclosing drug abuse among athletes and picturing big-time sports as a moral wasteland. Choosing his audience discreetly—the speech was made at a banquet honoring Alabama football players—Agnew made innuendoes about the title of Scott's book, *The Athletic Revolution*, and the fact that it contained a quote from Bernadette Devlin. Having subtly hinted that Scott and Meggysey were some sort of Lenin-Trotsky duo, Agnew fulminated at length on their attempt to undermine football with false accusations (the drug stories were true, however), the appropriateness of short hair in sports, and related subjects.

Historically, though, no question of propriety has seemed to fluster the sports establishment quite so much as matters concerning, uh . . . er, ah, sex. All baseball blushed brightly when, in 1973 spring training, two New York Yankee pitchers announced that—after serious contemplation—each would henceforth live with the other's wife and children. In the most predictable pronouncement in the history of the game, Commissioner Bowie Kuhn disapproved.

When Lance Rentzel (a pro football player who had been arrested for exposing himself to little girls and who publicized the fact that he was under treatment for the problem) was indicted for possession of marijuana, he was suspended from the National Football League. As in the Muhammad Ali case due process of law had not even begun. The *New York Times* reported: "There are those who suspect Rentzel's drug troubles provided a convenient excuse for the league to banish him so none of the millions of television viewers would be able to say, 'Look at that pervert.'" With just a few exceptions, suggestions of lust— legitimate or otherwise—have been anathema to the packagers and sellers of athletic entertainment.

As much as this sensitivity can be laid to prevailing community standards, it may also hark back to some extent to turn-of-the-century dime novels in which heroes expended all their passions on the field and courtship was restricted to tongue-tied, hands-off strolls with the girl next door. Far from oblivious to the success of the formula, nonfiction writers adopted the convention of representing ballplayers as Galahads in spiked shoes. Early chroniclers, particularly of Babe Ruth, seemed acutely conscious of the possibility that the young and/or impressionable might read their work.

Ruth, in fact, was the greatest beneficiary of the practice. Among the famous athletes of the period known as the Golden Age of Sport, only Bill Tilden had more shocking secrets. Tilden was a homosexual, the only prominent jock known to have been one, even up to modern times. During his prime (a long stretch when he dominated his sport to an unprecedented extent, going years without losing an important match), tennis officials silently prayed the truth would remain hidden. After Tilden's skills eroded he was ostracized; he died in poverty, and his story was not dealt with fully in print until 1975.*

---

*Homosexuality has remained the strongest taboo in sports. When a newspaper called *The Advocate* sent letters to major-league baseball teams in 1975 asking for interviews with "players living a gay lifestyle," the publicity director of the Minnesota Twins not only

FANS!

As for Ruth—whose renown at the time was so much greater than Tilden's or anyone else's, and whose image was proportionately more critical—it was not until decades after his heyday that anyone published an unexpurgated version of his life. Eventually, a spate of revisionist biographies *did* appear, churning out the hidden facts with now-it-can-be-told breathlessness: The Babe didn't know from table manners or personal hygiene; evidence suggests he sired an indeterminate number of illegitimate children; his "stomach ache heard round the world"—the episode that laid him up from a supposed overindulgence in hot dogs and soda pop—more likely was a coverup of syphilis; as the foregoing would indicate, his favorite recreation had to do with beds, but not necessarily those occupied by sickly children.

What made these disclosures possible and killed the fiction that an outstanding jock's only passion is for victory? Possibly the changes in consciousness that came to be known as the sexual revolution of the 1960s were influential.

After all, more than half a century had passed since the moral covenant between big jocks and small boys had been written in the press boxes of the land. Chastity and monogamy were down to their last few partisans, and people weren't so easy to shock anymore. Henry Ford II, discovered gamboling with a model while his wife was out of the country in 1975, earned a nationwide guffaw by cracking to reporters, "Never complain, never explain." And so, it was noteworthy for a man to be caught nude in a parked camper with a woman other than his wife only if the man was a big-league baseball player.

Cleon Jones, a New York Mets outfielder who'd had his glorious moments, had been injured during spring training; he stayed in Florida to work himself into shape when the team went north to start the season in May 1975. One evening he and a companion parked on a city street in

---

forbade the publication to mention the team but gratuitously denounced "your colossal gall in attempting to extend your perversion to an area of total manhood. . . ." The same year the *Washington Star* found in a survey that homosexual or bisexual athletes had to keep their preferences secret or give up sports and that female pro golfers had been told by sponsors that prize money was held down by the sponsors' conviction that the tour was dominated by lesbians.

St. Petersburg. A passing policeman who happened to look in the window arrested them for indecent exposure.

There wasn't much of a legal case. The charges were dropped on the theory that nothing had been exposed to anyone except the cop who looked into the van. That might have been the end of it, had the Mets' management not perceived a breach of the public trust. From the high office of Donald Grant, chairman of the board, this is how the situation looked: Since the last third of the nineteenth century—if not time immemorial—baseball had stood for all the virtues America believed in. To overlook the St. Petersburg Scandal, to appear to condone it, would be to risk losing the devotion of every clean-minded youth in Greater New York; gate receipts might well be at stake. Accordingly, Jones was fined $2,000—four times the previous team record.

Mere financial punishment seemed insufficient to the Mets, however. Something graphic was needed, perhaps something in the way of theatrical contrition. So Grant organized a press conference for Jones and his wife and read to the media a confession purportedly written by his erstwhile outfielder:

> *I wish to apologize publicly to my wife and children, the Mets'*
> *ownership and management, my teammates and to all Met fans*
> *and to* baseball in general [*emphasis added*] . . . *I am ashamed.*
> *Baseball is my life and I am pleading for a chance to get it back. I*
> *am basically a good man, and have no desire to be bad . . . I*
> *have promised management that if they permit me to rejoin the*
> *team, where I can regain the confidence of everyone and the*
> *support of my family, no one will regret having done so.*

A few months later Muhammad Ali declined to seek anyone's forgiveness when extramarital relations became a sideshow to his bout with Joe Frazier in the Philippines. Ali's infidelities were nothing new; sportswriters had known about them for years and had witnessed in Zaire, the previous summer, the first confrontation between Belinda, the wife, and Veronica Porche, the girl friend. The women had come out of that one unmarked, but Ali had sustained a few facial scratches. Some months later, in Kuala Lumpur, Malaysia, the trio appeared to be getting along peaceably.

FANS!

Until then Ms. Porche had been identified to the public only as the Ali family babysitter. In Manila no effort was made to conceal the fact that taking care of the kids was not her only duty. Ali escorted Veronica to a reception given by President Marcos, who took an admiring look at the statuesque lady and complimented Ali on his taste in the choice of a "wife." Apparently wishing not to confuse his host, Ali simply answered that Mrs. Marcos's appearance spoke well for the president.

The exchange of pleasantries led Manila newspapers to identify Veronica in photos as Ali's spouse. People started asking questions, and suddenly Ali's love life was a bigger story than the annual Fight of the Century. Within a single prefight week there were references to the Ali-Porche affair in *Time, Newsweek, Esquire, Rolling Stone,* the *New York Times*, and countless other papers. It was time to take a stand, and Ali did. "Hell," he said at one point, "do you think a man as pretty as me wouldn't have a girl friend?" He said he had several others and named them. Later he said, "I don't care what people think. I have a lot of lady friends. The main thing is she ain't white, so don't worry about it . . . You just tell people not to worry about who I'm sleeping with, and I won't worry about who they're sleeping with. I don't know any young men who are married in America who don't have girl friends . . . Why are they getting on me?"

This was confronting the issue squarely. Infidelity was at least as American as apple pie, maybe more American than prizefighting. Ali seemed to have struck the right chord; most observers were intrigued rather than outraged by his amours. There were scattered complaints—in New Orleans a shocked Archbishop Hannon ordered Catholic students to boycott a postfight visit by Ali—but the champ, certain of his exalted place in the cosmic scheme of things, flicked away this minor annoyance. He told a reporter, "I don't want to make some archbishop I don't know world famous," and likened Hannon to a dog baying at the moon. Besides, he said, the world had been taken in again by an Ali hype. The sex to-do was "just a put-on to boost ticket sales. I arranged it all. Tickets weren't going so good."

Friends in High Places

The Washington Touchdown Club's 1967 Mr. Sam Award—a prize conferred for services by a public official in the best interests of sports—went to Everett McKinley Dirksen, then Senate minority leader. His benefaction? A law allowing the National Football League and the American Football League to merge. Dirksen's colorful acceptance speech sounded calculated to show two things: the depth of his commitment to special privilege for pro football and his spiritual kinship with the Touchdown Clubbers. This is how he summarized events surrounding the bill's passage:

> *Congressman Celler, who was conducting hearings on the Senate-passed Merger Bill, had possession of the ball. While he was discussing a rule of order terminating the hearing until the call of the chair, the clock was ticking toward the end of the game and the Senate grabbed the ball. In the huddle I motioned to Sen. Russell Long that now is the time for the long bomb and for him to run like hell for the goalpost. Some people accused us of a sneakplay or an endaround play but it wasn't. I just faded back to pass to Russell Long heading for the goal line with Celler still watching the clock . . .*

The honoree amplified: October 13, 1966, had been "an unlucky day for Pete Rozelle, George Halas, the Murchisons, the Hunts . . . to name a few among the many fine owners . . ." With Congress planning to recess a week later, the House Judiciary Committee had hung up hearings on the special antitrust exemption the two leagues needed to become one. The owners were looking to this legislation to end their bidding war for college players. At the time the only protection the AFL and the NFL enjoyed against a graduate who was out to get as much money as he could was a mechanism called the *draft*. This was not to be denigrated as a money-saver, since it confined each greedy collegian's dealings to the team that had chosen him. But as long as there were two leagues and two drafts, many players would still have some bargaining leverage. Ultimately the Dirksen-to-Long touchdown pass took care of that, but the congressional quarterback was a little embarrassed that it took so long to seal the victory.

In 1961, when the NFL had asked Congress for an antitrust loophole for the specific purpose of negotiating collectively with the TV networks, the requested bill was signed into law twelve days after its introduction. Noting that "Congress can move the ball quickly when it makes up its mind to do so," Dirksen virtually apologized to the Touchdown Club for the fact that it took longer to push the merger bill across the goal line. But the House Judiciary defense had been tough until it weakened at the end of the game.

On October 14, the day after Celler had started his delaying action, Dirksen tacked the bill, as an amendment, to a tax bill the House had already passed. Within a week the package was safely on its way to the president's desk, having been shepherded through the Capitol by Russell Long in the Senate and Hale Boggs in the House. The merger became law.

The Louisiana legislators' zeal became understandable next time the NFL expanded. One of the new teams was awarded to New Orleans. But if anyone involved was abashed at the evidence of a quid-pro-quo, it didn't show; Dirksen chortled admiringly over the bargain Long and Boggs had driven. The whole thing had been conducted in a perfectly businesslike way, after all, and how else was Congress to cope with the knotty questions of what should or shouldn't be legal for sports tycoons?

The dilemma had been created nearly a century earlier, in the infancy of professional team sports. (The only one at the time was baseball.) The problem was rooted in the concept that a group of jocks "represented" the city in which they were paid to play. The industry had existed for just a few years before its entrepreneurs discovered a deplorable flaw in the average player's character: he could be persuaded to change teams for a bigger salary when his contract expired. Then, as now, franchise owners stood staunchly for untrammeled free enterprise, but they were uncharacteristically flexible in conceding that moderation must be practiced in this instance. And so they created the reserve system. Each team granted itself permanent options on the services of a specified number of ballplayers, who henceforth could either take what their respective owners offered at contract time or go home. A man became free to negotiate with other teams when he got his unconditional release, which happened when the legs weakened and the eyesight dimmed.

The system proved more than satisfactory in holding down payrolls. In fact, the owners were so delighted they soon extended it to cover all players, inspiring founders of latter-day football, basketball, and hockey leagues to adopt comparable measures.

While such systems are instituted to eliminate costly competition, owners regard them as defensible in other ways: The rules are meant to protect the fans' interests, they say. Since sports is not a business but a mystical blend of beauty, emotion, and chauvinistic expression, its followers can hardly be expected to tolerate the spectacle of jocks brazenly chasing a buck. Besides, pro leagues, whose preservation is *a priori* society's foremost interest, couldn't survive the economic strain of treating players as employees rather than chattels.

When baseball was given monopolistic *carte blanche* in 1922 an entirely different argument was used. In a case known as *Federal Baseball,* originating in a player's challenge to the reserve clause, the Supreme Court ruled that baseball was not subject to antitrust; Justice Holmes explained that baseball was neither trade nor commerce, and by no stretch of the imagination could be construed as interstate commerce.

Successive Courts declined to contradict the learned man. But neither did they have the gall, when the issue came up decades later, to make the same claims on behalf of football, basketball, and hockey. There being no way to avoid reference to the contradiction, Dirksen leaped over it in his Touchdown Club speech by saying, "I don't have time to explain the fine arguments why baseball was treated differently from the other sports." (Neither did members of the High Court "have time" to explain to President Eisenhower, as William O. Douglas recalled in *Go East, Young Man*. "Felix Frankfurter and I had trouble restraining ourselves when Ike asked Earl Warren what the difference in antitrust law was between baseball and football. Of course, there was no difference. . . .")

That didn't mean any league had been *prevented* from enforcing its version of the reserve clause. None had any trouble keeping players in line until a few lower-court decisions in the mid-1970s began going the wrong way. The NFL had gone to the trouble of creating an elaborate fiction by which players appeared free to better themselves: A man was entitled to "play out his option"—that is, stay with his old team for a season, without a contract, at a percentage of his previous salary, and then go job-hunting. Ostensibly superstar and journeyman alike, no longer indentured, could find boundless opportunity. But the owners added a safeguard against subjecting themselves to undue suffering because they weren't willing to pay as much as one of their employees might earn elsewhere. Called the Rozelle Rule (after Commissioner Pete Rozelle), it stipulated that the forsaken team had to be compensated—in money and/or flesh—by the seductive team, *at Rozelle's discretion*. By vigorous use of his powers, the commissioner was able to reduce attempted desertions to a minimum. It took a while before the outside world got the drift, but by 1975 a shocked Tom Wicker rhetorically asked his *New York Times* readers how they'd like it if they couldn't just work off their contracts and split, or how a General Motors honcho would feel if he weren't free to go across the street to Ford when the right offer came along.

The freedom to be competitive or noncompetitive, depending on the situation, has been enormously useful to pro leagues. It helped in 1975, for instance, when Bobby Orr, the Boston Bruins' superduperstar defenseman made it known that he was thinking of leaving his National Hockey League team to join the rival World Hockey Association. People paid dearly to watch Orr bash pucks and opponents, not only in the city he "represented," but in every arena in the league. His loss would mean less revenue for anyone with stock in an NHL team; with that fear in mind the league owners decided they would all subsidize his new Boston contract if necessary.

It went without saying that if Orr were an asset to the whole league, the whole league had a stake in making him look superduper on the ice, not to mention in insuring his bodily safety. With any luck, the public would never stop to think about such things. Meantime the question was, would the salary syndication play in Peoria? In a courtroom? "We have already explored the legality of such a venture as it would pertain to the antitrust laws," Clarence Campbell, the league president, said, adding that hockey's best legal minds were convinced the law would not be violated. Besides, the WHA, too, was ready to pool its money to put Orr on one of its teams.

A year earlier the supposed rival members of the American Basketball Association had also turned temporarily fraternal in an effort to put Bill Walton, graduating from UCLA, in the employ of one of its members. And in March 1976 the National Basketball Association acknowledged the accuracy of a *New York Times* report that said several stars—among them Rick Barry, Kareem Abdul-Jabbar, and Elvin Hayes—had been paid through a pooling arrangement in which all teams participated.

Along with the freedom to operate their leagues as cartels, pro teams enjoy federal subsidies, in the form of tax loopholes, and state and municipal subsidies, in the form of stadiums and arenas. Every team needs a place to play, and if the public isn't going to pay for it, who is?

"Build your own stadium?" Edward Bennett Williams, Washington Redskins' president, once exclaimed, recoiling from a reporter's horrifying question. "We would never do that. The economics of stadium operation are impossible unless you have an assurance of subsidies from the city or state governments."

Not many states or cities are naive enough to expect a man who's running a team to cut into profits by providing the ballpark too. Neither do they ignore the intangible benefit of having pro games played locally, namely the cultural enrichment of everyone with enough money or influence to get tickets. By way of introducing a $350-million stadium bill in 1973, Perry Duryea, speaker of the New York State Assembly, said, "Professional sports teams make immeasurable contributions to the good will and spirit of a community. Without this elusive thing called spirit no amount of economic well being can infuse a community with enthusiasm and a sense of common purpose." The only drawback is that while the profits are immeasurable and metaphysical, the losses are measurable and real. While annual interest obligations at Washington's RFK Stadium, for instance, came to $831,600, the largest remittance in any given year was $480,000. Every year the Treasury Department, hence the taxpayers, made up the difference so that a privileged few could continue to watch the Redskins.

But the RFK deficit was laughable compared to the public drain entailed by the erection of the New Orleans Superdome, a structure provided by the taxpayers of Louisiana for the New Orleans Saints football team and whatever baseball outfit might eventually turn up. The Superdome was built a decade after the Houston Astrodome, the first enclosed all-sports stadium, which was often called the Eighth Wonder of the World. If that was accurate, then the Superdome was unquestionably the Ninth. It was "the largest room ever built for human use." It was 27 stories high and covered 52 acres, and the whole Astrodome could easily fit inside it. It could seat 97,365. According to its boosters, the Superdome was "the depository of Louisiana's belief in itself . . . exhilarating, moving certainty that tomorrow can be now."

The project was authorized on the understanding that it would cost about $35 million. The Superdome ran into unexpected expenses, however. When it was completed, the original estimate was found to have been off by about $130 million. These things happen, and perhaps the public understood. But the Ninth Wonder wasn't cheap on the upkeep, either. It cost $38,000 a day to operate; the energy bill alone came to $1.75 million a year. (Besides which, the architecture made it possible for malicious types to drop food, drinks, and ice 17 stories onto spectators and players below, and an extra $60,000 had to be spent for a barrier.) As a partial measure the state imposed a 4 percent hotel tax in two counties and started renting parking space to shoppers on nongame days at the arena. Still, Louisianans would have to pay indefinitely.

This was no more the concern of the Saints' management than the cost of New York City's gracious refurbishment of Yankee Stadium has been to the Yankees'. The stadium, originally built for $2.5 million, would cost $24 million to renovate, according to a city estimate made in 1972. In two years that figure doubled. Then it went to $64 million and ultimately settled at about $75 million. "The city government is so broke it just shut down 43 schools," George Will wrote. "But . . . perhaps children learn more of lasting value in Yankee Stadium than in the typical New York public school."

Perhaps, but as Will knew perfectly well, that was not the issue at all. A sports complex was going up in the New Jersey meadowlands across the George Washington Bridge, under the direction of politicians who were just as eager as any others to acquire the only thing that can infuse a community with a sense of purpose. If New York wasn't willing to make the Yankees comfortable, they could always go elsewhere.

This was one of the eternal verities of pro sports. In 1975 Calvin Griffith, owner of the Minnesota Twins, told the business community of Minneapolis-St. Paul he expected more cooperation than he was getting. "I was wined and dined when they succeeded in getting me to move," he said, referring to his decision in 1961 that the Twin Cities public deserved baseball more than the Washington public. "I'd like to be convinced," Griffith added, "the business leaders in this area are as interested in keeping us here as they were in getting us to move here." He went on to say that he expected more effort by civic leaders in peddling season tickets. He wanted a better shake on his stadium deal—as rent he paid 7 percent of the gate minus the visiting team's share, plus 10 percent of the gross concessions. Better yet, he said, everyone would be better off if his hosts would just spring for a new domed stadium. "Every time it rains," he complained, "it costs us money."

As for the tax situation, teams are permitted to depreciate players as if they were pieces of machinery. On paper the value of the actual franchise (not depreciable, because it's regarded as having an indefinite life) is minimized. The cost of acquiring players is maximized, and their careers depreciated on a five-year scale. Thus the annual balance sheet shows huge (nonexistent) losses, which not only help owners avoid taxation on their teams' actual income but also provide deductions against profits from other enterprises.

A federal tax suit against the Atlanta Falcons in 1974-1975 illustrated the workings of the system. Five Smiths (the team's corporate name) had paid $8.5 million to join the National Football League in 1966. Only $50,000 was treated for tax purposes as the cost of acquiring the franchise. While that might seem a shamefully small pittance for membership in an organization like the NFL, the accounting staff of Five Smiths was well aware that nothing could be written off against the franchise fee. Five Smiths ascribed $7.7 million to the acquisition of player contracts and set up a five-year depreciation schedule for the whole amount.

Result: In its first two years the corporation was able to report tax losses while actually netting profits of about $1 million each year. The government's lawyers argued that, since the team's share of league television rights was worth $1.2 million immediately and since the owners had purchased the right to offer pro football exclusively in the Atlanta area, the depreciation allowance was excessive. The government further showed its inability to grasp reality by suggesting that no depreciation on humans should be allowed to buyers of existing teams or original owners (like Five Smiths) of expansion teams.

"If the court had agreed," an observer wrote, "the effect on sports economics would have been devastating." Most baseball franchises were worth at least $10 million by 1975, and many NFL teams nearly twice that, all because of the spectacular write-off possibilities. Take them away, and franchise values would collapse like the stock market on Black Friday. Not to worry: The tax court was most understanding, upholding the principle of five-year player depreciation and merely reducing the percentage Five Smiths could in good conscience represent as expended on the acquisition of human equipment.

Meanwhile, as the suit was contested, the National Basketball Association chose Lawrence O'Brien to succeed Walter Kennedy as commissioner. Some observers were offended. Editorializing on the surprise move, *Sports Illustrated* noted that "aside from the fact that he was born in Springfield, Massachusetts, where the game was invented, O'Brien's connections with basketball are nil."

But his connections with the federal government were extensive. He had been presidential adviser, cabinet member, chairman of the Democratic National Committee. The selection of a man who knew his way around Washington—at a time when pro sports leagues' special legal status was facing more determined challenges than ever before— showed that the NBA owners understood the situation perfectly. Their decision was entirely practical, the only adverse result being the important mutterings of purists like the *Sports Illustrated* editors, who continued, "Rather than choosing someone from within the sport . . . the owners have apparently agreed on what they think they want: a $150,000-a-year lobbyist whose job is to persuade congressmen and others of the righteousness of the NBA's position . . . Lobbyists may be all right in their way, but it is not encouraging that one of our major professional leagues should be headed by one of them."

On the contrary, it must have been comforting for O'Brien's employers to know they were represented by a pro politician. His exclusive concern, after all, would be the health of the industry, his chief responsibility preservation of the cozy arrangements that had been passing for governmental regulation. Nothing bore more directly on the continued prosperity of such enterprises than the continued indulgence of men in high places, and O'Brien could earn his $150,000 by doing his part to sustain the mood in which the Curt Flood lawsuit was decided.

Flood was a centerfielder for the St. Louis Cardinals whose legal problems began in 1969 when he was traded to Philadelphia. Being in some respects an average American, Flood preferred to live and work elsewhere. On the other hand, he didn't want to quit baseball. Exercising the only remaining alternative, he sued, claiming players were treated as chattels and that the standard player contract violated federal antitrust law. The Holmes precedent of 1922 was discouraging, to say the least.

But Flood and his lawyer, Arthur Goldberg, who expected the case to reach the high Court, had reason to hope: The Warren Court had shown a strong inclination to expand personal freedom. In the years between the filing of the suit and the final appeal, however, the Warren

Court became the Nixon Court. The ascendancy of personal rights was over; besides, jock talk was in, and the man in the Oval Office was nothing if not a baseball fan.

Flood's argument boiled down to this: Baseball's contractual practices deprived him of constitutional rights afforded citizens in every occupation but sports. Justice Blackmun's response, in the majority opinion, began with a three-page panegyric to the lore and legend of the Grand Old Game. "It is a century and a quarter," the learned man opened, with an acute instinct for the heart of the matter, "since the New York Nine defeated the Knickerbockers 23 to 1 on Hoboken's Elysian Fields, June 19, 1846, with Alexander Jay Cartwright as the instigator and the umpire."

Blackmun inexplicably omitted the line score and the identity of the winning pitcher, hurrying on instead into an affectionate sketch of those infant days of baseball. He cast a benevolent glow on the "outpouring of local pride" felt for the Cincinnati Red Stockings of 1869, "the ensuing colorful days," and "tinder for recaptured thrills, for reminiscence and comparisons, and for conversation and comparison in-season and off-season."

Scarcely pausing to munch his hot dog and sip his beer, the Bench-warmer rattled on, listing (in no apparent order) the names of every old-time great he could think of. He could think of eighty-six: Unforgotten were such trivia-session gems as Old Hoss Radbourne, an early perfect-game pitcher; Bill Wambsganss, whose claim to remembrance was the only unassisted triple play in World Series history; and even an umpire, Bill Klem, who (as every baseball-loving Justice must have known) "never called one wrong in my heart." Blackmun went so far as to apologize in the footnotes that "By mentioning some, one risks unintended omissions of others equally celebrated."

After the pantheon came a reference to one of the all-time great baseball poems, Ernest Thayer's "Casey at the Bat," an excerpt from Grantland Rice's incredulous "He Never Heard of Casey," and the entire text of Franklin Pierce Adams's "Baseball's Sad Lexicon," better known in saloons as "Tinker to Evers to Chance."

Legal sticklers were a bit taken aback, as if the Court had prefaced its decision in a civil-rights case with a paean to the joys of life in the antebellum South, tossed in the lyrics to "Dixie" and "Massa's in de Cold, Cold Ground," and wrapped up the whole thing by telling the plaintiff, "Frankly, my dear, we don't give a damn." But as far as most red-blooded Americans were concerned, this was the perfect foreword to a ruling on an issue that purportedly threatened the status quo of baseball.

Besides, if it wasn't exactly what Flood had been hoping for, it was downright evenhanded compared to the lower-court decision. Drawing on the legal theory that guided Blackmun, Judge Irving Ben Cooper of New York District Court had determined that, "Baseball's status in the life of the nation is so pervasive that it would not strain credulity to say the Court can take notice that baseball is everybody's business. To put it mildly and with restraint, it would be unfortunate indeed if a fine sport and profession, which brings surcease from daily travail and an escape from the ordinary to most inhabitants of this land, were to suffer in the least because of undue concentration by any one or any group on commercial and profit considerations. The game is on higher ground; it behooves every one to keep it there."

Hockey Means Never Having to Say You're Sorry

The refinement of promotion techniques in American team sports advanced to a new level in spring 1974 with the creation of the National Box Lacrosse League, soon known as the National Lacrosse League. Unabashedly and without mincing words the NLL appealed to the potential customer's enthusiasm for bloodshed—an historic point of departure. Predecessors in the industry had used violence—with varying degrees of subtlety—as a selling point but had never presented it as a game's *raison d'être*. Never had a team "sport" advertised by saying, "Come on out and watch men mangle each other!"

This, in so many words, was the NLL message. The Maryland franchise took the lead, with a campaign designed around a cartoon ogre named Crunch Crosscheck, whose motto was "Ya gotta be mean ta play box lacrosse!" Along with Crunch's print ads, there were radio spots done as interviews with Attila the Hun (and Genghis Khan and Ivan the Terrible), who remarked on box lacrosse's striking similarity to the sacking of a city. The Philadelphia Wings sought to benefit from the local hockey team's image; would-be spectators were urged to think of box lacrosse as a kind of hockey in which every team was the Philadelphia Flyers, which was to say something approaching a collection of sadists and homicidal maniacs. The genius of this approach was confirmed when the Wings' opening game drew 12,841 on an evening when the Flyers had already used up many spectator dollars in a championship game in the same arena earlier in the day.

At no point—before *or* after opening night—were the NLL flacks accused of using hyperbole. Box lacrosse, already established commercially on a much smaller scale in Canada, was the evolutionary perfection of standard (outdoor) lacrosse, a heinous pastime in its own right, descended from a paramilitary activity of North American Indian tribes. (In the United States, however, the game first became popular not among ill-bred ruffians but at fashionable eastern prep schools and colleges, where it remained fairly exclusive until the second half of the twentieth century.) Historical accounts suggest its inventors used the game as a divertissement, as well as an amusing way to desecrate the severed head of a war captive, which was often the source of a ball.

Considering both its antecedents and its public promises, the NLL had a lot to live up to. It didn't fail. After a first look, one observer wrote that the game combined "the best features of outdoor field lacrosse with elements of basketball, hockey, soccer, and thermonuclear holocaust." Another sportswriter said, "Box lacrosse makes first-degree murder seem like a church outing." Another was reminded of "the battle of Stalingrad indoors."

Hockey, whose shining example had lighted the way for box lacrosse, catered to appetites for gore only slightly less brazenly throughout its half-century of existence. Individual teams cultivated images of brutality, the most notable being Philadelphia. Local news outlets there cooperated, calling the team the Broad Street Bullies, and management adopted an advertising theme stressing that the Flyers' gratuitous savagery was worth the price of a seat. Commercials and promotional films showed fistfights instead of hockey, and the Flyers experienced spectacular success at the box office.

The National Football League, too, had exploited in not-so-oblique ways the fact that the game often had gruesome effects on players. There were commercials showing horrifying collisions, documentaries called "The Violent World of . . ." There was an ever-growing martial lexicon: *blitz, bomb, trenches, suicide squad.* And the NFL was regarded as a paragon of marketing success among pro leagues. Still, football and hockey had never abandoned descriptions of themselves as entertainments that offered drama and beauty and fostered civic, national, or institutional pride.

Now the National Lacrosse League had dared to ignore that tradition, and hockey, suddenly a follower instead of a leader, was beginning to shake off its inhibitions as well. Then, only a few months after box lacrosse had rampaged onto the scene to fulfill its vows of carnage, a pro athlete was criminally indicted for an act committed during a game. It was a first in the United States. The scene of the alleged crime was an arena in Bloomington, Minnesota. A hockey game was in progress at the time, and sparks were flying between Dave Forbes of the Boston Bruins and Henry Boucha of the Minnesota North Stars. Jostling each other with a belligerence worthy of the game, they wound up simultaneously in the penalty box, where their exchange of epithets continued. Back on the ice, they moved directly toward each other, and Forbes rammed the butt end of his stick into Boucha's face.

Boucha crumpled to his knees, gushing blood. In the spirit of the hockey axiom that an advantage must be pursued, Forbes pounced on his back and flailed away with both fists until the referees and other players, perceiving that a mismatch had developed, pulled him away. Boucha's poor account of himself in the fight was attributable to the fact that the bone structure around one eye had been shattered by the stick blow. He needed delicate, lengthy surgery just to save the sight in the eye, and several months later had another operation to complete the repairs. Forbes was disciplined in the traditional way by the National Hockey League commissioner. Clarence Campbell sentenced him to sit out ten days of the season.

Hockey people were genuinely solicitous about Boucha's health. They were also angry about Forbes's punishment—ten days seemed awfully harsh. But the thing that really shocked them was the decision of the Hennepin County grand jury to indict Forbes for aggravated assault. Within the fraternity, it seemed not only a monstrous overreaction to your normal, everyday hockey tiff, but also an outrageous intrusion into an area where civil authorities didn't belong.

The indictment raised an intriguing question: Was there a

difference, legally speaking, between bashing someone's head with a hockey stick on the street and doing the very same thing during a regulation league contest? Or as Jim Murray, a syndicated sports columnist, put it—was murder permissible so long as you sold tickets to it?

In the inbred councils of jock journalism, certain philosophers were ready with their answer for all such damning questions: Sports are special. "The laws which apply to most of us cannot rationally be applied to professional sports," wrote Dick Young, who wielded great influence, thanks to his column in the *New York Daily News,* a sports-oriented paper with the highest circulation in the country. Young said each sport should be responsible for policing itself (an option the National Hockey League had long since rejected, on the theory that it could only hurt attendance). The *New York Times* took the opposite view in an editorial: "There is no excuse for using the bloodlust of hockey fans, football buffs and other assorted sportsmen to immunize behavior which, had it not occurred on the playing fields, might be categorized as felonious assault or assault with a deadly weapon."

No United States court had yet addressed the issue, but a similar case had been tried in Canada. During an exhibition game in 1969 Ted Green and Wayne Maki had chopped at each other's head with their sticks until Green was felled with a fractured skull. (He recovered sufficiently to play hockey again, although with a metal plate in his head and without his former ferocity.) Both players were indicted in the Ottawa Provincial Court, in whose jurisdiction the game had been played. In *Regina* v. *Maki* Judge Edward C. Carter acquitted Maki on grounds of self-defense, but added—without elaboration—that "professional hockey is within the bounds of criminal prosecution." Carter died before getting a chance to expand on his theory. In the case of Green, who had instigated the fight, there was a series of postponements. Ultimately, he was tried by another judge, Michael Fitzpatrick, who dismissed the case with the observation that "Hockey cannot be played without what normally are called assaults."

That spare body of opinion comprised the total of precedent at the time of the Forbes indictment. Other sports offered no basis for comparison. No football lineman had been held legally accountable for smashing the quarterback after the whistle had blown, no basketball player hauled into court for using his hip to ricochet an airborne opponent into the third row of seats, no jockey indicted for swerving deliberately so as to drive another horse and its rider into the rail. Considering the frequency with which such things happen, it seemed implausible that the issue hadn't come up before January 1975. But, then, most district attorneys probably understood that the prudent thing was not to interfere with an entertainment beloved by constituents.

The history of baseball, however, included an incident that, handled differently, might have established a precedent. During a 1963 game San Francisco's Juan Marichal, while in the batter's box, had turned around and pounded the skull of Los Angeles catcher John Roseboro with his bat. Marichal later explained he thought Roseboro was teasing him dangerously; he felt the ball had been passing too close to his ear on return throws to the pitcher. As far as baseball was concerned, this was no excuse. Despite Marichal's protestations, he was fined and suspended by league officials. He was also sued for damages by Roseboro (the case was settled out of court), but civil authorities apparently had taken no notice of the attack.

This was unfortunate, since a criminal trial might have focused on a principle that seems the standard in most sports. Baseball players accept as part of their working conditions the fact that base runners sometimes come at infielders with their spikes high, and pitchers now and then aim a fastball at the patella, just as basketball players expect an occasional well-aimed elbow and football players a knee-searing clip. So why were hard-bitten competitors sincerely horrified at the sight of Marichal taking batting practice on a competitor's head? Because the act of wielding a bat, rather than the ball, against an opponent was regarded by all as beyond the baseball pale—as a tactic which, even stretching the point, couldn't possibly be considered relevant to the strategic and psychological requirements of the game.

With hockey, that was the rub. Nobody (presumably) was buying baseball tickets in anticipation of seeing heads split open. Hockey's

FANS!

appeal to onlookers, on the other hand, had always been in its crisp, bruising action, which had the tendency to provoke fights among players. Nobody was suggesting the lads should be allowed to take switchblades or tire chains onto the ice; people simply pointed out that the sticks were already out there—part of the game—and besides, this wasn't any sport for sissies. In fact, the whole debate surrounding the Forbes issue was colored by the preconception that gore is to hockey as mustard to the hot dog. "Violence," declared Stan Fischler, an eminent hockey writer, "has been part of the woof and warp of hockey since the first game was played in Montreal on March 3, 1875."

Most players feel their manhood is at stake whenever they lace up the skates. Few pros wear helmets. The general reluctance stems partly from vanity (headgear diminishes individuality and obscures handsome visages) but mostly from fear of being thought unmanly. Helmets are for players who have already had their craniums splintered, such as Ted Green of the celebrated Green-Maki battle. For similar reasons goaltenders resisted wearing facemasks for decades; consequently, the face of every old time goalie was a collage of scars, and most had noses like prizefighters'. Generation after generation of players has come to accept the willingness to fight as the ultimate test of machismo.

The age at which that ethic is established was one subject of a report the Province of Ontario commissioned in 1974. William McMurtry, the Toronto lawyer who did the study, found, for instance, that the Ontario Hockey Association had suspended for two years a junior team because its adult leader had withdrawn the team from a playoff series in which the brawling was so wild he feared for his players' lives. The most poignant story in McMurtry's report concerned a seventeen-year-old boy named Paul Smithers, who was the best player and only black in his league in the Toronto suburbs. One of his rivals, Barrie Cobby, made a habit of showering Smithers with racial insults when their teams met; in the climatic game the antagonism reached a new peak. "It was not a hockey game," according to Ross T. Runfola, a sociology professor writing in the *New York Times*. "They were waging war, a war orchestrated by a crowd that at times appeared to be emotionally deranged. The crowd reaction assumed an increasingly ugly character almost in perfect cadence to the illicit violence and racist baiting on the ice . . . At one point the game threatened to get completely out of hand when the entire Applewood team and parents in the arena started to taunt Smithers and yell, 'Get the nigger.'" When, on top of all that, Cobby speared Smithers with his stick, Smithers' self-control ran out. The code of hockey demanded a response. Smithers waited until after the game, accosted Cobby in the parking lot and challenged him to fight. Four of Cobby's teammates grabbed Smithers and held him against a car; then Cobby lunged. Smithers, his arms pinned, kicked out and struck Cobby in the groin. Cobby crumpled to the ground and died within minutes, choking on his own vomit.

The sickening irony, Runfola wrote, was that "if Smithers' attack on Cobby had occurred during the game, Smithers would have been liable for a five-minute major penalty. Off the ice he was liable for a term in prison. . . ." Smithers *was* convicted of manslaughter and sentenced to six months in the Brampton Adult Training Center, but the sentence was suspended. Nevertheless, his life had been shattered and another teenager's had been lost. Arthur Maloney, Smithers' lawyer, told the *Washington Post* that if he had his way, he'd "close every arena and collect the hockey sticks and set fire to them. We're creating a stable of animals." Judge Barry Shapiro, who sentenced Smithers, suggested he not quit sports but learn to hold his temper: "You should learn to seek redress in a nonviolent manner."

But one hockey player could become nonviolent only if all of them did. And that was not about to happen, if comments on the Forbes indictment were any indication. The official spokesman of hockey took the lead in explaining to the outside world why a legal case should not be made of the game's internal affairs. Noting that 95 percent of seating capacity was being sold, Commissioner Clarence Campbell said (at various times), "Without violence it wouldn't be hockey . . . If people could have bought tickets to the Vietnam war, they probably would have . . . Fighting is a well-established safety valve for players against other types of violence which would be more vicious and damaging. Insofar as it is part of the show, certainly we sell it." Campbell's comments caused Canada's chief mental health official to call for his

FANS!

immediate firing, but the game's foremost philosopher, Coach Fred Shero of the Stanley Cup champion Philadelphia Flyers, backed up the commissioner: "You need the fight in hockey. It has to be there . . . Two guys fighting, that isn't violence. Listen, you throw the puck in the corner and two teams go after it. Hard. If they don't, you don't have a game, do you? All those people who complain about the violence, do you ever see them run out of the building when it gets rough? The players aren't complaining. The fans aren't complaining."

Lefty McFadden, an executive of the Washington Capitals, picked up where Shero left off: "The last time I heard Vince Lombardi speak, I heard him talk about violence. He talked about all the violence in football and violence in hockey. Take away the violence and he said you could take away football and hockey. I realize that it isn't what we like to teach our youngsters, but it is a fact of life in hockey. You have to have some violence . . . The fans enjoy violence. It is what draws them to the sport, what will keep them interested. The people I talked to are not shocked at what goes on. They prefer to see *more* roughhousing at the Capital Centre." Bobby Clarke, player: "If they cut down on violence, people won't come out to watch." Harry Sinden, Boston executive: Penalizing violence would "absolutely mean a demise of pro hockey attendance." And the man quoted most throughout the affair, an old-timer who had given all of hockey words to live by, Conn Smythe: "We're going to have to do something about all this violence or people are going to keep on buying tickets."

Of course, on the point that blood-and-guts was what made the league thrive, there was little argument. "Ask a fan to pick his five most memorable games," Robert Fachet of the *Washington Post* wrote, "and the list almost assuredly will be dominated by violence. It is the bench-clearing brawl or the savage stick duel that leaves a lasting impression. My hockey memories are dominated by the swinging fist or the swinging stick." It is pointed out repeatedly that many teams flogged tickets with fight film clips, that NBC had done the same to plug network telecasts and had even hired as commentator Ted Lindsay because he'd been known in his playing days as a goon. "That's laying the old lumber on 'im," Lindsay had exulted on the air. "The hockey stick is the great equalizer."

152

Never Having to Say You're Sorry

Detractors could not in good conscience claim that gore wasn't extremely marketable; they merely deplored that it was on the market. Syndicated columnist Garry Wills reasoned, "Defenders of hockey player Dave Forbes think they are also defending the sport. Actually they make the strongest possible case for abolishing hockey . . . The thing is barbaric . . . Can I kick a man in the groin because we happen to be playing tennis at the time? . . . That makes athletes gladiators, for whose blood we can cry at will. That is an insult to more people in our country than to the hockey fans." Or as Jim Murray put it, "If it's in the guise of a game is it all right for the victors to eat the vanquiehed? If so, bring back the lions."

Actually the lions never have been taken away, except in the most literal sense. Modern boxing, hockey, football, and auto racing still offer as recreation the prospect of watching someone get killed; all that's changed over two thousand years is the narrow definition of what should be called "sport." When Arthur Beisser, a psychiatrist, finds in the National Hockey League "a new use of violence . . . not as a means to an end, but for recreational purposes, for pleasure . . . an end in itself," he might just as well be describing ancient Rome. It doesn't stretch the imagination to picture the commissioner of the Coliseum League protesting, "Without violence, it wouldn't be gladiating." Accounts of goings-on at the Coliseum speak of blood flowing so copiously that gladiators had trouble keeping their footing (a problem that would have been short work for today's stadium drainage specialists), and promoters never had a bit of trouble selling out the place. The slash-'em-ups were challenged, in the rivalry for the public's entertainment *sesterce*, only by the Circus Maximus chariot races, with their omnipresent promise of a spectacular collision or the fatal trampling of a fallen driver. Speaking of the games a scholar wrote, "No 'basketball' or 'football' of another era can so monopolize the popular mind." Maybe yes, maybe no; there is, nonetheless, such a thing as the Super Bowl, compelling enough to command 80 million TV viewers and stop the commerce of a nation in its tracks. Nit-picking aside, though, it's inarguable that the more gory the game, the more merrily the turnstiles sing.

Sport, Thorstein Veblen said, is "an expression of the barbarian temperament." In more ways than one. Most of the activities that fit into the category of sports derive from the arts of war. Greece's ancient Olympic Games were a collection of soldierly skills (true also of the medieval tournaments), encompassing running, throwing javelins and heavy weights, and several forms of hand-to-hand combat, including no-holds-barred wrestling in which the loser often wound up dead. The modern Olympics include many of the same events and reserve their greatest glory for the winner of the decathlon, ten contests that cumulatively are the test of the perfect soldier.

But sensibilities have changed over the course of history. The gladiatorial games (which reached a peak of popularity during the time of Julius Caesar, when the season lasted one hundred days and three hundred pairs of combatants competed) eventually had to go, as Western civilization grew squeamish about staging human slaughter so blatantly. At least, this conclusion can be drawn from the fact that nothing quite so raw as the Coliseum fare has survived to the present and that even the most savage contemporary entertainments—except boxing—claim to have some competitive objective other than bodily harm.

The same can't be said for another ancient pastime: watching animals tear each other apart. The Romans and their contemporaries were smitten with bearbaiting, in which the bear or the dogs (and sometimes both) wound up disemboweled; its appeal was so durable that it stayed high in the ratings for a couple of millenia. In England it wasn't outlawed by Parliament until 1935.

Dogfighting and cockfighting, both sources of delight to the masses in antiquity, still flourish in many parts of the world. Where banned, they are preserved sub rosa by devotees who periodically go public to protest the stupidity of their suppression. In the early 1970s it became apparent that dogfighting was enjoying a renaissance in the United States. Training had become sophisticated, with dogs harnessed to treadmills, angled upwards, so that they were forced to develop massive leg muscles. Dogs in training were fed live cats; killing them was calculated to sharpen the combative instincts. In 1974 the *New York Times* reported that about one thousand matches a year take place in this country. Every match had a loser, of course, and the *Times'* source explained that the ideal way to finish off man's best friend once he had been wounded was to thrust an icepick through his heart. Cockfighting, dear to the American colonists, was eventually legislated out of sight but not out of existence. Since it's still legal in some Latin countries, North American enthusiasts regard themselves as victims of discrimination. "Do you realize we don't have a decent pit?" a Baltimore practitioner once complained to the *Washington Star*. He also pointed out that "You'll find very few alcoholics among cockfighters. It takes too much time to rear and care for your cocks properly. . ." Using similar logic, Rep. John Monks of the Oklahoma state legislature supported legalization by observing, "In every country the communists have taken over the first thing they do is outlaw cockfighting."

In China, where dogs and chickens have never been expended so frivolously, cricket fighting was the rage from olden times until the revolution. A 1927 booklet by Berthold Laufer, an anthropologist, gives some idea of the seriousness with which the pastime has been treated over the centuries. For one thing, there was Kia se-tao, thirteenth-century general and a passionate cricketeer who had written his era's definitive treatise on the subject. Couriers reporting an important city's fall to the Mongols found him on the lawn, watching a fight. "In this manner you look out for the interests of a nation!" he was scolded. Kia paid no heed and kept his attention on the crickets. Laufer described the care of crickets: they were kept out of drafts and in smoke-free rooms, since smoke was considered hazardous to their health. Links between their diets and diseases were studied, and they were nurtured through training with everything but chicken soup. Then the little warriors were sent into battle in a jar in a public square. Though it's hard to imagine how anyone more than three feet away could follow the blow-by-blow, crowds packed the square to cheer their choices and bet enthusiastically. Wagers totalling $100,000 a match were not unusual in Canton in the 1920s. A fight ended when the stronger or more agile cricket brought its weight down on its opponent and severed its head.

With crickets, as with other sacrificial athletes, morality was in the eye of the beholder. Laufer wrote, "Cricket-fights are not so cruel as cock and quail fights . . . but the three combined are not so revolting as the bull-fights of Spain and Latin America." These exceedingly fine distinctions could just as easily be reversed by partisans of the bullfight or any of the other bloody spectacles. All that can be said for Laufer's view is that it admits to comparative degrees of horror at the things people inflict on their fellow creatures, each other, and themselves in the name of sport. The antecedents of soccer and rugby apparently were only a step removed from the diversions of the Coliseum. A sixteenth-century English essayist, Philip Stubbes, wrote about them, "I protest unto you, it may rather be called a friendly kind of a fight than a play or recreation, a bloody and murdering practice than a fellowly sport or pastime. For doth not everyone lie in wait for his adversary, seeing to overthrow him and to pitch him on his nose, though it be upon hard stones . . . so that by this means sometimes their necks are broken, sometimes their legs, sometimes their arms, sometimes one part thrust out of joint, sometimes their noses gush out with blood . . . and a hundred such murderous devices, and hereof groweth envy, malice, rancor, choler, hatred, displeasure, enmity and what not else? And sometimes fighting, brawling contention, quarrel picking, murder, homicide and great effusion of blood. . ."

Three centuries later the same concerns creased the brows of some who had seen American football. It was a terribly bloody sport; equipment and rules had not yet been refined enough to compensate for the ferocity of the participants. After seeing his first game John L. Sullivan, the heavyweight boxing champion, said, "There's murder in that game." And there was. In 1905 alone there were eighteen deaths. As rough a rider as he was, Teddy Roosevelt was appalled. He called football "a blight on humanity" and threatened to outlaw it, until Amos Alonzo Stagg invented the forward pass, which reduced the amount of close-quarters brutality. (Several years earlier the Massachusetts legislature had banned football in the state after the death of a player, but the law was vetoed by Governor Bigham, who said, "I am sure a much greater harm, even loss of life, results from over-study or dissipation." Since most of the players were WASPs, a meeting of the Harvard Club at about the same time was told "even death on the playground is cheap if it educates boys in the characteristics that made the Anglo-Saxon race preeminent in history.")

But society does change, and in the twentieth century those sports found it necessary to grow (ever so slightly) tamer. Boxing too changed, sort of. As traced by Rex Lardner in *The Legendary Champions*, it had been relatively static since ancient days. Even the custom by which the rich and highborn sponsored fighters for their own glory dated to that time; Caligula imported boxers from Africa to compete on his behalf. English nobles in the eighteenth and nineteenth centuries had their own stables of bare-knucklers, and in the antebellum South plantation owners took as much pride in their boxing slaves as in their racehorses. From time immemorial until 1866 a boxing match had been an ordeal that went on until one man was insensible, with continuous action and little or no heed paid to fouls.

Then John Sholto Douglas, 8th Marquess of Queensbury, drew up rules that made boxing seem—by its previous standards—humane. Matches were divided into rounds, with rest periods in between, fouls were recognized and made punishable, gloves were brought into use, and the 10-count knockout was instituted, eliminating the need for the loser to be knocked completely unconscious. There things have stood, more or less, until now. The object of the game is still to administer a concussion that temporarily paralyzes the central nervous system, a circumstance that continually keeps a few critics on boxing's back. In 1974 a neuropathology research team reported in a British medical journal its study of cerebral damage in fifteen former boxers, two of whom had been world champions. In twelve of the fifteen the partition between the two sides of the brain had been turned, and there was irreparable damage to cerebral tissues that might lead to loss of memory, speech disturbance, and lack of balance. The term "punch drunk," first used in 1928, now was considered fact.

What worried the people who ran boxing was the appearance of violence, not the real thing. They were embarrassed by incidents like the fabricated tussle between Muhammad Ali and George Foreman at a prefight publicity luncheon. Ali, his suit coat torn away, started throwing rolls and pats of butter at his opponent. A female guest rushed up with a candlestick and said, "Here, Cassius, hit him with this." Ali replied, "Oh, thank you, ma'am, but I'm just playing." Before Ali's previous fight, he and Joe Frazier had grappled on the floor of a videotaping studio. They were each fined $5,000 by the New York State Athletic Commission, whose chairman, Edwin Dooley, said the incident "did severe damage to boxing and its image. Thousands of kids are going to see that, and they'll think there's no sportmanship in the sport. They'll think it's a sport of hooligans instead of gentlemen."

Meanwhile, *inside* the ring men were being maimed and killed. Boxing produced several deaths every year. Watching Frazier beat Jerry Quarry senseless in June 1974, Burling Lowrey, an English professor, was reminded of the bout in which Emile Griffith's blows had killed Benny (Kid) Paret: "Griffith got off the hook because violence in sports, even if it results in permanent injury or death, is sanctioned by strict rituals that perhaps have their origin in the mythology of the human race."

Legitimacy seemed only a question of how far the myth would stretch. Auto racing, with all its dismemberments and deaths by fire, bore society's stamp of approval, except on occasions when a popular driver was killed and many sportswriters recognized in unison the unsportiness of their deceased friend's occupation. Demolition derby, with its intentional collisions, on the other hand, was beyond the pale. In between came marginal entertainments: roller derby, contact karate (the promoter's view—"I don't care what the implications for society are, people . . . want to see two guys knock the crap out of each other. . ."), shark fighting (proposed contest in an underwater cage between a scuba diver with a spear gun and a great white shark), and Evel Knievel.

Whether Evel Knievel's performances could be called sport was widely debated. He made his living jumping a motorcycle over rows of cars or trucks. Since motorcycles were also used in races, and races were sporty, Knievel by extension had something to do with sport. Accordingly, the athletic media embraced him. The secret of his success, as *Sports Illustrated* put it, was "to combine the grotesquerie of death with the attention of millions." At first it was only thousands. The car-leaping routine, bloodcurdling as it was, was stupefyingly repetitive. But

Never Having to Say You're Sorry

Evel had a vision: the Grand Canyon. According to myth, Paul Bunyan had inadvertently created it by dragging his gargantuan axe along the ground; now a nonmythological hero would deliberately vault it astride a mighty machine.

The landlord, the U.S. government, objected. There were ecological issues, and besides, it would be unseemly to lend a national monument to an individual's commercial project and to sanction in advance his likely death. Instead, Knievel got permission to use a less-celebrated canyon and laid plans to zoom across the gorge of the Snake River in Twin Falls, Idaho, on September 8, 1974, on a rocketlike machine called Sky-Cycle X2. Knievel's flacks rose to new heights of rhetoric: "His life is no more governed by the clock than the Mississippi River is held in check by the battered levies which bear the scars of old defeats . . . a project which would make Buck Rogers blush . . . he speaks about Death, an old traveling companion of his who has shadowed him in so many places that Evel has come to accept his presence as damned near routine . . . in a sense, Evel Knievel and Sir Edmund Hillary are brothers under the skin. . ."

Millions around the country made plans to trek to Twin Falls or take in the jump at a closed-circuit theater, at ten dollars a seat. As it turned out, September 8 diminished Evel's presence rather than enlarging it. First, he was upstaged by politics; that morning Gerald Ford had pardoned Richard Nixon, thus distracting some Americans from the drama at the Snake River. Then the jump itself fizzled. Sky-Cycle X-2 malfunctioned, and Evel wound up bouncing on his impact-absorbing nose cone along the near shore of the Snake.

If the gloss had been dulled, it was none too soon for many Americans. Knievel imitators had been popping up everywhere. In a show at Ocala, Florida, Bob Pleso, twenty-two, landed his motorcycle on the twenty-eighth of thirty cars and was killed. Another minor-leaguer, Wicked Ward, was forced into retirement after breaking his neck on a jump. Previously he had broken his feet, ankles, legs, shoulders, arms, wrists, rib cage, and back. José Cesteros, a Ft. Lauderdale social worker, barely failed to kill himself in a ten-car leap.

While many people saw nothing wrong with allowing consenting adults to behave that way, most were opposed to imitative daredeviltry among children, with whom Knievel was hugely popular. His licensing agent claimed that revenue generated by Knievel items—toys, hobby kits, and the like—amounted to $100 million a year. A spokesman for the Ideal Toy Company acknowledged three-year sales of $75 million on fourteen Evel Knievel toys and noted that no other living male sports star had ever had a successful line of toys named after him. While his unsavoriness was definitely worth mentioning (a typical description: "onetime hubcap thief and bank robber, a hard-drinking heartbreaking bar fighter. . ."), it wasn't the main worry. Jack Anderson reported in his syndicated column the results of a national survey of fifty children's hospitals, showing that countless youngsters of all ages were trying to emulate Knievel's tricks and winding up maimed or dead. Conjuring epidemic injury and paralysis, Rep. John Murphy tried to dissuade ABC from televising the Snake River extravaganza. He might just as well have asked Las Vegas casinos to shut down the crap tables.

Why should the TV people take the responsibility? If people wanted to self-destruct in homage to some lunatic on a motorcycle, that was their business. Besides, the world had long since learned to live with the expectation that certain events would cause a certain amount of agitation in their audiences.

Until they were abandoned, weekly boxing programs at Madison Square Garden, the high temple of athletic culture, were accompanied by weekly riots. The *New York Times* issued battle helmets to reporters covering fights and often editorialized on the tendency of pugilism to brutalize both the participant and the spectator. Sober attempts were made by jock-journalists to chalk up the phenomenon to ethnology. They explained: Matches usually pitted a Puerto Rican against another Spanish-speaking national. The injuries dealt regularly to persons and property were the result of nothing other than the overheating of all that Hispanic blood, which was a little too warm to begin with.

This theory's only shortcoming is its failure to explain the barbarity of the cold-blooded, white, middle-class Americans who monopolize pro football season tickets and comprise the majority of big-league baseball attendance. How to explain why centerfielder Pete Rose was so preoccupied with dodging missiles that "I'm always out of position because [spectators are] throwing things at me. I don't want to get hit by a bottle." Why would a special fence have to be built above the players' tunnel at Kezar Stadium in San Francisco to protect quarterback John Brodie from beer cans (often full) and worse? For the last few years the end of the World Series and the pennant playoffs has more often than not been a signal for fans to descend into the field, tear up as much of it as possible, and generally terrorize the fleeing players. There have also been death threats to players occasionally, and after the end of the sixth game of the 1975 World Series umpire Larry Barnett, who had made a controversial call, needed an armed guard to get off the field safely. Basketball players have gotten used to being showered with ice, cans, and bottles every time something displeases the home crowd.

And those are the sports that don't rely on brutality as a gate attraction. Wrestling feeds on the hatreds of the spectator to fuel the fighting in the ring. What goes on there is usually promoted like a morality play of the Middle Ages: The good guy, who is virtuous and plays by the rules, suffers at the hands of the dirty, devious, evil villain while the hapless referee looks the other way. Against all odds the hero finally wins out.

As if the formula weren't explosive enough, promoters light the fuse with advertising and gimmicks to enhance the impression of violence—which in pro wrestling is entirely fictitious. Infected with the Christmas spirit in 1975, one arena billed a Holiday Holocaust—20-man Yuletide Wrestling Free-for-All. It featured Haystacks Calhoun, "600 pounds of meanness and muscle," and Ivan Putski, "nastier than a swarm of bees." Another card offered André the Giant, "7'4" tall, weighs 444 pounds and can destroy people with his hands, his feet, his elbows and his breath . . . See André the Giant do terrible things to Cowboy Bob Duncum . . ." Occasionally The Cage is put into use. The Cage is 19 feet long and wide and 9 feet high. The wrestlers are put inside, the door closed, and the "rules" suspended; the one "who can walk out on his own" is the winner.

It took decades of synthesizing hatred before pro wrestling finally got what it was bargaining for. In January 1975, marking a milestone in

FANS!

the history of American sports arenas, a spectator opened fire with a pistol. His two shots struck a total of five other spectators (none of whom were killed). At the time of the incident, theatrics in the ring had reached a climax. The villain had the hero tied up in the ropes and appeared to be working him over, while the referee ineffectually waved him away. Apparently, the gunman misinterpreted the scene and thought the match was being awarded to the scoundrel. In their investigation the police put surrogates in the seats that had been occupied by the five wounded. They discovered all had been on trajectories between the gunman's seat and the place where the referee had been standing. Witnesses told a reporter they had talked wrestling all evening with the man; he was a real aficionado.

The National Hockey League—as yet—had nothing to match this outburst of passion, but it still had no reason to be ashamed. Unarmed fans had often mixed it up not only with officials, but with stick-bearing players. One brawl involving the Philadelphia Flyers started when St. Louis fans dumped beer and debris on the Flyers' coach, who had gone to the side of the rink to complain to an official. Two Flyers rushed up the ramp to avenge him, and when the spectators fought back, the whole team charged in. Stan Fischler called it "one of the worst brawls in the history of the NHL." Another started when a Vancouver fan reached over the glass barrier and pulled the hair of Philadelphia's Don Saleski, who at the time was throttling Barry Wilcox of the home team. Substitute goalie Bob Taylor of the Flyers (who later explained, "I couldn't let him do that to Donny") plunged into the stands, and to no one's surprise, was joined quickly by his teammates. Serious injury was avoided as fans in the invaded section retreated before the stick-wielders. The tables were turned one night in Philadelphia when Boston's Derek Sanderson, tired of being taunted, tried to climb the wall separating the stands from the penalty box. Rising to the challenge, the spectators reached down and tried to pull him over. Soon the stands were full of Bruins in hand-to-hand combat with civilians. When it was all over, this message appeared on the scoreboard screen: "THE FANS INVOLVED IN THE FIGHT ARE ALIVE AND WELL . . . 18 BRUINS COULDN'T HURT THEM."

So now game violence was merging with fan violence. Distinctions were becoming blurred—where did the intrinsically bruising game of hockey leave off and the breakdown of civil order begin? And wasn't this what the Dave Forbes case was about? And wouldn't its outcome be a comment on society?

After all the journalistic debate, the trial was an anticlimax. Gary Flakne, the district attorney who had asked for the indictment, researched lawbooks in vain for precedents on athletic assaults. Lo, these many years of mayhem on field, court, and ice, and nothing yet on the books. Flakne accused Forbes of "knowingly" assaulting Boucha "with a dangerous weapon, to wit a hockey stick," and inflicting more harm by "hitting the face and head of said Henry C. Boucha upon and against the ice surface."

The defense argued that hockey was not financially equipped to survive the imposition of real-life rules and regulations—the ever-replayable trump card of organized sport. Implicit in this appeal is the assumption that society's main interest lies in preserving the league in question. Time after time, from the trial level to the Supreme Court, judges had swallowed this. Here, however, a jury still had to determine whether Forbes had in fact assaulted Boucha. So the defense also argued that in the context of pro hockey Forbes was a sort of automaton, conditioned to behave in a certain violent way and not responsible for his actions. Forbes became the "Lieutenant Calley of hockey," taking the punishment his superiors—if anyone—deserved.

Ronald Meshbesher, the defense attorney, hoped to show the jury the Minnesota team's promotional film, promising "rock 'em, sock 'em hockey." The judge ruled it inadmissible, but Meshbesher was allowed to bring out the fact that most of the filmed highlights were fistfights. He explained that hockey players learn brawling as early and as naturally as they learn skating. In his summation he declared that the trial would never have taken place if Forbes had been in a Minnesota uniform instead of the visiting Bruins' garb. The outcome was a hung jury, deadlocked 9-3 in favor of conviction. It was "those hockey fans" who caused the mistrial, one juror told the press. Flakne, accused by hockey lovers of bringing the original charges as a political ploy, weighed the possibility of a retrial, then dropped the idea. Issue closed, at least until another player got skulled.

Propaganda

The implications of Muhammad Ali's international significance made Norman Mailer contemplative and a bit concerned for the boxer. As Ali held forth to the foreign press after his fight in Zaire in 1974, Mailer wrote, for *Playboy,* "Out there, the new champion is giving a press conference to a hundred African reporters and media men, who gather round him with the solemnity and respect they might once have offered to Gandhi . . . With what an immensity of anxiety must Ali live at the size of his world role and his intimate knowledge of his own ignorance."

From afar the observation seemed partly worthwhile. It was certainly possible Ali had some familiarity with the extent of his own ignorance. But neither was there any sign the awareness ever got the best of him.

Consider, for instance, his contributions to Zaire's effort to rid the outside world of its preconceptions. The people of Zaire, Foreign Minister Bula Mandungu had drily noted on a prefight visit to the United States, "don't live in the jungle as most of you think." At the same moment, at the same press gathering, Ali was gleefully conjuring an image of George Foreman, his opponent, in a cannibal stewpot. He had already christened the bout the Rumble in the Jungle and enjoyed the sound of the sobriquet so much he used it whenever possible, right up until fight time. When he saw Foreman, he warned him, "My African friends will put you in a pot!"

Half a year later in Malaysia Ali was well on his way to stirring up a

FANS!

religious war until told to stop proclaiming that the fate of Islam hung on the outcome of his match. Still later, in the Philippines, which, like the other countries, was promoting a fight to dress up its international image, Ali's chant was, "It's gonna be a chilla and a thrilla and a killa when I get the gorilla in Manila." (The "gorilla" was Joe Frazier.) Within earshot of newsmen he told President Marcos, "You ain't as dumb as you look—I saw your wife."

If dignity had been bartered away, Marcos still seemed to feel he got the best of the deal. Ali had served the purpose for which he had been imported: to put a relatively obscure nation on stage before the rest of the world. Hosting a heavyweight championship fight had become the acknowledged solution for an underdeveloped country that wanted attention but didn't feel like declaring war on anybody. Ali's incalculable symbolic value was what virtually guaranteed the success of such a venture. Lesser jock heroes, no matter how famous, embodied at most the pride of a single ethnic group or geopolitical area; Ali was the idol not only of Americans of all prefixes but also nonwhites and Muslims (not to mention connoisseurs of fancy prizefighting) everywhere.

In an interview with *Sports Illustrated*, Marcos said, "Ali symbolizes success in that part of the world which sees white men as colonialists and the like. The old voices against colonialism are all over Asia again because of the Vietnam debacle, and Ali symbolizes a continuing protest against this racism and dominance because of color and birth. And while this may not be fascinating to the Western world, it is to Asians a highly-charged matter." As to gains from staging the fight, "We have benefited already. The fight publicizes our country. Many people do not know where the Philippines are, and don't know what the situation is here. They think that the military runs the government, tanks are in the streets. Have you seen any tanks? They think people are arrested on any pretext. that there is oppression, tyranny, and the civil government is nonexistent or inoperative. That there are no judges. But whatever you fellows say, you must see that the fight can be held here in peace and order."

And it was. Marcos couldn't have been happier with the outcome;

next he was prepared to put up $5 million to host the world chess championship. He even sent for Bobby Fischer, suffered the grandmaster's bumptious presence overnight at the presidential palace, and paid him $20,000 to show up at some government-sponsored tournaments. Three more months of worldwide publicity—a delicious prospect to Marcos—were in the offing, until the match was canceled when Fischer irked the international chess hierarchy and was stripped of his title.

In Zaire the previous year things had gone less smoothly. Part of the fault lay with Ali's unfortunate locutions (an ever-present risk), but the caucasian-in-the-cauldron theme got even more of a working over than was warranted by his antics. Rumble in the Jungle was such a handy tag it found its way into the most dignified journals. The tabloid *New York Daily News* headlined a story about slow tour sales with "Bongo, Bongo . . . They Don't Wanna See the Congo," above a cartoon that showed a white man dropping his suitcase and running while Ali ranted about native dietary habits. Promoter Don King was quoted: "If he says it's gonna happen in Africa, some people believe it . . . You do scare people . . . When I went to Africa the first time, I was apprehensive myself."

Whatever fears *were* justified were over President Mobutu's unabashedly antiwhite politics. Television programming each night in Zaire began with a picture of a map of Africa, all black except for South Africa and Rhodesia, which were colored white. To the accompaniment of war music, bayonets swept down the screen, turning the whole continent black, after which the president's voice invited viewers to help him throw the whites into the sea. Mobutu had personally launched an *authenticité* campaign, giving up his original Western name (Joseph) and urging his countrymen to do likewise, ordering that everyone in the French-speaking country be addressed as *Citoyen* (citizen), forbidding neckties, and encouraging the elimination of all Western influence.

Mobutu had come to power in 1965, after one hundred years of Belgian colonial rule. By 1970 he felt secure enough to hold elections and won the presidency with over 10 million votes for and 158 against. As the personification of the country, he was now telling the people that the

FANS!

Foreman-Ali bout was his "gift" to them. All over Kinshasa, the capital, there were roadside signs in French and English proclaiming, "A fight between two blacks in a black nation, organized by blacks and seen by the whole world: that is a victory of Mobutuism. The country of Zaire, which has been bled because of pillage and systematic exploitation must become a fortress against imperialism and a spearhead for the liberation of the African continent . . ." But beyond presenting itself as capable of dealing with oppressors, Zaire wished to give the impression of being a peaceful, efficient, modern land that had left its revolutionary furies behind and was ready for large-scale export of its copper, cobalt, and other vast resources, as well as development of its negligible tourist trade.

The investment began with $5 million for each boxer. Tremendous sums were also spent in anticipation of the expected ten to fifteen thousand foreign visitors. Buses were bought to ferry tourists around Kinshasa; street lights were installed; university dormitories were refurbished and fitted out with ultramodern kitchen equipment; arrangements were made to fly in food from Europe. The media, of course, were accommodated as lavishly as possible; most representatives were put up outside of town at a retreat nicknamed the African Grossingers.

Nevertheless, there was friction over the quality of prefight reporting. Some of the American journalists who had come early had discovered defects in Zairian society, and Mobutu's press adviser, Tshimpumpu-Was-Tshimpumpu, had found it necessary to call them together for a dressing-down. "We are a young nation," he told them, "and we have our problems just like you do. But some of you lack sincerity and a sense of the truth." To those who had written that the bout was staged solely for the greater glory of Mobutu, he said, "I would like to know if there is a rule that all world championships must take place in the United States. Why not in Africa?" The clincher was his assertion that the writers were safer at night on the streets of Kinshasa than New York or Washington, D.C.

Things might have improved thereafter but for a bit of bad luck: Foreman suffered a gash above his eye in training. It happened while

Propaganda

most of the American reporters assigned to cover the fight were still en route on a charter plane and had stopped over in Trier, West Germany. When the medical report from the Foreman camp—that a long postponement was likely—reached them, most made plans to turn around. They were begged not to; Mobutu offered to send his personal 747 jet for the last leg of the journey. Shirley Povich of the *Washington Post* reported the efforts of Bob Goodman, a fight publicist, who argued, "Don't pay any attention to what Foreman's doctor is saying. Never believe a camp doctor or a camp spokesman. They all lie. I wrote their stuff for too many years."

Meanwhile, in Kinshasa, the government was trying to keep the cut and the postponement from being blown out of proportion. Within thirty minutes after Foreman had been injured, telephone and Telex lines in the capital mysteriously went out of order. The foreign minister tried persuasion on the media: "You must not publicize this. It will be improperly understood in your country. This cut is nothing. I suggest you forget about this story. Go for a swim." When he found out later that the cut had not been kept a fraternal little secret between Zairian bureaucrats and American sportswriters, he protested, "Americans are hysterical; they always dramatize things. The fight won't be delayed more than a day or so. I tell you that Foremen should be able to train tomorrow." By way of buttressing his argument he asserted of the boxers, "Nobody forced them to stay."

George Foreman gave a slightly different account several months after the fight, when at a safe distance from his former hosts: "Right then [after the accident] is when I should have left. But Don King and some of the other promoters came around and asked me to stay in Africa. They told me it would have a terrible effect on all the closed-circuit TV distributors and exhibitors . . . But if that wasn't bad enough, I also started getting this spooky feeling that I wouldn't be *allowed* to leave. Everywhere I went a dozen guys with guns were all around me, pushing people out of the way." Several visitors who approached Foreman's villa in hopes of interviews were turned away by soldiers with sub-machineguns. Reporters who included this and other unflattering details in their copy.discovered later that Telex operators who supposedly spoke no English were uncannily excising the most damaging passages.

Despite the tensions and the month-long delay, the promotion wound up a huge success. The fight itself, scheduled for 3:00 A.M. local time to accommodate viewers in the Western Hemisphere, went off beautifully, with Ali winning by a knockout. His reclamation of the title from Foreman set off rejoicing around the globe. Television-by-satellite, as well as more prosaic media, had given Zaire enormous, unprecedented exposure.

Now—particularly with Ali champion again—Third World countries stood in line for chances to match the publicity coup pulled off by the obscure native government that so recently had replaced Belgian control. For a sum that was piddling in almost any nation's budget, an audience in the hundreds of millions was available, as well as the opportunity to present a considerable amount of self-glorification on the closed-circuit screen. Don King now was able to boast that he dealt with governments, not other promoters. There was talk after the Zaire fight of future matches in Cairo, Teheran, or Tibet, and the sites chosen were no less exotic. The first challenge to Ali, by Joe Bugner, was staged in Kuala Lumpur, Malaysia, a place that considered no sacrifice was too great to impress the outside world. City officials ordered hotels and nightclubs to cancel striptease shows and substitute "performances of Malaysian culture." Then it was on to Manila, which was on its best behavior for the Ali-Frazier fight. That series of triumphs complete, King began negotiating with Turkey, Monte Carlo, Guatemala, and others.

Meanwhile, Montreal, Canada, was engaged in a more grandiose kind of athletic self-promotion. Montreal was to host the 1976 summer Olympic Games, an incredibly costly undertaking but one that offered a chance of substantial direct revenue along with the usual intangible gains in prestige. Skeptical residents were reassured when Mayor Jean Drapeau declared, upon affirming the city's commitment, "The Olympics can no more have a deficit than a man can have a baby." At the time, the estimated cost of the games was $310 million. By the time it reached $550 million, Drapeau was the butt of every conceivable obstetrical wisecrack. Eventually costs passed $1 billion. If expectations of the planners' expense had been an understatement, their revenue projections were not. Montreal merchandised the Olympics as never before: Marketing licenses were peddled aggressively to businesses interested in selling the official soft drink, ballpoint pen, or toilet paper of the Olympics. Mints turned out set after set of commemorative coins, hustled through mass mailings by authorized agents. "I am writing you personally," a typical form letter read, " . . . to help keep alive the Olympic ideal."

Interest in preserving the ideal was far more subdued than the coin-gimmick enthusiasts had suspected. And the deeper into the hole Montreal got, the more people began noticing the inconsistencies of the modern games. Nationalism had long since replaced the individualism that had been the classical focus. Theatricality was now the first concern. "Athletes are little more than actors in a gaudy show," *Sports Illustrated* scolded, "the primary purpose of which seems to be to entertain crowds and generate publicity and revenue for the host country." Even the ceremonies had become futuristic parodies of ancient symbols; in 1976 the eternal flame on Mt. Olympus was transmitted to Montreal by use of a device that turned genuine flame into ionized particles that were transformed into coded electrical impulses that were then relayed to Canada by satellite and restored to recognizable combustion by a laser beam. More and more the once-sacred observance was regarded as a propaganda circus. George Will, the syndicated columnist, wrote about the planned 1976 and 1980 games, "Montreal politicians are like most municipal politicians, only perhaps more so: they will fight to their constituents' last dollar for a publicity bonanza. Brezhnev, like Hitler, understands the propaganda value of having the world's television cameras tightly focused on the Games, without a glance at the Gulag."

It seemed unfair, however, to compare Canada to the Soviet Union (1980's host would be Moscow) in this regard. The worst thing Drapeau could be accused of was trying to puff himself and the glories of his city. The Brezhnev-Hitler analogy was more accurate; both Nazi Germany and Soviet Russia had presented the world with strapping jocks as evidence of the virtues of their socioeconomic systems. Athletes can be,

FANS!

as Robert Lipsyte noted, "a country's best propaganda tool . . . an example of socialism in action or a testament to the vitality of democracy or living proof that the people love the junta."

That's why the Soviet Union subsidizes full-time athletes for the Olympics and other competitions that are supposedly for amateurs. In the days before sex tests, there were also accusations that some women competitors from Communist countries were really men. Charges and countercharges about drugs were common, too, and in 1974 several European countries' swim teams accused the East Germans of using male hormones to make their women bigger and stronger. It may or may not have been their galling superiority that made the Flying Frauleins look masculine to their opponents, but a French sports-medicine specialist attested, "These swimmers have, in fact, muscle and fatty development that is unusual in girls of their age. Also a special skin quality, a bit of hairiness . . . rather curious voices and certain signs in their step."

East Germany's swimmers lived well—their reward for the glory they brought the homeland. So did Russia's stars. At a time when the average monthly wage for a doctor was 150 rubles and a coal miner 200, world champion weightlifter Vasili Alexeyev was paid 500. He was classified as a "mining engineer," but the position didn't seem to interfere with his training. Soviet jocks could expect other perquisites— extra living space, cars, vacation homes—as long as they avoided embarrassing the regime with either their performances or their behavior. The government was so disappointed by chess player Boris Spassky's defeat by Bobby Fischer in 1972 that it stripped him of countless privileges he'd enjoyed as world champion. It was three years, however, before the Kremlin got complete satisfaction for the national insult. Spassky announced his intention to marry. He was living quietly in Moscow, having been snubbed by the regime, denounced by *Pravda*, and denied visas for travel abroad. He got permission to wed on November 11, 1975, but the bride-to-be, a Frenchwoman working at the embassy in Moscow, was ordered to leave the country by the end of September. After Spassky had been sufficiently embarrassed by publication of his troubles, the government relented and allowed the wedding.

Propaganda

In January 1975 the national youth newspaper, *Komsomolskaya Pravda,* unloaded on a hockey player named Aleksandr Marltsev. "Glory has made your head spin," the star center of the Soviet Union's international team was told. Marltsev was also accused of drinking too much, wearing his hair too long, and missing a flight to a game in Sweden for frivolous reasons. Vladimir Snegirev, author of the article, hinted that the authorities were contemplating action. "You know the consequences," he wrote ominously. This was taken by Russia-watchers as a warning not just to Marltsev but to any jock whose conduct might reflect badly on communism. When Martina Navratilova, a teenaged tennis player, defected in 1975 from Czechoslovakia to the United States, she explained, "Once I got too famous I had to behave perfectly . . . My government thought I was getting too Americanized. . . ."

The Soviet Union had plunged into Olympic competition in 1952, making no bones about the fact that its participation was intended to prove superiority to the United States. From then on the major preoccupation during the games was the respective medal totals of the two superpowers. In a contretemps that was to be matched time and again in succeeding Olympiads, there was a charge of bias in the judged events—in this case Soviet diving judges were accused of seeing the competition through red-colored glasses: Gary Tobian of the United States was getting high marks on his dives from all but the Russian and Hungarian judges. The pattern looked strange to almost everyone involved; gold-medalist Joaquin Capilla of Mexico volunteered that ideology might have given him the winning edge. Two days before the games ended, Russia finally took the lead in total points. *Komsomolskaya Pravda* proclaimed "the golden Thursday of Soviet Sport. The American lead has been liquidated."

Disposed as they are to accepting such a challenge, Americans nevertheless have had problems matching the efficiency of the Soviet sports machine. While genuine amateurism is nonexistent in the United States, too, central management of athletic resources is nowhere near as efficient as behind the Iron Curtain. Efforts to correct this have consisted mostly of congressional hearings to affirm the necessity of locating youths who can prove once and for all that nobody can heave a hunk of lead farther or run a quarter-mile faster than a properly trained capitalist. Invariably, the senators and representatives are blocked by insoluble conflicts between the various amateur athletic organizations. And there matters stand for another four years. What little can be done by the government is done. Example: a waiver by Congress of the five-year citizenship waiting period for Jana Ledvinkova, a former Czechoslovakian skier, so that she could represent the United States in the 1976 winter games at Innsbruck. The bill was signed into law by another skier, Gerald Ford, in keeping with his belief that "a sports triumph can be as uplifting to a nation's spirit as, well, a battlefield victory . . . if we want to remain competitive, and I think we do, we owe it to ourselves to reassess our priorities, to broaden our base of achievement so that we again present our best in the world's arenas. From a purely political viewpoint, I don't know of anything more beneficial in diplomacy and prestige."

Adolf Hitler's creativeness in this area of philosophy led to an observance of the games that will be known forever by the subtitle the Nazi Olympics. They were held in Berlin in 1936, a time when the Third Reich was eager to demonstrate its racial superiority and the fitness of its people. Athletics presented a perfect opportunity.

Germany's allies were just as eager to show that they, too, were to be reckoned with. Even before Hitler got around to using sport as a propaganda tool, Mussolini had beaten him to the punch. Primo Carnera, an Italian, had become world heavyweight boxing champion, largely through manipulations by the American underworld. It mattered little to his countrymen that Carnera had reached the top because his opponents faced a choice between taking a swoon in the ring or receiving a bullet in the head after the fight. (Only one had been imprudent enough to reject the first alternative, but he had been done in by his cornermen with a debilitating nasal spray.) Carnera was champ, and by virtue of that circumstance, the epitome of Fascist manhood.

And so his 1935 bout with the up-and-coming black American, Joe Louis, was promoted as a racial and nationalist confrontation. At the time of the prefight publicity buildup Mussolini had sent troops to Italy's northeastern African colony to intimidate Abyssinia, as Ethiopia was then called; he claimed Abyssinia had threatened him and his possessions. Against this backdrop there were fears that a victory by Louis over Carnera might be used as an excuse to persecute Africans. A professor at a black college said, "I am afraid that the defeat of Carnera by Louis will be interpreted as an additional insult to the Italian flag which will promote Mussolini to start again the recent attempt by Italy to annihilate Abyssinia."

At home Carnera was pliantly playing the role of symbol of his nation's martial prowess. Il Duce ordered him a specially tailored uniform (Carnera stood 6 feet 6 inches) of the Fascisti. Before long newspapers around the globe were running wirephotos of a Blackshirted champ exuberantly delivering the Fascist salute.

Patriotic feeling ran high as fight time approached. Fears of ethnic violence were serious enough to warrant a force of thirteen hundred policemen around Yankee Stadium on the night of June 25, 1935. Some three hundred plainclothesmen mingled with the crowd, and emergency forces waited outside the ballpark with teargas bombs and grenades. As it turned out, the serious violence was confined to the boxing ring. Louis blasted the inept Carnera, and Il Duce's campaign on the sporting front was over.

Der Führer was just beginning. He, too, had a prizefighter, and the master heavyweight of the Master Race seemed to be the real thing. At first, though, Hitler was cautious about embracing Max Schmeling, and the Nazis made little show of affiliating with the fighter before his first bout with Louis in 1935. Had they known what Schmeling knew, they needn't have hedged. A serious and brilliant student of pugilism, Schmeling had analyzed Louis's style from every angle and discovered a single flaw: Louis sometimes left himself vulnerable to a righthand punch.

A timely right stopped Louis. After the fight Schmeling got a telegram from his government's minister of propaganda, Joseph Goebbels: "Congratulations, I know you won for Germany. Heil Hitler." The pace of Schmeling's Nazification picked up when he returned to the Fatherland. He was hustled off to the Bavarian resort of Berchtesgaden, from which pictures of him socializing with the Nazi elite were distributed. Schmeling by now was just about as symbolic as a pug could be, and when plans for another Louis bout, in June 1938, were announced, serious opposition developed in the United States. Boycotts were threatened. The American Jewish Committee lobbied for cancellation of the match on the theory that, should the championship pass into the hands of a German (Louis had acquired the title since his defeat by Schmeling), the Nazis would have a new propaganda weapon with which to assault American morale.

The White House had a different idea, however. Franklin Roosevelt was of a mind to beat Hitler at his own game; he invited Joe Louis to his office. "The meeting between the Harvard-educated, polio-afflicted aristocrat and the black, 25-year-old sharecropper's son creaked with artificiality," Gerald Astor wrote. "About the only common ground lay in the development of the upper torso and arms. Compensating for the loss of lower-limb strength, the president had built up his pectorals and biceps in order to support his body. Toward the end of the tête-à-tête FDR supposedly said, 'Lean over, Joe, so I can feel your muscles.' Having satisfied himself of their mass, the president continued, 'Joe, we need muscles like yours to beat Germany.'" Years later, in an oral history of boxing called *In This Corner . . .* Louis confirmed the substance of the quote.

The Nazi propaganda machine was in top form. Caustic quotes attributed to Schmeling (Astor says it's still unproven that they were actually the words of the German boxer) kept showing up in the sports sections: "I would not take this fight if I did not believe that I, a white man, can beat a Negro . . . The Negro will always be afraid of me . . . the black amateur . . . the dumb animal . . ." In return, Louis purportedly declared his zeal to show what a black man could do. Nazi radio hedged its bets; Arno Helmers, sent to New York to do the blow-by-blow on shortwave, reported that Gov. Herbert Lehman of New York (who was Jewish) was involved in a plot to ensure Schmeling's defeat. Two days before the bout Der Führer weighed in with a cable of good wishes.

That public identification with Schmeling by Hitler marked the high point of boxing bravado in the Third Reich. Louis chopped Schmeling down in a performance so ferocious and efficient it exhausted the ringside reporters' supply of adjectives. Damon Runyon was moved to write what became one of the most famous leads in American sportswriting: "Listen to this, buddy, for it comes from a guy whose palms are still wet, whose throat is still dry, and whose jaw is still agape from the utter shock of watching Joe Louis knock out Max Schmeling . . . Louis was like this: He was a big lean copper spring, tightened and retightened through weeks of training until he was one pregnant package of coiled venom . . . Schmeling was . . . a man caught and mangled in the whirring claws of a mad and feverish machine." Naturally no small amount of jingoism inspired the American writers, just as it dictated the Nazis' response. Fight films shown in Germany were tricked up to make it look as if Schmeling had been kidney-punched. As for on-the-spot radio reports to the Fatherland, the broadcast power was mysteriously cut off as soon as Schmeling appeared to be in trouble. It didn't come on again until the fight was over, and Helmers concluded his broadcast with consoling assurance to Schmeling: "We will show you on your return that reports in foreign newspapers that you will be thrown in jail are untrue."

Between the two Louis-Schmeling bouts the Olympics of 1936 were celebrated, and they offered more opportunity than the prize ring for a broad tribute to Nazi culture. As with the second fight, detractors of the Reich opposed letting it use sports to show the world the glories of Nazism. But the critics had to reckon with Avery Brundage, president of the International Olympic Committee and, more importantly, self-appointed guardian of some fuzzy ideals, concerning amateur and politics-free sport, that everyone but Brundage recognized as ludicrous in the modern world. Brundage stood firm on allowing the games to be held in Berlin; he insisted that only sports were at issue and that others should emulate his ability to rise above concern for smaller questions like the steadily increasing persecution of Jews. "Frankly," Brundage said, "I don't think we have any business to meddle in this question. We are a sports group. When we let politics, racial questions, religious, or social disputes creep into our actions, we're in for trouble." On another occasion: "Certain Jews must now understand that they cannot use these games as a weapon in their boycott against the Nazis."

The Nazis seemed to compromise their principles temporarily.

FANS!

They distributed a pamphlet noting, "Among inferior races, Jews have done nothing in the athletic sphere. They are surpassed even by the lowest Negro tribes." But they also put token Jews on a few of their teams as if to disprove charges of bigotry. Some of the more virulent propaganda placards in the Olympic district of Berlin were removed, and the whole city was spruced up. The competitors' "village" was built on an unprecedentedly grand scale. Germany not only spent $30 million to make the athletes' quarters lavish, but also installed in the village one of the bungalows used four years previously in Los Angeles so that the world could see how piddling it looked by comparison. Brundage was impressed. "No nation since ancient Greece," he declared, "has captured the true Olympic spirit as has Germany."

How this statement squared with the plain desire to prove through athletics the supremacy of National Socialism was a mystery. At any rate, the games began like a Teutonic fairytale. The first event—the shot put—was won by Hans Woellke, a sergeant in the Nazi police. It seemed an omen for the Master Race. No German had ever won the Olympic track-and-field event before; now the gold medal had been captured in an event that called for brute strength. Woellke was promoted on the spot to lieutenant by Hermann Goering.

Next, Willie Schroeder, world record holder in the discus throw, was expected to duplicate Woellke's feat on behalf of Aryans. Schroeder was urged on by a chant from the grandstand: "Take the discus in your hand and throw it for the Fatherland." He did, but not far enough, and finished fifth.

Schroeder's defeat wasn't the worst blow to Hitler's genetic theory. "The Master Race met its master," Richard Schaap wrote. "He was American. He was black." Jesse Owens and nine other American blacks—"the black auxiliaries" in the lexicon of German journalism—destroyed the distinctively Nazi Olympic spirit that Brundage had found so admirable. Every time Owens won an event Hitler left the stadium to avoid acknowledging, much less congratulating, the living refutation of his ideology.

If there was ever a quintessential moment delineating real sport from the ulterior political and commercial strivings that bear the name, it came during those 1936 games, with a small, almost negligible act of comradeship between competitors. Jesse Owens had won gold medals in the sprints, but now was having trouble in the broad jump. Unable to gauge his approach to the takeoff point correctly, he had fouled twice and was likely to foul out altogether on his third try when a jumper from another nation volunteered a hint: Place a strip of tape safely behind the foul line and use that as a guide. The suggestion worked; Owens went on to qualify for the finals and win a third gold medal. The man who had given him the opportunity, knowing that to help an opponent as talented as Owens was to ensure his own defeat, was Lutz Long, a son of the Fatherland.

Munich's Legacy

Thirty-six years after the Nazi Olympics the summer games were again held in Germany. The host city was Munich. Never before had such effort been invested to make the games look festive and peaceful. If there was any theme, it was beery Bavarian jollity. In the opening parade of teams, the athletes were welcomed by thousands of Munich schoolchildren who sang and danced with wreaths of flowers and strewed petals in the path of the competitors. People began speaking of "the Serene Olympics."

Then, on the eleventh day of the Olympiad, September 6, 1972, a small group of Palestinian terrorists infiltrated the compound of athletes' quarters and launched an attack on the Israeli team. Yossef Gutfreund, a wrestling judge, awoke early in the morning to the sound of pounding on the door of his dormitory room. He instinctively rushed to barricade the door with his body, at the same time shouting a warning to his teammates. Some escaped, leaping from second-story windows. Gutfreund and another Israeli were killed, cut down by submachinegun fire, and nine others were taken hostage. The Arabs issued ultimatums, threatened executions of their prisoners. Negotiations were conducted at the highest level—Willy Brandt, the West German chancellor, had rushed to Munich—and a safe-passage deal was made; the Arabs and Israelis were taken by helicopter to the airport, which was surrounded by police and special guards. In the shoot-out that developed, some of the terrorists and all of the hostages were killed.

Elie Wiesel later wrote, "Munich: a past charged with hate and

181

death; it brings to mind the downfall and shame of an entire civilization. Munich evokes Hitler. Precisely what contemporary Germany was trying to make us forget with the 1972 Olympic Games. By investing great effort and energy it hoped to erase the memory of the previous games, under triumphant swastikas, in 1936. An ambitious project reduced to dust, or rather ashes, by a few messengers of violence."

The ironies of the failure were overwhelming. First: That Jewish blood should be again shed heinously in the country whose previous Olympiad had been, by implication, a foreshadowing of the "final solution." After covering the memorial service in Munich for ABC, Jim McKay wrote, "When last the Olympics were held in this country, men in yarmulkes were being beaten and thrown into concentration camps. Now, they stood like mankind's conscience, reminders of the past as they were symbols of the terrible present." Second: That the country where an earlier regime had so relentlessly used sport as a propaganda tool should also be the place where international politics dealt sport its worst blow.

This specific terror, this murder, was far removed from exalting the glories of a culture on the basis of a few individuals' physical prowess, but it was still the logical conclusion of Nazi Olympics, American-Russian jock rivalry, and Duce-glorifying pugilism. It was the final step in the use of the arena to contest international issues, and there could never again be a guarantee that a sports event with the whole world's attention focused on it would be safe from a repetition of Munich. Stricken at the injustice of the deaths, Jim McKay had reasoned, "The murdered Israelis were not representatives of their government. They were sportsmen. . . ." Neither was golfer Gary Player a representative of the South African government when anti-apartheid demonstrators harassed him at tournaments in the United States and Australia, nor Manuel Orantes of Spain when he was heckled by his government's detractors during tennis matches in Sweden; nor Russian basketball players when they were subject to a Jewish Defense League demonstration in Madison Square Garden.

Theoretically, the Olympic Games are innocent of political implications. The Olympic movement, in fact, is thought of—at least by the industrial and hereditary nobility who have controlled it in modern times—as a celebration of individual achievement (despite obvious delight in ceaseless flag-waving and anthem-playing). This is a philosophic carry-over from the ancient games, in which the separation of sport and state apparently once was a reality. The games originated in Greece, sometime around 1370 B.C. (the first officially recorded celebration came about six hundred years later), stimulated by the classical ideal of combining the highest possible development of both mind and body. In the beginning they consisted only of foot races; eventually, contests less purely athletic—boxing, chariot racing and the like—were included, and with them, in time, came corruption and commercialism. Likewise, the competitors came to be regarded less as individuals and more as extensions of the city-state.

Since the games at first were considered sacred, all mundane matters were subordinate. During wartime soldier-athletes were allowed to pass safely across enemy lines to compete, and some historians maintain that truces were declared during Olympiads. The modern Olympics, founded by a Frenchman, Baron de Coubertin, in the hope of reaffirming the ancient ideals, haven't fared as well; twice the games have been called off in deference to the uninterrupted conduct of world wars. And when most of the world was at peace, observances have been used to aggravate tensions that, with any sort of luck, might ultimately result in shoot-outs.

The 1956 summer Olympics at Melbourne actually took place in November of that year, since Australia is in the Southern Hemisphere. At the time there was turmoil in Europe and the Middle East. Russian troops and tanks had brutally cut down Hungarian revolutionaries. Israel, with the support of France and Britain, had moved into the Gaza Strip. Together the conflicts accounted for the decimation of the Olympic roster. In protest of Israel's actions, Egypt, Iraq, and Lebanon withdrew. Spain, Switzerland, and the Netherlands pulled out over the invasion of Hungary. The People's Republic of China also made indignant exit in reaction to the mistaken raising of the Nationalist Chinese flag over their camp.

The Hungarians stayed and competed. They probably had little choice; reprisals against families were a sanction they didn't dare risk. Quiescent they weren't, however. They took down the Communist symbol and flag over their camp and raised the flag of free Hungary. When Russia and Hungary met in water polo, the goings-on in the pool looked like a form of warfare. Hungarian expatriates shouted insults from the stands while blood flowed in the water.

That episode was in the defiant tradition established in 1908, when the American team deigned not to defile its flag by lowering it to the head of state of the host country during the opening parade. That Olympiad, staged in London, boasted unusually prominent flag tensions. Ill feeling was generated by several factors, not the least of which was that British-American friendship had not yet flowered to the extent it someday would. Beyond that, many of the American athletes were of Irish descent, and the British and Irish weren't getting along all that well. Instead of being allowed to compete as a nation, the Irish had been merged into a consolidated United Kingdom team, and many quit rather than run and jump in partnership—however contrived—with Englishmen. Meantime, Finland and Russia were having it out, with the Finns finally getting permission from the czar to compete as a separate team but not to march under their own country's flag. The choice between hoisting the czar's banner or none at all was an easy one: They marched without a flag.

On opening day no American flag was displayed along with the other nations'; the British explained they hadn't been able to find one. Sweden's flag was missing, too, and the Swedes later pulled out of the games over a disagreement with British wrestling judges. By parade time, the resourceful Yankees had scared up a few American flags to carry. As each national contingent marched past King Edward VII, its banner was lowered in deference to His Majesty. Old Glory, however, remained upright, and Martin Sheridan uttered what became America's Olympic watchword: "This flag dips to no earthly king." Presumably until the games were held in heaven, the Stars and Stripes were safe from humiliation.

The rarity of an Olympics without overtones of hate makes it all the more incomprehensible that anyone should regard sports as a medium for fostering better relations between countries. Yet the United States has never abandoned the ideal and has often deployed jocks diplomatically, in exercises as routine and relatively apolitical as "goodwill" tours of baseball teams to Japan, Latin America, and Europe and as seemingly strategic as the "Ping Pong diplomacy" of 1971. What this amounted to was permitting American players to accept an invitation to matches with the Chinese team in Peking after the world championships in Tokyo. The Ping-Pong games were played without provoking nuclear warfare. In fact, a good time was had by all, a circumstance credited for "breaking the deadlock" that had been keeping the two nations from embracing each other in nonathletic spheres. A Ping-Pong ball, it seemed, had breached the figurative Great Wall, blasting the opening through which Richard Nixon passed on his historic visit to a land that for decades had held itself aloof from official dealings with the U.S. government.

China and the United States continued trying to promote frendship through sports. In May 1975 dual track meets between the national teams were held in Canton, Shanghai, and Peking, with every effort made to soft-pedal the appearance of contention; no flags were displayed, no anthems played for winners of events, no scores kept. Responding as they often do, the athletes fell right into the spirit of competition for its own sake. "Amity among the athletes was indisputable," dispatches said. Wirephotos of the finish of one meet showed members of both teams with hands joined and held aloft and huge smiles on their faces as they jogged around the track. The tenor was not unlike that of the table-tennis matches. Then, everyone had tacitly agreed it was irrelevant to compare the merits of the teams. The Chinese reigned, while the United States—Ping-Pongwise—was a Third World country, and everyone including the American media was willing to regard the games as exhibitions. With the degrees of skill reversed in track and field, Americans in general and the media in particular couldn't refrain from treating the meets as a confrontation. Headlines in American newspapers read, "Runaway in China . . . U.S. Routs China . . ." United Press International's correspondent wrote, "The meet was a friendly affair. No point score was kept, which was just as well, because if it had been, the total would have come to 22 events for the U.S., compared to only one for the Chinese over two days . . . The Chinese accepted each of their defeats with uncommonly good grace and appeared almost oblivious to the fact they couldn't even get on the board today." The Associated Press version: "The Americans had no more trouble with the Chinese national team than it had with the provincial teams in Canton and Shanghai."

No government's relations with other nations and its own minorities have been more profoundly affected by sport than South Africa's. In an article datelined "Capetown," in the *New York Times* of June 9, 1975, Anthony Lewis wrote, "The big political news in South Africa this past weekend was a football game. A visiting French rugby team played one from South Africa—and there were four blacks on the home team . . . Not to make too much but . . . symbols do matter, and it means something when there is a beginning of change in rugby—the biggest sport in a sports-mad country . . . A cabinet decision was required to clear the way for the match . . . Changes in sport here, such as they are, have come about entirely because of outside pressure. . . ." Regarding the same rugby match, the *Wall Street Journal* said, "To appreciate the significance of this one must realize the devotion of the Afrikaner, traditionally an apartheid hardliner, to the sport of rugby. Indeed, it is probably only through sport that foreign pressure on apartheid may be having any impact. South Africans are a vigorous lot who love their tennis, soccer, cricket and rugby. Being boycotted, cut off and threatened with cutoffs from international competition probably carries more weight than all the arms embargoes, economic sanctions and liberal handwringing put together."

The outside world's disapproval of apartheid had led to South Africa's expulsion from the Olympic Games in Mexico City in 1968. At the same time, white South African athletes competing outside the country—notably Gary Player, who played a lot of golf in the United States—were being taunted in organized demonstrations. After the Olympics South Africa made the first hesitant changes in the monochromatic sports scene within its borders; it began not by integrating its own nonwhites but by bringing in outsiders established in the world's eyes.

Munich's Legacy

What helped was the availability of a pioneer too young, too ignorant of politics, and too cuddly to be perceived as a threat to the whites. Evonne Goolagong's skin was the wrong color, but a sufficiently light shade of it; she was partly descended from Australian aborigines. She was only a teenager, and the extent of her activism was exactly what South Africa had in mind when it invited her to compete in the 1971 South African Open tennis tournament at Johannesburg. "I'm a nonpolitical person and I'm not ashamed of that," she later avowed."More race. Always race. Couldn't I be treated merely as a promising young Australian tennis player?" Before she had emerged as a world-class nonwhite player, only Arthur Ashe, a black American, had been available, and he had rendered himself ineligible by being something more than a political cipher. Ashe, in fact, had begun trying to integrate South African tennis in 1969, but had been refused a visa every time he applied. As he freely admitted, his case may have been damaged by his observation in 1968 that "They ought to drop an H-bomb on Johannesburg."

"I was considered safe," Goolagong wrote. "They weren't sure about Arthur." But her very safeness offended many Australians, who considered it demeaning for her to entertain white racists with her tennis playing and tacitly accept their social system. The rumor that she would receive "honorary white" status for purposes of the visit didn't help. And if Goolagong herself was oblivious to the political pressures that made South Africa break down and let her in, the people around her weren't.

In 1971 the South African cricket team's traditional tour of England was canceled because of a boycott started by an English university student in protest of the exclusion of nonwhites from South Africa's national teams. Soon the corresponding soccer and rugby relationships with England also were suspended. South Africa, already kicked out of the Olympics, was now expelled from Davis Cup tennis competition. Also in 1971, the pace of demonstrations against South African jocks abroad picked up. In one of the more prominent incidents, an NAACP group picketed the U.S. Pro Championships of tennis in Boston, demanding that Frew McMillan, Cliff Drysdale, and Rob Maud—all South Africans—be excluded from the tournament. The picketers said that if Arthur Ashe was kept from practicing his profession in South Africa, the same prohibition should be applied to South Africans in the United States. Some of the NAACP people bought seats in the Longwood Cricket Club grandstand and heckled the South Africans during their matches.

Somehow Evonne Goolagong hadn't noticed a thing. " I couldn't believe the furor that erupted in Australia when it was announced that I'd been invited to play," she said. "I'd heard of apartheid, but I guess I didn't realize at first how historic my entry into the tournament would be. . . ." So much the better. She competed without agitating caucasians or fomenting any uprisings. In 1972 she played again and won the singles championship. The Republic failed to crumble, and a new era began. Together with some diplomatic maneuvering, the Goolagong goodwill opened South African tennis the following year to Ashe. He struck a bargain: He would refrain from denouncing the country while in it and immediately before arriving; in return he would be treated as a human being (i.e., a white man) and would be free to move about the country for observation purposes.

Ashe's account: "The South African government knows I'm using them and I know they're using me. They can say, 'See, we've allowed Ashe to play.' But I've gone there with three preconditions. I can come and go where I please and say what I want to. I won't play in front of segregated audiences, the stands must be integrated, and I wouldn't go if I have to accept an honorary white status, which is the way they can get around things." In *Arthur Ashe: Portrait in Motion* he quoted a toast made at a party by a black South African lawyer: "You can make us or break us, Arthur. You are the pride and idol of us all . . . God bless you for coming, Arthur, our Arthur." Bearing that responsibility, Ashe could see only one course. "Arthur Ashe is not going to topple a government, but the very nature of sports is such that I believe that progress can be made in this frivolous area first. Perhaps if I were a politician or a businessman or a clergyman or whatever, there would be compelling reasons for me not to go, but I am a tennis player and it seems proper to me . . . Look at it in the United States. The white guy who will sit next to a black spectator at the ballpark and root for a bunch of black athletes wearing his city's name across their chests may have a conniption fit if you asked him to sit next to a black at work or in school or in church. But maybe next time, after the ball game, it won't seem so bad or unusual."

Once it had a basis for the claim that it was capable of change, South Africa started a propaganda campaign. Large block ads appeared in American publications, signed by the information counselor of the South African embassy:

Could the next Olympics be in Pretoria, South Africa?

There's no reason why it couldn't—except that South Africa itself is barred from the Olympic Games.

We were expelled a few years ago at the insistence of some nations who claimed equal opportunity in sport for the different races did not exist in South Africa.

(In golf, South Africa has more black players competing in professional tournaments than even the United States.)

Responsible voices in the Olympic movement objected to this irrational ouster but were soon drowned.

With our black and white merit teams denied access to the Olympic Games in Mexico City and more recently Munich, we had to find another way of providing them with international competition.

In 1973 we staged our own mini-olympics attended by more than 2,000 sportsmen from all over the world. In Pretoria they competed for gold, silver and bronze regardless of race, color or creed.

Since then we have hosted many other international events and world championships. There is no reason why South Africa should not host the next real Olympics—providing she is accepted back into the Olympic community. And why shouldn't she be?

Before readers had time to answer that one, a more sophisticated campaign was launched in *Sports Illustrated*—a three-page series of ads, each with a photo of a black hand holding a piece of sports equipment and a message like "In South Africa, more black golfers play on the PGA circuit than anywhere else in the world." There was subtle detail—the tennis racket pictured in the grasp of a noncaucasian was the Arthur Ashe Head Competition Model. "So if somebody tells you progress isn't being made in South African sport, you can tell them they're ignorant of the real facts," the text said. "Put the facts together and you'll realize we all deserve to play together."

The progress and the praise notwithstanding, South Africa continued to be a pariah. Abroad its white athletes were still regarded as symbols of inequality. At the Wills Masters golf tournament in Australia in 1974 Gary Player was heckled by people carrying signs that read, "Player lies—apartheid thrives." As he bent over his putt on the last hole someone shouted, "Go home, racist." On the same day, in Nice, France, an anti-apartheid group of 100 had met a South African rugby team at the airport wearing black masks and carrying a banner that said, "Rugby, yes—racism in sport, no." The next year when Player went to Australia he left his black caddy at home, to avoid the heckling and humiliation that had been directed at the man. He did bring a black South African golfer, who was hooted at and called "black dog." Black golf officials who had come along, too, pleaded with the crowd and argued that no one had done more than Player to integrate golf in South Africa.

Opposition seemed most stubborn in the sport in which South Africa had tried hardest to change its image. By 1974 Davis Cup eligibility had been restored, but the All-India Tennis Federation declared its team would not be allowed to play South Africa. Among participants and tennis lovers there was some adverse reaction. Vijay and Anand Amritraj, outstanding players, said they wouldn't play for India again. *Tennis* magazine decried the "inclination of governments to use the game as a tool of national policy." *Sports Illustrated* editorialized on "India's lamentable decision . . . Follow India's thinking to its logical conclusion and there would be almost no international competition. Communist wouldn't meet capitalist, Scottish nationalist would refuse to compete against the English . . . the South Africans' extraordinary devotion to sport might yet prove the undoing of the insidious policy of apartheid . . ." India's refusal to play in the final gave South Africa the Davis Cup by default.

In 1975 authorities in both Mexico and Colombia refused to let their teams play South Africa, and in France the Rhodesian women's team was banned from Federation Cup competition. The extent of Mexico's revulsion became apparent when the World Championship Tennis doubles tournament was held in Mexico City. WCT officials had obtained a letter of agreement from the Mexican government stating that nobody would be barred from the tournament, but the pledge was no help to Frew McMillan and Bob Hewitt, defending champions, who hailed from the sports world's least favorite country. Hewitt was wakened at his hotel, shortly after arriving, by Mexican immigration officials. Told to pack immediately, he was taken to an airport motel where he temporarily shared a room with two immigration men. Customs officials detained McMillan and his wife and children at the airport; then they were taken to the motel where Hewitt was being held. The Mexican government had determined that the two players were in the country illegally, traveling on tourist permits, and therefore ineligible to win the tournament prize money. After a few hours of detention they were put on a flight to Dallas. Arthur Ashe protested, "With the exception of 18 million black South Africans . . . no one is more anti-apartheid than I. I am all for pressure on South Africa, and lots of it, but I draw the line at the shotgun approach." Two months later at the annual meeting of Davis Cup participants in London, a vote to exclude South Africa again was defeated. According to one report, the American delegate said the United States was fed up with political interference with the Davis Cup and would have withdrawn had any nation been excluded for political reasons.

This hardly meant the trend was being reversed or that nations and individuals were losing their enthusiasm for airing issues in the arena. On the contrary, it seemed that more and more countries were finding reasons not to play with each other, and terror was on the verge of becoming a commonplace in international sport.

In the spring of 1974 the lives of two Scottish soccer players were threatened by the Irish Republican Army before a game in Frankfurt, West Germany. Reason: they were Protestant. At about the same time authorities in Hamburg got warning of a planned rocket attack by urban guerrillas on Volkspark Stadium in protest of the normalization of relations between East Germany and West Germany, whose soccer teams were about to meet for the first time. Neither threat was carried out, but sportsmen were getting jumpier all the time. The next year Jack Nicklaus refused to play on the United States team in the World Cup golf matches in Bangkok, Thailand. His explanation: fear for his life. Nicklaus cited his station in life, vis-à-vis that of the oppressed classes, and the political turmoil in Thailand. "With all the things going on over there now, it just wouldn't be fair to my family if I played. Golf has a reputation as a rich man's game. It's a rich, capitalistic sport. I think I would be a natural target . . . My playing there at this time as a representative of the United States, well, it could be a very unpleasant and potentially dangerous thing." The State Department, forced into an unaccustomed need to take an official position on a golfer, "took exception" to Nicklaus's opinions.

Within a week the Nicklaus statement was punctuated by a situation that developed elsewhere in the world. Jaime Fillol, a member of the Chile Davis Cup team, was told he would be shot to death if he took part in a match against Sweden in Baastad. At issue was his political affilation; left-wing Chilean exiles living in Sweden were unhappy about his support of the military junta ruling their homeland. Fillol took the threats seriously, and when the provincial police in Baastad announced they weren't prepared to guarantee the safety of the Chilean team, its members asked that the match be switched to a neutral country. There were meetings of international tennis officials in London and Forest Hills, New York. Ultimately, the Chileans were told to play or default; at the same time, the Swedish government declared its willingness to try to keep its guests alive.

"Sweden is girding itself for an unaccustomed state of siege," Martin Walker of the *Manchester Guardian* wrote in the days before the match. He pointed out there were elusive operatives trying to blow up the Spanish embassy in retaliation for death sentences against Basque terrorists. There were Japanese terrorists whose deportation had brought a declaration of war against Sweden by the Japanese Red Army. "And then," Walker added, "there is the almost prosaic threat to the Chilean tennis match, which the Swedish left has vowed to stop."

Prosaic or not, the precautions were elaborate. An Australian tennis team had once spent twelve days training under armed guard in India because of threats, but that was nothing compared to what was going on in Baastad. Bjorn Borg, the most famous of the Swedes, practiced with a bodyguard. Instead of traveling openly direct to Sweden, to what might be an unpleasant reception, the Chileans laid low in Denmark for a while and then were secretly escorted across the border. The security net drawn around Baastad may have been the tightest ever for a sports event. Much of the town itself, a fashionable coastal resort, was closed off with a fence. Two gunboats guarded the coast. The tennis court was fortified with a 35-foot-high wire fence, and there were 1,200 policemen, 107 police dogs, 43 mounted police, two helicopters, and a battery of spotlights to ensure that tennis would be played in safety. Swedish law forbade a forced search of spectators. Instead, those who refused to submit "voluntarily" to being searched were denied entry.

As the time to play drew near, it became apparent that more than a few extremists were angry with the Chilean tennis players. Someone took out a newspaper ad in which the match was described as a show of support for the junta and the players as open supporters of dictatorship. The provincial police chief reported his department was receiving an average of two threats of violence an hour. An estimated 6,500 demonstrators pressed in on the barriers a few blocks from the tennis club, shouting wildly and setting off firecrackers, the sounds of which carried to the courts. According to the Associated Press, "Fillol . . . appeared unsettled while playing on the red clay center court as the first firecrackers went off. Borg indicated that this could have been the reason why the Chileans, considered one of the world's top doubles pairs, were so easily defeated in the second set."

The question of who was fit to host or participate in the Olympic Games kept growing knottier. The International Olympic Committee awarded the 1980 Summer Games to Moscow, but only on certain conditions: The Russians must behave nicely to everybody. The press and foreign spectators must be less than totally restricted in their movements. Political archfiends like the South Koreans must not be excluded. Israeli athletes must not be baited by rigged audiences. This last was not exactly a hypothetical prohibition. In 1973, the year before the IOC meeting in question, the Soviet Union had sponsored the World University Games as a sort of showcase of its qualifications for staging the Olympics. The Middle East was a hot issue at the time, as was emigration of Soviet Jews to Israel. Israeli athletes became the object of Russian Jews' hopes and Russian non-Jews' hatred. During basketball games they were baited savagely. Soviet Jews who rooted for the Israelis were attacked by other spectators, and uniformed Soviet soldiers ripped up an Israeli flag they carried. After that incident Russian athletes competing in the United States could be sure of encountering demonstrations by American Jews. During one basketball tour a game was interrupted at the University of Maryland when someone in the stands threw oil—later claimed to be Arab in origin—onto the playing floor. The Washington chapter of the Jewish Defense League took credit for that incident, which it called a protest of the persecution of Soviet Jews.

The conclave that deemed Soviet Russia an appropriate place for the games found Rhodesia unfit to compete with decent folks. Before this ouster, South Africa had been the only country excluded; now, by a vote of 41-36, the committee ruled Rhodesia—in which sports were not integrated—also had failed to conform to the ideals of the movement. This was the culmination of a campaign by black African delegates to eliminate the continent's white supremacists from the Olympics. The Supreme Council of Sport in Africa, representing forty-five black and North African countries, called the vote "a victory for the world," and the council's head, Abraham Ordia of Nigeria, proclaimed a rejection of "the pernicious philosophy of apartheid." But the de facto rejection had actually occurred two years earlier when Rhodesia had been kept from taking part in the Serene Olympics in Munich. At first the IOC had decided to welcome the Rhodesians, so long as they entered under the flag of Great Britain. This was not only monumental illogic but gross hypocrisy, heightened by the fact that Rhodesia had broken away from Britain over apartheid. While American blacks bandied the idea of a pullout, the black Africans united in the threat of a boycott, and the IOC responded by revoking Rhodesia's welcome; in the land of the Master Race, the Olympics had been purged of white supremacists.

Epilogue

A t Innsbruck, Austria, for the 1976 winter games—a relatively tiny gathering, limited to entrants from countries with cold weather and mountains—a force of five thousand policemen and soldiers was required to guard the Olympic village, hotels, and the competition sites. The newly built village, designed compactly to reduce chances of another Munich, was surrounded by a high fence with built-in electronic alarms.

As for the 1976 summer games in Montreal, by the previous fall authorities were already investigating rumored terrorist plots against the Israelis. According to a Toronto newspaper, Canadian nationalists with access to the Olympic organizing committee's plans were conspiring with foreign terrorists. Security presented a staggering problem. To begin with, there was the "world's longest unguarded frontier," the Canada-United States border. The U.S. Customs Service wanted Congress to appropriate $23 million to install sophisticated traps for terrorists trying to sneak across the border; part of the plan called for airplanes, boats, helicopters, radar, infrared photography equipment, and sensors buried in the ground—all considered essential to cover isolated areas. The budget office reduced Customs' request to $2.7 million, leaving questionable whether enough security could be bought. Canada's expenses were about $100 million, much of it for a force of thirteen thousand guards. Visitors were screened at airports. The village was surrounded by a ten-foot fence, and its grounds were under scrutiny at all times on closed-circuit TV. A helicopter was kept available in the village, and a team of sharpshooters on hand.

FANS!

For two weeks before the games there was bitter squabbling about which countries had the right to take part and which banners they had the right to raise. The Canadian government had refused to allow the team from Taiwan to identify itself as "Republic of China." Rather than submit, the Taiwanese pulled out the day before the games began. Meantime, many black African nations threatened to boycott if the International Olympic Committee refused to bar New Zealand because it had allowed its rugby team to play in South Africa. The IOC did refuse, and when the parade for the opening ceremonies formed, twenty-six teams were missing, and another withdrew the next day.

I believe none of those things would have happened if the Olympics were conducted without teams, uniforms, flags, anthems, or any reference to athletes' nationalities. But without those trappings the games would be nothing but athletic competitions, which is to say it would hardly be worth anyone's while to show up. What country would be willing to finance sport for its own sake?

In *Ends and Means* Aldous Huxley wrote: "Like every other instrument man has invented, sport can be used for either good or evil purposes . . . Used badly it can encourage personal vanity and group vanity, greedy desire for victory and even hatred for rivals, an intolerant *esprit de corps* and contempt for people who are beyond a certain arbitrarily selected pale."

That, of course, is merely the beginning of the "used badly" list. Sport has been the source of more shameless propaganda, the subject of more nonsense beliefs, and the instrument of more disreputable purposes than any institution but government or religion. And sport seems to be gaining.

Index

FANS!

income, 76-81, 83; influence on children, 160; international relations, 165, 167, 185; management and promotion, 92-94; morals and public expectations, 121-132; mystique, 61, 63-64; political endorsements, 97-101; post-retirement activities, 73-74; propaganda value, 166-170, 182; religion, 109-119; salary, 80, 81, 137; stardom, 32, 71-72, 75-76; stereotyping, 20, 21; tax depreciation on, 139-140

Athletes for Sale (Denlinger and Shapiro), 38, 40, 42

Athletes in Action, 115

The Athletic Revolution (Scott), 128

Atlanta Braves, 14, 65, 66

Atlanta Falcons, 140

Atlanta Journal, 67

Austin Peay, 51

Austria, 35

Auto racing, 153, 158; advertising and, 85-86, 87

Bacon, Mary, 92

Bad Nigger—The National Impact of Jack Johnson (Gilmore), 23

Baker, Russell, 90

Baltimore Colts, 119

Baltimore Orioles, 110

Barnes, Marvin, 81

Barnett, Larry, 161

Barrie, Richard, 91

Barry, Rick, 137

Barton, Gene, 50

Baseball, 25-26, 27, 30, 63, 121-122, 135; commercialism, 84-85; contracts, 141-143; Hall of Fame, 65, 67-68; homeruns, 64-65;

political use of, 100, 101-102; stadiums, 139; violence, 149, 161

Basketball, 12, 26, 63, 89, 97, 127, 135, 140-141; college, 43, 44, 45, 50-51, recruiting, 37-39, 41, 42; high school, 31; salaries, 80, 81; violence, 149

Baugh, Laura, 93

Baylor University, 19-20

Bearbaiting, 154

Beisser, Arthur, 153

Belgium, 34-35

Bell, Marty, 88

Bench, Johnny, 74

Benitez, Frankie, 23

Bergerac, Michel C., 80

Berra, Yogi, 122

Beyer, Andrew, 12

Bicycle racing, 34-35

Bigham, Gov. (Massachusetts), 156

Biletnikof, Fred, 74

Bisher, Furman, 127

Black athletes, 23-26, 123-127, 186-191, 194

Blackmun, Justice Harry, 142

Blancas, Homero, 56

Blankers-Koen, Fanny, 35

Bleier, Rocky, 125

Blomberg, Ron, 21

Blount, Roy, 53

Boggs, Hale, 134

Bond, Alan, 86

Borg, Bjorn, 35, 193

Borman, Frank, 41

Boston, Mass., 27

Boston Bruins, 28, 162

Boston Red Sox, 27, 62, 102, 110

Boucha, Henry, 147, 163

Boxing, 21-25, 112-115, 123-125, 153, 157-158, 165-170, 174-177

Boycotts, 176, 177, 186, 187, 190,

198

Index

Index

Index

FANS!

Index

National Football League, xiv, 1, 7, 8, 9, 57, 58, 62, 83, 95, 129, 133, 134, 136, 140, 146; *See also* individual teams and players
National Hockey League, 27, 136-137, 148, 153, 162
National Lacrosse League, 145
National League baseball, 30
Nationalism, 32-35, 57-58, 171
Navratilova, Martina, 173
Nazi Germany, 171, 174, 175-179
Nebraska, University of, 16
Nelson, Byron, 56
Netherlands, 35
New Jersey, 139
New Mexico, University of, 38
New Orleans Superdome, 138
New Times, 56
New York, 24
New York City, 139
New York Cosmos, 75, 76-77
New York Daily News, 148
New York Giants, 30, 62, 69
New York Jets, 79
New York Mets, 62, 69, 102, 130-131
New York Post, 3, 21
New York State Athletic Commission, 158
New York State Boxing Commission, 126
New York Times, 27, 71, 76, 129, 136, 148, 150, 154
New York University, 40
New York Yacht Club, 87
New York Yankees, 21, 80
New World Christian Youth Center, 116
New Zealand, 196
Newcombe, John, 88, 94
Newsweek, 19, 108

Nice Guys Finish Last (Gardner), 12, 31, 62
Nicklaus, Jack, 54-56, 83, 104, 192
Nixon, Richard, 2, 47, 60, 97-99, 100, 103-107, 159, 185
North Carolina State University, 39, 46
North Carolina, University of, 43, 45
North Dallas Forty (Gent), 118
Northrop Corporation, 5
Norton, Ken, 74, 113
Notre Dame, University of, 49-50

O'Brien, Lawrence, 81, 140-141
Offen, Neil, 62, 104
Ohio State University, 45, 46-48
Oklahoma, University of, 40, 45
The Old Ball Game (Coffin), 26, 60
Olivier, Sir Laurence, 90
Olympic Games, 35, 154, 171-179, 181-184, 189, 193-196; 1936, 174-179, 182; 1972, 181-182; 1976, 170-171, 174, 195-196; 1980, 171, 193; advertising opportunities, 90-91; ancient Greece, 17, 154, 183; ideals, 183; security, 195
The Olympics (Schaap), 84
On God's Squad (Evans), 119
116 Club, 5
Ontario Hockey Association, 150
Orantes, Manuel, 182
Ordia, Abraham, 194
Oregon Journal, 128
Orr, Bobby, 136-137
Owens, Jesse, 100, 178, 179

Palmer, Arnold, 72, 77-78, 94, 105
Palmer, Jim, 20
Paret, Benny, 158

FANS!

Parseghian, Ara, 49
Patterson, Floyd, 112, 126
Payson, Joan Whitney, 69, 105
Pele, 75-77
Pepitone, Joe, 71
Philadelphia Flyers, 26-28, 145, 146, 162
Philadelphia Wings, 145
Philip, Prince (England), 75
Philippines: Ali-Frazier fight, 114, 166, 170
"Ping Pong diplomacy," 185
Pittsburgh Steelers, 28
Player, Gary, 93, 94, 182, 186, 190
Pleso, Bob, 159
Plimpton, George, 60, 66, 67, 115
Politics and sports: national, 73, 97-108; world, 181-182, 185, 186-194, 196
Portland Trail Blazers, 128
Povich, Shirley, 169
Powell, Adam Clayton, 100
Powell, Justice Lewis F., 60
Prefontaine, Steve, 61
Puckett, Tommy, 12

Quarry, Jerry, 22, 74, 127, 158

Racism, 23-25, 26, 123, 124, 127, 186-191, 194
Radbourne, Old Hoss, 142
Rafferty, Max, 57
Ralbovsky, Martin, 26
Randle, Sonny, 46
Raspberry, William, 3
Recruiting: college teams, 37-42; draft, 134
Regina v. *Maki*, 148
Religion and sports, 19-20, 109-119
Rentzel, Lance, 129
Reynolds, Grant, 100

Rhodesia, 167, 194
Rice University, 39
Richard, Maurice, 29
Richardson, Bobby, 116
Richler, Mordecai, 61
Rickey, Branch, 25
Riggs, Bobby, 18-19, 86, 126
Rizzo, Frank, 28
Robbie, Joe, 7
Robert F. Kennedy Stadium, 4; annual losses, 138
Roberts, Oral, 38
Robinson, Frank, 108
Robinson, Jackie, 25, 99
Rockefeller, Nelson, 99
Roddenberry, Seaborn A., 123
Rohan, Jack, 41
Roller derby, 158
Roosevelt, Franklin Delano, 68, 176
Roosevelt, Theodore, 156
Rose, Pete, 160
Rose Bowl, 1961, 47-48
Roseboro, John, 149
Ross, Barney, 22
Rossman, Mike, 21-22
Roth, Philip, 60
Royal, Darrell, 105
Royko, Mike, 79
Rozelle, Pete, xv, 7, 9
Ruffian, 18
Rugby, 186
Runfola, Ross T., 150, 151
Runyon, Damon, 176
Russell, Bill, 89
Russia, 184
Ruth, Babe, 59, 61, 64, 74, 85, 100, 129-130

Saint Louis, University of, 45
St. Louis Cardinals, 6

Index

Index

Printed in Times Roman by the New Republic Book Company, Washington, D.C. Bound by Halliday Lithograph, West Hanover, Massachusetts.
Designed by Gerard Valerio.